T0023122

"*Dirt Road Revival* is exactly what you want it to be: a fast-moving political road trip, through the winding back roads of deep-red rural America to a joyful destination that will have you leaping to your feet and lunging for the collection plate. Maxmin and Woodward share the driving as generously as their hard-won wisdom. Along the way, they lay out a detailed and powerful map for transforming electoral campaigning in the United States. If enough insurgent politicians follow them down the road they're traveling, it could lead to a progressive super-majority across the country."

—NAOMI KLEIN, author of *On Fire* and *The Shock Doctrine*

"In a story told with urgency and passion, Maxmin and Woodward offer a practical playbook for anyone who wants to get into politics to achieve a better future for those who have been left behind. They show us that rural communities are moral communities that respond more to personal stories and values over policies. Building trusting relationships is the key, and this takes time and effort and demands humility and a willingness to learn, but the future of American politics depends on it. The Democratic Party—indeed, all America—must take heed, and *Dirt Road Revival* offers us a path forward. This is a wonderful, powerful book—and one of the most hopeful I've read about a possible future for American politics."

—ROBERT B. REICH, former US secretary of labor and author of *Saving Capitalism: For the Many, Not the Few*

"Rural white America has gone red. So how do two rural-born, Harvard-educated, Bernie-minded activists—one the candidate, one her campaign manager—win big in the most rural county in the nation's most rural state? And how might others do the same? Knock on many doors. Get up potluck suppers. Listen more than talk. Recycle old campaign signs. Talk about climate change as hurting winter ice fishing on the lakes. Don't write off people who voted for Donald Trump. This is a beyond-timely tough-love letter to the Democratic Party, helpful, consequential, brilliant. Read it and pass the book and message on—quickly!"

—ARLIE HOCHSCHILD, author of *Strangers in Their Own Land: Anger and Mourning on the American Right*

"Chloe and Canyon did not win because they knew it all—they won because they listened to and believed in rural voters and the stories they told them at the doors and along the many dirt roads they traveled. *Dirt Road Revival* explains how we got here as a party—losing ground every cycle—and the road we can take to start connecting with rural voters again. It's our job as Democrats not to come in with capes but rather to do exactly what *Dirt Road Revival* lays out: deeply care about the voters you are looking in the eye, advocate with them, and never back down from a fight. It is exactly that fighting spirit that earns respect from rural folks and starts to win back their hearts and their votes."

—JANE KLEEB, author of *Harvest the Vote: How Democrats Can Win Again in Rural America*

"As someone who's spent almost his whole life in rural America, both red and blue counties, I'm not sure I've read a more loving and realistic account of dirt road country. And as someone with a keen interest in American politics, I'm *certain* I've never read a more gripping (and practical) account of how to win elections than *Dirt Road Revival*. Not many political books make you both weep a little and then stand up and cheer—but this will!"

—BILL MCKIBBEN, author of *The Flag, the Cross, and the Station Wagon: A Graying American Looks Back at His Suburban Boyhood and Wonders What the Hell Happened*

"If bridge builders like Chloe and Canyon could be cloned, rural America would experience a political renaissance. Their empathetic, homespun 'politics as unusual' depicted in *Dirt Road Revival* is exactly what our country needs."

—ERICA ETELSON, cofounder of the Rural Urban Bridge Initiative and author of *Beyond Contempt: How Liberals Can Communicate Across the Great Divide*

"*Dirt Road Revival* offers a unique and compelling blend of rigorous research, political expertise, and personal storytelling. Maxmin and Woodward open up about their own experiences and adventures, showing their passion for rural America and the people who sustain it, generation after generation. *Dirt Road Revival* builds bridges across fractious political divides, combining clear-eyed, practical reasoning with honest assessment and empathetic observation. This book will inspire readers to believe in the possibility of rural revival and motivate them to act now."

—JENNIFER M. SILVA, author of *We're Still Here: Pain and Politics in the Heart of America*

DIRT
ROAD
REVIVAL

DIRT
ROAD
REVIVAL

HOW TO REBUILD
RURAL POLITICS
AND WHY OUR FUTURE
DEPENDS ON IT

CHLOE MAXMIN AND
CANYON WOODWARD

Beacon Press
BOSTON

BEACON PRESS
Boston, Massachusetts
www.beacon.org

Beacon Press books
are published under the auspices of
the Unitarian Universalist Association of Congregations.

25 24 23 22   8 7 6 5 4 3 2

This book is printed on acid-free paper that meets the uncoated paper
ANSI/NISO specifications for permanence as revised in 1992.

Text design and composition by Kim Arney

Library of Congress Cataloging-in-Publication Data

Names: Maxmin, Chloe, author. | Woodward, Canyon, author.
Title: Dirt road revival : how to rebuild rural politics and why our future
   depends on it / Chloe Maxmin and Canyon Woodward.
Description: Boston : Beacon Press, 2022. | Includes bibliographical
   references. | Summary: "Dirt Road Revival lays out a roadmap for
   progressive politics in rural America based on two young campaigners'
   successful races in the most rural county in the most rural state in
   America" —Provided by publisher.
Identifiers: LCCN 2021054427 | ISBN 9780807007518 (hardcover) |
   ISBN 9780807007563 (ebook)
Subjects: LCSH: Democratic Party (U.S.) | Rural population—United States—
Attitudes. | Politics, Practical—United States. | United
   States—Rural conditions—21st century. | Political
   campaigns—Maine—Lincoln County.
Classification: LCC JK2316 .M28 2022 | DDC 324.2736—dc23/eng/20211216
LC record available at https://lccn.loc.gov/2021054427

For our communities.
For our homes.

CONTENTS

A HANDSHAKE

The headlines indicated something unprecedented taking place on the dirt roads of Maine. In November 2018, Katrina vanden Heuvel, editorial director at *The Nation*, wrote in the *Washington Post* of the surprise winner of a Maine election: "Her victory stands out even more because of where she was able to win: in a district that contains the most rural county in America's most rural state." Two years later, the *Bangor Daily News* front page announced "Maine Democrats Oust Top GOP Lawmaker as Republicans Erode House Majority in Mixed Election." Presenting its 2020 Buster Douglas Award, named after Douglas's surprise boxing upset over Mike Tyson, the *Daily News*, Maine's second-largest newspaper wrote, "This year it goes to Chloe Maxmin for taking out Maine Senate Minority Leader Dana Dow. . . . Not since 1992 has an incumbent Senate leader been knocked out."

In 2018 and again in 2020, candidate Chloe Maxmin and campaign manager Canyon Woodward, two mid-twenties climate activists raised in rural red America, won grassroots campaigns in conservative rural districts where Democrats struggle to get elected. Chloe became the youngest woman in the Maine House of Representative in 2018. Two years later, she became the youngest woman state senator in Maine's history.

This book tells our story and lessons learned on the campaign trail. From the beginning, we approached our campaigns determined to figure out a new theory and practice for a Democratic resurgence in rural America. We've watched since 2009 as the Democratic Party abandoned rural Americans—our communities—allowing the rural vote to trend red, with little effort to stop the bleeding. The 2016 presidential election made clear that the consequences of these choices have produced an existential threat to American democracy, plainly illustrated in Donald Trump's ascendancy and the 2021 US Capitol attack. Rural red districts like the ones that we grew up in have become a decisive force swinging national politics toward an extreme right-wing agenda. Reuniting our country depends on forging a new political paradigm for Democrats in rural America.

Since 2018, we have chronicled each step of the learning process as our methods and beliefs are tested every day against the tough realities of Maine's dirt roads. Our aim has not been just to win and create change but also to learn. Our conversations with Maine's rural voters educated us. Shake enough hands and the hands shake you—each one a teacher. We let our campaigns transform us. We emerged from two campaigns and four years of lawmaking with a powerful, credible, honest, practical, detailed, and dirt road–tested playbook to share with you.

This book is also a tough-love letter to the Democratic Party. As Republican politicians consolidate around autocratic values and the principles of minority rule, all those who cherish democracy look to the Democratic Party—despite its shortcomings—for the qualities of courageous leadership that can steer our nation through this divided time. Democrats will need sustainable political power if we are to build a robust, citizen-led, twenty-first-century America based on our core values of social and economic justice, opportunity, and inclusive prosperity. These values are on the line as we navigate the defining decade of our time for citizens' rights, strong democratic institutions, equality, racial justice, climate action, debt-free education, affordable healthcare, equal pay, broadband access, citizen (as opposed to corporate) power, and more. Democrats cannot succeed with the radical urgency that is required unless we lead a dirt road revival to rebuild political power in rural America. *Dirt Road Revival* is the grassroots primer for a profound renewal of the Democratic Party's vision and strategies for rural America.

Before we dive fully into the stories of our campaigns and the framework for a Democratic revival, part 1 zooms out to ground ourselves in rural America's recent history and often harsh realities. These first two chapters draw heavily on the work of sociologists and other authors to provide a brief yet critical foundation to understand the context in which we are living and campaigning. How did rural America become such a politically potent force for Republicans? What drove so many rural Americans away from the Democratic Party in recent years?

Part 2 is our first-person story of successful rural campaigns in Maine. In 2018, we ran for State House District 88, which had never been held by a Democrat. In 2020, we ran for State Senate against the Senate Minority Leader, the highest-ranking Republican in Maine. Senate District 13 voted for Trump in 2016. In 2020, District 13 voted for Joe Biden, but it also voted by a double-digit margin for Republican US senator Susan Collins. Our campaigns ground Democratic politics in the rural spaces that have been left behind and in our commitment to work with our community in ways that are positive, creative, hopeful, enduring, and even joyful. We took a leap of faith and dove headfirst into campaigning on the dirt roads of rural Maine.

In part 3, we share the lessons distilled from our combined decades of organizing work and our two successful campaigns. These chapters cover the strategic principles that guide our work, the process that structures our campaigns, and our approach to the day-to-day tasks of an election cycle. These are the real-world lessons that blossomed as we built a movement on the campaign trail. Our goal in these chapters is to translate our vision and experience into something that will be useful for you and your community, whether you're a first-time candidate or campaign manager (as we were in 2018), a veteran political organizer, or a door-knocking volunteer.

But first, we want to say hello. We always start our campaign meetings with what we call our preamble, a life check-in before we get to work. This is our preamble to you, our handshake, our introduction. This practice is rooted in how we were raised. Things move at the speed of relationship in rural America. You don't jump straight into business and take care of things as quickly as possible. An essential part of the culture of living and organizing in rural America is slowing down and building relationships. It is the touchstone on which our future—and all hope of transforming how we relate to politics and one another—depends. And a good relationship starts with a handshake. This small gesture is about establishing a modicum of trust and human connection. To show up, look someone in the eye, and shake their hand is to plant the seeds of possibility and connection. It's also what is lacking in today's politics. A voter told us one day, "I don't identify with either party. I vote for the person. I vote for whoever has the firmest handshake."

CANYON

Raised in the beautiful backwoods of Southern Appalachia in a small town where political activity was mostly confined to local issues, I was largely a stranger to public protest. Attending Harvard on need-based financial aid, I certainly didn't anticipate confronting the institution that made my continued education possible. Yet I could not in good conscience study climate change without confronting the fact that Harvard was investing its billions in companies driving climate catastrophe.

My understanding of the climate crisis began at the age of sixteen, after I lived for a short time with a family in Phyang, a small village in a deep green valley of northern India surrounded by the barren mountains of the Himalayan highland. Life in Phyang, and for the more than one billion people who inhabit the Himalayan river basins, is sustained by meltwater harnessed by the intricately designed irrigation systems that conserve this precious resource. As the glaciers melt and dry up due to global warming, the whole region will likely be forced to grapple with severe water insecurity. Much as day-to-day life in rural America is affected by decisions made in faraway Washington, DC, climate change is driven by industrial superpowers far removed from hamlets like Phyang. Still, the decisions of those with power affect the water supply of the Himalayas and much of the world.

I began to wrap my head around the injustice of human-caused climate change and reflected on what actions I could take personally. I took steps to reduce my own carbon footprint and water use. I organized 5K races in my town to raise money for clean water projects in developing countries. At Harvard, courses in environmental science and public policy furthered my understanding of climate change as a systemic crisis requiring systemic solutions. I came to understand that individual behavioral change—becoming vegetarian, recycling, efficient lightbulbs, and so on—would not be enough to prevent climate catastrophe. I joined protests on campus against the Keystone XL pipeline proposal and bused to Washington, DC, to surround the White House with thousands of others calling for President Obama to reject the pipeline.

I fell in love with organizing and soon joined Divest Harvard, a budding campaign on campus that Chloe had created with a handful of other students. As students before us had done in the face of Big Tobacco, apartheid in South Africa, and genocide in Darfur, we built a divestment campaign on campus to get Harvard to sell its fossil fuel stocks and reinvest in affected communities. The Harvard Corporation—the university's governing body—is the oldest corporation in the Western Hemisphere. Harvard and its culture epitomize the status quo. Activism was not popular on campus.

Despite this culture, our campaign grew quickly. We organized the first student vote on fossil fuel divestment in the world: 72 percent of students voted in favor, landing Divest Harvard on the front page of almost every major newspaper. Then 67 percent of Harvard Law School students voted for divestment. Over four thousand alumni and one thousand faculty were also on board. We sued Harvard University for failing to divest, organized an international fast, and launched a twenty-four-hour sit-in inside Massachusetts Hall, the location of the president's office. We then organized "Harvard Heat Week" to shut down Massachusetts Hall for six days and six nights. So many people were trained for this action that, when administrators moved their operations to University Hall, we were able to shut down that building too. Dozens of famous alumni, including Desmond Tutu, Natalie Portman, Cornel West, and Al Gore, voiced their support. Divest Harvard has continued through the years. It even became a litmus test for 2020 presidential candidates on the left, garnering endorsements from Bernie Sanders, Elizabeth Warren, Julian Castro, and Tom Steyer.

It was while doing climate justice organizing that I met Chloe. A high-key visionary, she radiated contagious confidence and had an endearing habit of correcting people who called her a freshman—she was actually a freshwoman. We bonded one day in 2011 as we traveled across Boston to gather supplies for an anti–Keystone XL pipeline art installation. Growing up in small towns, Chloe and I had never ridden a public bus before. We knew that our stop was next, and we were ready to get off. But the bus kept going. We looked at each other, confused as heck. As it turns out, you need to press the button to alert the driver that you need to get off at the next stop. We had no idea. From there, we developed a deep and enduring friendship.

Our campaign at Harvard grew to over seventy thousand people, and the divestment movement exploded across the world. But, as time went on, we worried that divestment wasn't enough. The purpose was to weaken the fossil fuel industry's political influence by making it toxic for politicians to associate with them. In turn, the people could reclaim politicians' attention to usher in climate policy. The problem was that, while the divestment movement created incredible grassroots momentum, we had no effective game plan to bring that energy to bear on electoral politics. We weren't running candidates, supporting electoral campaigns, pushing legislation forward, or getting students out to vote. The path to electoral politics remained blocked.

At Harvard, Chloe and I puzzled over the climate movement's lack of political power. But during visits home over breaks and holidays, we connected with the people in our rural communities whose struggles had been ignored by politics. We witnessed the degradation: rural hospitals bought out by private companies and services cut; slashed local budgets that forced schools to lay off teachers; Republicans refusing to expand Medicaid; small-town banks bought out by big financial institutions only to close branches and tighten credit; Main Street businesses that had defined our towns for decades forced to close, unable to compete with Amazon; small farmers struggling to compete with Big Agriculture; drug epidemics; lack of basic services, including high-speed internet and reliable cell phone reception. The examples are endless.

Even amid these systemic challenges, the rural America that Chloe and I grew up in is beautiful, resilient, and rooted in strong values. It called both of us home. Home, where we were raised to appreciate the benefits of living in community and looking out for one another in times of need. Home, where we learned the necessity of self-sufficiency and resourcefulness. Home, where we developed strong connections to the land and to each other. Home, where we gained faith in the basic goodness of our neighbors and learned to respect and listen to them, even when we didn't agree.

At Harvard and at home, it became clear to us: the Left needed to radically rethink how we build political power in rural America. Our rural communities needed a voice. The years of organizing at Harvard had given us the tools not only for analysis but also for action. The foundation for our life work in politics together began to take shape. We imagined working on campaigns at home that could empower overlooked rural communities to define a new political era. We bucked the tide of our peers heading off to big cities and work on Wall Street or in Silicon Valley, opting instead to return to our rural roots and invest in our home communities. Chloe returned to Maine, and I returned to the Carolinas.

I moved back to the rural South and brought my Divest Harvard organizing skills with me. I worked as a regional field director for Bernie Sanders's 2016 campaign in South Carolina, opening a campaign office and managing four full-time field organizers and three paid interns in the most rural corner of the state. Together, we built a high-performing team. While we didn't win, our rural South Carolina region garnered a higher percentage of votes for Bernie than any of the other six regions in the state.

I learned an enormous amount about campaigning. I was lit on fire by the potential of the powerful marriage of movement politics and electoral politics that Bernie's campaign cultivated. I also had my first glimpse of the toxic campaign culture that was nearly ubiquitous across the Democratic campaign world. We worked at a breakneck pace every single day of every week with the exception of Thanksgiving, Christmas, and New Year's Day. The only days I took off the entire campaign were a few days to visit Chloe when she was going through a hard time. My boss told me that it would be best for me to lie about where I was going and say that it was an immediate family member in crisis. I told her she could tell the state director what she wanted, but I wasn't going to lie. If our campaign wasn't able to make space for us to show up for one another as full human beings and practice community care, then how could it be expected to actualize the broader vision of collective humanity that we were fighting for?

After the campaign, I returned to North Carolina's southern Appalachians to organize in my rural home district for the rest of the 2016 cycle as a field director for State Senate candidate Jane Hipps. Similar to my work on the Bernie campaign, we applied the organizing frameworks that I learned at Harvard to organize local Democratic Party bodies and progressive organizations. We mobilized over a hundred volunteers to contact over forty-five thousand rural voters. Our campaign could not overcome the Koch-funded incumbent in our very conservative district, but we built communities of volunteers at the county level and planted the seeds of hope for a political shift in the mountains.

Through these campaign experiences, I began to see firsthand how rural communities were being left behind by the Democratic Party. Democrats invested disproportionate resources on statewide races and urban turnout, often siphoning resources from rural races. Funding that was promised to our campaign in rural North Carolina by the state caucus in 2016 was shifted at the last minute to pay for TV spots in metropolitan markets. In another election, rural volunteers in the North Carolina Eleventh Congressional District were redirected from local efforts to make phone calls to boost urban turnout in Charlotte. This singular focus on metropolitan politics weakened the party in rural areas.

Following the 2016 election, I devoted months to reflecting on the campaigns and organizing locally in the North Carolina Democratic Party to pass platform resolutions and elect progressive Democratic leaders at the precinct, county, and district levels. I was elected as the second vice chair for my home congressional district and coordinated trainings and organizing resources for county leaders and volunteers. Investing in hometown Democratic politics felt meaningful and rewarding on many levels. Yet, with unconstitutionally gerrymandered districts still in place in the mountains heading into the 2018 election, I struggled with the question of where to focus my energy. Then came Chloe.

When Chloe told me that she was running for state representative in 2018, I thought it was a little absurd. She was a twenty-five-year-old progressive candidate in a staunchly conservative district that had voted Republican by an average of 16 percentage points over the preceding three elections. It is also the most rural county in Maine and the oldest (by age) in the country. I had a strong enough grasp on basic math to know that electing a Democrat in District 88 was improbable at best. Plus, neither of us had ever run our own campaign before. Yet I could tell that she had made up her mind, and I knew that there is no turning back once Chloe commits to something.

At the same moment, I had received an offer to manage a high-profile State Senate campaign in North Carolina with much higher odds of success—and get paid well to do so. I struggled with which path to take: the leap of faith in Chloe's town of Nobleboro, Maine, or the more straightforward path in North Carolina. I agonized for days over the decision but finally decided to land in Nobleboro. I kept coming back to the immortal words of Maimonides so often quoted by our Harvard mentor, Marshall Ganz: "Hope is belief in the plausibility of the possible, as opposed to the necessity of the probable." I told Chloe that I believed it was possible. By March, I had uprooted from the mountains of my North Carolina home and moved to Lincoln County, Maine, to build the campaign with her.

CHLOE

I was on break one night in 2018 during a shift at the brewery where I worked near my home in Maine. I had texted Canyon a week before, telling him that I was moving back to Nobleboro (population 1,600) to run for state representative. I asked him if he would move there with me, manage the campaign, and help me create a new vision for rural progressive politics. On that fateful night, after days of reflecting, Canyon texted back: "I'm in."

Growing up in rural Maine, I cannot remember politics being an issue. At least not one that we talked much about. If I shared the same politics with someone, we might chat about that. If we had different politics, we would be respectful of each other's perspectives. Almost all the people who raised me are Republicans. There's Uncle Dick, my honorary uncle who came to all my birthday parties and taught me how to ride a lawn-mower. Bruce, a die-hard Republican, taught me how to shoot guns. Dr. Olson, or "Awesome" as we called him, taught me how to ride a snow-mobile. This place has always had my heart. I have always known that I would live here and use my existence to fight for my home.

This gut feeling was first put to the test when I was twelve years old and learned about a proposal for a massive development in the beautiful North Woods. Led by Plum Creek, one of the largest development corpo-rations in the country at the time, this project would disrupt the largest tract of undeveloped woods east of the Mississippi River. It was a bad deal for Maine. I could see the need for economic development in Maine's ru-ral places, but did we have to destroy the land to do that? I connected with advocacy organizations and started to testify at public hearings, write letters to local papers, and do whatever I could to get engaged.

Next, I started the Climate Action Club (CAC) while I was in high school to provide opportunities for students, faculty, and community members to get involved with environmental and climate change work. We were the first student-run club at my school. To reduce plastic pol-lution, we worked with local businesses to sponsor a community-wide reusable bag that featured businesses' logos and was for sale at stores across town. The CAC tapped into national networks of youth organiz-ing and started to win grants for projects. We eventually won $5,000 in a national competition to put solar panels on our school—the first time a school in Maine got solar panels without government support. Word of our work spread, and we were featured on the Sundance Channel in one of their docuseries.

My work with the CAC was transformative. It was in meetings with those students, in the halls of that school, in my rural town that I learned the power of a small group of young people to do something good. It also showed me the power and potential of work that is rooted in community.

Next stop was Harvard. I knew that I wanted to study climate change and activism. Two critical things happened during my freshman year. First, I met Canyon Woodward. Tall, blond, skinny, and known for his charisma, Canyon was an icon of our class. Our friendship blossomed through activism, but we quickly found camaraderie in our love for our rural hometowns, our desire to return to them, and our motivation to fight for where we grew up.

The other turning point was when I learned about a plan to pump tar sands through a defunct pipeline that crossed through Maine. It ran within hundreds of feet of Sebago Lake, the drinking water source for 20 percent of Maine's population. The line ended in Casco Bay, a huge port, fishery, and economic center. The pipeline is nominally owned by the Portland Pipeline Company, which sounds like a nice local company but is 76 percent owned by ExxonMobil. Blame it on naïveté and growing up in a tiny, safe, rural town, but I had no idea that a corporation like Exxon-Mobil had roots in Maine. This project opened my eyes to the coercive power of the fossil fuel industry. In one big flash, I began to realize that deeper strategies were needed to confront the hidden, manipulative, and threatening behaviors of fossil fuel corporations.

The summer after my first year at Harvard, I interned with the Maine Sierra Club to stop the pipeline. Then 350.org founder Bill McKibben wrote an article for *Rolling Stone* titled "Global Warming's Terrifying New Math," in which he alluded to a new tactic to confront the fossil fuel industry: divestment. I went back to Harvard that fall to cofound Divest Harvard alongside Alli Welton and Eva Roben. It was my way of fighting for Maine even though I was in Massachusetts.

Harvard's endowment is around $53 billion, with very little ethical screening. Any pot of money that big needs to be held accountable in some way. If Harvard divested from fossil fuels, that would send a huge signal to the world that the fossil fuel industry's destructive actions would no longer be condoned. (Harvard actually did divest just a few days before we finalized this book! On September 9, 2021—about nine years to the day that Divest Harvard was born—Harvard University announced that its endowment would no longer invest in fossil fuels.) I also saw that almost everyone is part of an institution that has some means of participating in a call for fossil fuel divestment—whether a school or religious endowment or a city or state pension fund. What compelled me most about the divestment movement was the theory of change that drove it. Getting schools, churches, states, cities, and individuals to divest from fossil fuels sent a loud message that the people no longer wanted to associate with the fossil fuel industry. The idea was that politicians would take note, stop taking money from these corporations, and start listening to the people. And if politicians listened to the people more than corporations, maybe we could pass meaningful climate legislation at the national level. As a Harvard student, I could think of no better way to spend my time.

During our junior year, Canyon and I found ourselves co-coordinating Divest Harvard. Our friendship was forged in the fires of campus activism and grew from there as we began to talk more deeply about politics. But we knew that it would take a host of new strategies and tactics to engage our rural hometowns in the climate fight. Neither of us had grown up attending big marches or rallies. They were always far away from our homes, and the thought of being in a big noisy crowd just didn't jibe with where we came from. We didn't know how exactly, but we knew that a climate movement in rural America needed to look different from what we were seeing at Harvard.

We also noticed the huge gaps between movement power and electoral results. In 2013, thirty-five thousand marched in Washington, DC, to protest the Keystone XL pipeline. In 2014, three hundred thousand people flooded the streets of New York for the People's Climate March. It seemed like the momentum was growing so quickly. But in 2014, there was another big red wave that led to a Senate Republican majority and more Republican victories in state legislatures across the country, widening a gap between people power in the streets and electoral politics. This gap had emerged slowly, over decades. But during those years, global warming had become a climate catastrophe. We could no longer afford a politically ineffective climate movement.

The day after I graduated from Harvard in 2015, I packed my stuff into my dad's truck and drove home to Nobleboro. I wanted to build my life in Maine and understand how to build a new kind of political power that could translate all that good movement energy into real political power. I became a fellow for *The Nation*, where I explored this topic in my writing. I supported myself with jobs at bars and restaurants while interning in Bernie Sanders's 2016 campaign and later volunteering on Hillary Clinton's campaign. In 2017, I was an organizer for a progressive mayoral candidate in the city of Lewiston, Maine. Although I learned so much about political organizing from these campaigns, I knew deep down that the strategies that I was seeing would not resonate in my rural hometown. Something was still missing even though I couldn't quite put my finger on it.

In February 2018, I visited Canyon in North Carolina. As always, politics filled our conversations. We reflected on the 2016 presidential election and how the rural vote was responsible for the election of Donald Trump. We saw a deep need to prioritize rural America and build long-lasting political power, to root young people in their rural hometowns, and to create political campaigns filled with community, hope, and inspiration instead of divisiveness, exhaustion, and monotony.

When I came back to Maine, I knew it was time to run for office. I had always imagined running when I was in my thirties. I thought that I needed a couple of graduate degrees, a settled life, and maybe a family to welcome me home. But in 2018, I realized that there was no need to wait. There was no time to wait. Two weeks after my visit with Canyon, I filed to run.

THIS BOOK

This book is rooted in our firsthand experiences campaigning in rural red America, the same districts that Democrats have abandoned and that contributed to Donald Trump's victory. But we're not just going to criticize or mourn past failures. The issues of our age are too urgent. This book is about paving a new way forward for long-lasting political power. We're going to share success stories and real-world lessons that we can all use in our communities to launch a dirt road revival that fights for people and planet.

We read every book and article that we could to substantiate our observations and give you the best sense of what is happening in rural towns across the country. There is more complexity to it than we could fit in the pages of this book. We are neither historians nor academics, and we don't profess to have all the answers. Who are we? We are two young people who grew up in rural America. The rural-urban divide is something that we understood intuitively as rural kids who went on to college in the city. We lived the consequences of Democrats leaving our communities in the dust, and so we set out to cut a new path for progressive politics in rural America. This book is our way of sharing that path with you.

A couple of quick housekeeping notes before we begin. We critique the Democratic Party quite a bit in this book.[1] As we navigate the most important decade of this young century, we see the Democrats as our best hope for progressive political power. For us, party *is* values. We are Democrats because of our values of equal access and opportunity. But right now, the party is not translating those values into a rural context, leaving our hometowns behind.

You'll also notice that we frequently talk about our deep, meaningful, inspiring relationships with Republicans even though we recognize the toxic bankruptcy of the Republican Party. This distinction is key to everything that we do. We will never write off individual Republicans even though we recognize that the Republican Party has coalesced around the deeply antidemocratic principles of minority rule and autocracy that present a grave threat to our collective future. In personal conversations with folks in our community, we discovered an enormous space of shared values, respect, mutual disagreement, and willingness to listen. We've built common ground and real relationships from these conversations. While the Republican Party will not fight for people and planet, there are many Republicans in our community who do and will. In our view, this is the living proof that Democrats must build bigger broader movements that welcome rural voters, including those who do not appear progressive in traditional ways.

Lastly, aside from our personal introductions in this chapter, we write in the first-person plural, using "we" to share our experiences and the third-person singular when referring to just one of our perspectives. This is intentional. The book is coauthored, and our work is truly an equal partnership. Our singular voices cannot capture the riveting reality of our collaboration and campaigns. These grammatical choices are intended to convey both the facts and the spirit of our shared work.

Hope exists only in the shadow of uncertainty. As 2016 made clear, we can never be sure about the outcomes when we undertake political work. Our charge is to embrace the unknown, lean into self-doubt, and dive in without having all the answers. We know that we won't win every time. There will always be setbacks and temporary defeats that are hard to swallow. But the difficult work of bringing people together to organize and strive for a better world is valuable in and of itself. Transformative change is not the work of an election cycle or two. It is a constant striving over years and decades that falls to each generation. Right now, hope lies down the beautiful, uncertain, and sometimes harsh dirt roads. This journey, like all great journeys, begins with taking the first step.

PART I

TAKE A BACK ROAD

*Rural America and the
Democratic Party*

CHAPTER 1

DOWN THE DIRT ROAD

What's Up with Rural America?

Rural America decisively entered center stage of US politics as the majority of the country scrambled for answers in the aftermath of the 2016 election that thrust Donald Trump to power. One need only take a cursory look at a map of the results to see the great divide that carried Trump to the White House: Hillary Clinton won almost every urban center as Trump swept the vast stretches of less populated country in between. The greatest support for Donald Trump came from small rural towns like our own.[1] Exit polling revealed that Trump won nearly two-thirds of the rural vote, while losing by a similar margin in cities and evenly splitting the suburban vote.

What's more, millions more people cast their ballots for Democrats than for Republicans in 2016. Republicans did not win a majority of votes for president or for Senate. Nevertheless, the GOP managed to emerge from the election with control of the White House and both chambers of Congress.

A hundred years ago, winning by large margins in rural America also would clinch the national vote in a landslide. Why? Because a majority of the population was still rural. When our democratic and electoral systems were created, over 95 percent of people lived in a rural community. Since then, the percentage of the US population living in rural areas has slowly but surely plummeted, hitting 55 percent a hundred years ago and falling below 20 percent today.[2] This seismic demographic shift has thrown the balance of power in our country wildly askew, as our electoral system has failed to evolve to reflect the geographical shifts in our population. The consequence of this imbalance is that each rural voter has—by several magnitudes of power—more influence over the presidency and the composition of our state and federal legislative bodies than their non-rural counterparts.

Trump rose to power, with a two-to-one margin in rural areas that was insufficient to win the popular vote, because of the all-important Electoral College. With his shocking victory came renewed scrutiny of our antiquated electoral system and the disproportionate power that rural America continues to wield in it. Although Democratic presidential candidates won the popular vote in seven out of the past eight elections dating back to 1988, Republican candidates have been elected by the Electoral College in three of them.

As a result of these minority presidential victories, the same unrepresentative imbalance of power has become firmly enshrined in our federal judiciary. Most notably, conservative presidents who have failed to win the majority vote have gone on to appoint five of nine of our sitting US Supreme Court justices.[3] The federal bench was also loaded with ultra-conservative justices by Trump due to the unprecedented refusal of Mitch McConnell's Senate to confirm many of Obama's appointees. This left 103 federal court vacancies for Trump to fill—the most in a generation.[4] We will be dealing with the repercussions for decades to come.

Worthwhile efforts to correct the structural imbalance of power between rural and urban voters have gained modest ground since the 2000 presidential election, when Al Gore won the popular vote but lost the Electoral College. A huge majority of citizens, steadily hovering around 60 percent since 2000, believe that the Electoral College should be replaced via a constitutional amendment to implement a national popular vote system.[5] Despite this popular support, such a constitutional amendment is a nonstarter in Congress. It would require support from the GOP, which derives much of its power from this unequal system. Individual efforts across the country are yielding some progress in getting states to join an interstate compact, which would allocate states' electoral votes to the candidate who wins the national popular vote. This too is unlikely to reach the critical mass of states necessary to go into effect until Democrats are able to rebuild legislative majorities in rural states.

A brief survey of the composition of the US Senate and state legislatures, as well as the history of the national popular vote, paints a stark picture of rural America's outsized influence in the electoral systems that we have in place. Today, the ten most populous states in the union are home to one half of the US population, but their cumulative twenty senators make up only one-fifth of the US Senate. Meanwhile, the other half of the population, spread out through forty smaller states, elects eighty senators. Let that sink in. One half of the country gets four times the number of US senators per person than the other half. Former US labor secretary Robert Reich points to the problem when a state like California, for example, with forty million people, has an equal number of senators to one like Wyoming, with 579,000.[6] Because so many senators are elected by less populous states, Democrats must be able to compete in rural areas to maintain political power.

State legislatures and the US House of Representatives are—at least on their surface—designed to better reflect the changing population patterns of their states with more proportional representation. Yet partisan gerrymandering by Republican-controlled state legislatures has yielded a similar imbalance between rural and urban voting power. The result is that many states that elect Democratic candidates to statewide office send overwhelmingly Republican delegations to the US House and have legislatures with Republican majorities or supermajorities. "This helps explain why Republicans have controlled the Pennsylvania State Senate for nearly four decades, despite losing statewide votes about half that time," writes Emily Badger for the *New York Times*. "It explains why Republicans are routinely overrepresented in state legislatures, even in blue states like New York. It explains why Hillary Clinton carried only three of eight congressional districts in Minnesota—districts drawn by a panel of judges—even as she won the whole state."[7]

Jonathan Rodden lays out some more glaring examples of rural America's political influence in his book *Why Cities Lose: The Deep Roots of the Urban-Rural Politics Divide*. "In 2012, for instance, the Democrats received around 54 percent of the total votes cast in elections for both state legislative chambers in Michigan, but they came away with only 46 percent of the seats in the Michigan House of Representatives, and 42 percent of the seats in the state senate." This example is duplicated in many other states, including Michigan, Wisconsin, Minnesota, Missouri, Ohio, Wisconsin, and Pennsylvania.[8] Democrats routinely leave rural votes on the table while running up huge margins in the most densely populated parts of states. The result is that Democrats simply do not win as many seats as they ought to, given their popular support.

This leaves us with a simple truth. For everyone's sake, Democrats must reckon with the significant disadvantage of a geographically consolidated base and recognize the profound influence of rural voters. This reality continues to be a tough pill to swallow for Democrats. Many argue that the party should spend less time and resources on rural voters in favor of investing even more in urban and suburban voters. "For Democrats still traumatized by Trump's victory, it's a vexing question," reports Holly Bailey for the *Washington Post*.[9] "For a big faction of the party, [pursuing rural votes] is crazy. Rather than tie themselves in knots chasing a deeply conservative electorate that loves guns, opposes abortion and is firmly in the GOP camp, Democrats need to focus on driving up enthusiasm among people who share their values, this group says."

For years, mainstream Democratic strategists have promulgated a mindset in the party of abandoning rural America to focus on more densely populated areas. In the lead-up to the 2016 election, Chuck Schumer proclaimed: "For every blue-collar Democrat we lose in western Pennsylvania, we will pick up two moderate Republicans in the suburbs in Philadelphia, and you can repeat that in Ohio and Illinois and Wisconsin."[10] This mindset has become ingrained in the strategic thinking of the party establishment. It is reflected in the common refrain that "demography is destiny," referring to the misguided belief that any year now the swelling suburbs and urban centers will hit a tipping point enabling Democrats to overcome the lopsided votes from our declining rural communities. Even the 2020 election barely moved the needle. Trump maintained his wide margin of victory in rural areas overall. As political commentator Ezra Klein noted in the *New York Times*, "In 2020, Trump lost by about seven million votes, but if about 40,000 votes had switched in key states, he would have won anyway."[11]

All of this is to say that our democracy is a relic of the time in which it was created. It rewards the party that can capture voters spread out over large geographic areas. If the Republican Party has these voters locked down, the Democrats will continue to fight on uneven terrain. We are no longer an agrarian society with the geographically diffuse population that our electoral system was designed to represent. But these are the rules of the game, and Democrats are at a distinct disadvantage.

Beyond the strategic imperative of reconnecting with rural America to win elections, there is something deeper. We need the perspectives of rural people to help inform in our policymaking. Rural organizer and author Jane Kleeb points toward this in her book *Harvest the Vote: How Democrats Can Win Again in Rural America*: "The Democratic Party needs rural voters because they are part of the American fabric; they can contribute ideas and solutions that will help us confront the many issues facing our country today."[12]

We couldn't agree more. Think about this: As we navigate a world transformed by climate change, whose voices do we want animating our response to climate change? Those of Tesla-driving Silicon Valley technocrats and wealthy suburbanites? They can only take the conversation so far. We need the wisdom of rural folks in those discussions—the rooted wisdom of those who grow our food, who live every day in the natural world, who are profoundly more connected to the land. As extreme wealth inequality pushes our society toward its breaking point, are wealthy suburbanites the political bloc over which the Democratic Party should be obsessing?

The perspectives and lived experiences of working-class rural people are much more likely to bring the political scales back into balance than are those of the suburban and urban elite. Wealthy establishment Democrats have bought so many seats at the policy table that they have begun to think that the table belongs to them. As we enter the most important decade of this young century, Democrats must reckon with the consequences—electoral and societal—of abandoning rural America. It's time to do the deep work of rebuilding trust on the dirt roads.

THE LAY OF THE LAND

Although it may not feel like it, there was a time—not long ago—when neither party had a meaningful advantage over the other in rural America. Something of a rural-urban divide stretches back decades in the sense that urban voters have long aligned with Democrats, but the Republican Party's advantage among rural voters only materialized in the second decade of the twenty-first century, according to Pew Research.[13] Although Democratic presidential candidates have chronically underperformed, survey data from Pew shows that, from 1999 to 2009, rural voters were evenly divided in their partisan leanings such that neither party held a material advantage. Democrats lost their competitive foothold in rural America in a remarkably short stretch of time at the close of the 2000s and suffered the significant political consequences throughout the 2010s.

After the election in 2000, there was much ado over the starkly divided electoral map. It revealed Al Gore's dismal under-performance among rural Americans, who, just a year prior, were evenly divided in their partisanship, with 45 percent leaning Democrat and 44 percent leaning Republican.[14] Rural Americans voted overwhelmingly for George W.

Bush in 2000 and once more in 2004. By 2008, many had grown weary of the Republican agenda that was not serving them.[15] While Barack Obama continued the tradition of Democratic presidential candidates underperforming based on the even partisan split of rural voters at the time, he won a greater share of the rural vote in 2008 than either John Kerry in 2004 or Al Gore in 2000.[16] Obama's rural vote haul in 2008 was almost 50 percent greater than the tiny share that Hillary Clinton won in 2016 and that Biden won in 2020. [17]

It was over the course of Obama's presidency that Democrats ceded an unprecedented amount of power in rural America. In 2010, Republicans opened up a statistically significant advantage in partisan preference among rural voters for the first time, while flipping US Senate seats in North Dakota, Arkansas, Wisconsin, Illinois, Pennsylvania, and Indiana. By the end of Obama's second term, Republicans had widened that budding rural advantage to 16 points.[18] During those years they flipped a slew of crucial US Senate seats in Nebraska, Montana, Colorado, Louisiana, North Carolina, Alaska, South Dakota, Iowa, Arkansas, and West Virginia.

Bad as the losses were at the federal level, nowhere was the growing rural divide more visible and devastating than in the results of state legislative races across the country. Over the course of Obama's eight years in office, Republicans flipped an astounding 965 state legislative seats, while Democrats flipped only 15. A shift of this magnitude in legislative seats had not occurred since World War II.[19] As Republicans took hold, unprecedented gerrymandering, relaxed environmental regulations, voter-ID laws disenfranchising citizens, decreased funding for public schools, climate denial, rejection of Medicaid expansion, and other items on the powerful American Legislative Exchange Council wish list swept the nation.

The vast majority of the Republican gains that enabled this shift were in rural areas.[20] The GOP's ascendance in rural America over this period is also starkly reflected in county-level statistics. By 2016, Republicans had increased their vote share in an overwhelming majority of counties compared to before Obama was president. In the 2016 election, Republicans continued to see a decreased vote share in over 80 percent of the 137 large urban counties compared to 2004. However, Republicans won a greater share of the vote in all but a tenth of the remaining 1,501 smaller counties that stretch across most of the country.[21]

Following the 2016 election, data showed a clear trend of rural people voting more Republican over the 2012 and 2016 presidential elections, with smaller population size and larger distance from cities correlating with increasing likelihood to vote Republican.[22] In 2016, the GOP increased its rural advantage in the presidential election by 20 percentage points over the high-water mark for Democrats set by Obama in 2008.[23] This trend flattened out in 2020, with Trump maintaining large margins in rural America but only increasing his overall margin of victory by 0.4 percent in rural areas.[24] Notably, even while losing the rural vote, Biden won a slightly higher percentage than Clinton did in 2016 in a number of crucial battleground states, including Georgia, Arizona, Michigan, and Wisconsin.[25]

Liberal pundits have long pointed to the Democratic Party's nomination of Obama in 2008 as the turning point for rural voters they insinuate—or state outright—abandoned the party because they are racist. But this is not the whole story. The racism of rural America is a complex and critical issue. We are not academics who study it, though we have seen its violence in our communities. Certainly racism, fueled vigorously by right-wing media personalities and conservative activist groups, had an outsized impact on our politics and society during the Obama years. Our point is simply that the nomination of Obama alone is not what drove rural voters from the party, as evidenced by the fact that he won a greater share of the rural vote than any other Democratic nominee since the twentieth century.

So what is happening in rural America? To understand the political leanings of rural voters, we first have to understand the on-the-ground reality. In rural America, there is deep struggle. The people who live here are mostly working class and aging, a mix of teachers, farmers, factory workers, health professionals, meat processors, miners, fishers, service and retail workers, retirees, tourism-dependent workers, and small-business owners. Strong threads of independence and interdependence form the thick fabric of these communities. Folks are divided politically but share an overwhelming frustration and disillusionment with a politics that has failed to support their basic needs.

Rural Americans, like so many, cannot rely on any of the conditions that might allow a decent or flourishing life: good jobs, affordable healthcare, a healthy planet for current and future generations, strong public schools for our kids, debt-free college educations, the right to age at home, basic transportation, high-speed internet, secure retirement, and a living wage. The rising cost of healthcare in rural communities is overwhelming. Rural hospitals have been closing across the country, leading to nearly a 6 percent mortality increase.[26] Small-town schools and colleges suffer from a dire lack of funding, putting the pressure on property taxpayers to make up the difference.[27] Farms, once the hallmark and foundation of rural communities, are in peril. While there were nearly seven million farms in the United States less than a hundred years ago, today there are only two million.[28] According to the Center for American Progress, in 2019 the projected farm income was in the bottom quartile of all of the years since 1929.[29] Almost 60 percent of rural Americans see lack of broadband access as a problem in their community, as many parts of the country lack internet access and cell coverage.[30] A devastating opioid crisis is filling the void in many parts of these left-behind communities.

Driven by the loss of jobs and empowerment, middle-aged white people without four-year college degrees are dying of drugs, alcohol, and suicide at unprecedented rates—what economists Anne Case and Angus Deaton have termed "deaths of despair."[31] In addition to purely economic factors, Case and Deaton argue that these deaths are driven by a related—yet distinct—"decline of family, community, and religion." As these communities struggle, inhabitants lose hope for their future prospects. Too many fall into patterns of addiction that further deteriorate their own health and the health of the community.

Drawing on a recent report by the Brookings Institution's Hamilton Project, the *New York Times* reported that "the fifth of the American population living in counties with the highest share of rural population suffer the lowest levels of vitality—by a long shot. Americans in these low-vitality counties are far more likely to live in poverty, suffer health problems, die early and lack a job."[32] Those who choose to build their lives here face overwhelming challenges, and those who leave rarely return.

Although the population of rural America is not declining in absolute terms, it is shrinking as a percentage of the overall composition of the country. Unlike urban areas, which benefit from high rates of immigration, most of the rural growth is simply due to births replenishing the population. According to a 2018 Pew study, the meager growth of rural counties after 2000 fell to 3 percent, less than half of their 8 percent growth rate in the 1990s. Meanwhile, urban and suburban counties have been on an upward trajectory, with growth rates increasing to more than 13 percent since 2000.[33]

Rural America is getting older and older.[34] For example, Maine has the second-highest percentage in the country of seniors living in rural towns. In addition to being the most rural state in the US, it is also the oldest state (by age) in the country.[35] Nowhere is that more evident than in Lincoln County, where our two campaigns were based, where the median age today is over thirteen years older than it was in 1990.[36]

Most of the people living in rural America have been there for a long time. In fact, 80 percent of rural residents were raised in a small town or rural area (though not necessarily the one in which they currently live).[37] The median age of rural adults, fifty-one, is six years older than that of their urban counterparts.[38] According to writer and sociologist Robert Wuthnow, who has spent decades studying rural America and conducting countless interviews in small towns across the country, people born in rural places are much more likely to remain in their home state than those in urban places.[39] Many of the folks who do leave are young adults who head off to college and never return.

This "brain drain," as sociologists Patrick J. Carr and Maria J. Kefalas write in *Hollowing Out the Middle: The Rural Brain Drain and What It Means for America*, has played a big role in these demographic shifts.[40] Bright, motivated young people who leave their small towns to attend college too often choose not to return to rural America. As more and more students have taken this path, their hometowns have suffered from a dearth of young leadership and innovation. Rodden lays out some of the data behind the brain drain in *Why Cities Lose*. "In the 1970s, county-level rates of college graduation were only weakly correlated with population density," he writes. "The share of college graduates in the population has grown everywhere over the subsequent forty years, but the growth has been far stronger in metropolitan counties. The gap between rural and metropolitan counties was around 10 percentage points in 1970, but by 2010, it had grown to over 20 percentage points. Far more than in the past, college graduates are now clustered in city centers, suburbs, and college towns."[41]

This tracks with the partisan education divide that has opened up over the past decade, one of the biggest political shifts we've seen in recent years. White voters with only a high school education have moved to the GOP, according to Pew: "White voters who do not have a four-year degree now constitute just a third of Democratic voters, down from 56% two decades ago. By contrast, non-college white voters continue to make up a majority of Republican and Republican-leaning registered voters (59% now [2018], 66% in 1997)."[42] What is going on with this non-college-educated voting bloc? The short answer is that, like rural America in general, they have been left behind by today's economy. Whereas throughout much of the twentieth century a non-college-educated rural worker could reasonably expect to find a good job that paid well enough for an entire family to get by, that is no longer the case. So many of the good jobs in rural America dried up as Big Agriculture and free trade undercut small farmers and manufacturing jobs were shipped overseas in the neoliberal economy.

Prosperity generated by America's recovery from the Great Recession of 2007–2009, overseen by a Democratic administration, was concentrated in the knowledge economy of our big cities that left Main Street reeling. These cities have accounted for 72 percent of employment growth in the United States since the financial crisis, according to a study by the Brookings Institution.[43] Rural areas, on the other hand, have stagnated, with employment levels remaining lower than they were before the recession in many rural communities. All of a sudden, if you didn't have a college degree, you were shuck out of luck as your options started to look more and more like Dollar General, Walmart, or McDonald's. All the while, Democrats, siloed in cities that were reaping the rewards of neoliberalism and an economic recovery that privileged Wall Street and big corporations, promised to deliver more of the same—seemingly oblivious to the struggles of rural workers and people without a degree.

So in rural communities across America, young people left to find education, jobs, and opportunity, leaving behind aging workforces and communities.[44] And the youth who stay around too often find themselves in a hopeless reality. "Drugs and crime that resulted from drugs were an outlet for people in their communities who felt they were stuck and going nowhere," writes Wuthnow. "I think a lot of it has to do with the hopelessness and the lack of opportunities young people feel here in this community," said a rural resident he interviewed in a southern community of eleven thousand that is 90 percent Black.[45] Tara Westover, author of the memoir *Educated*, points to the effects of this inertia that has settled into the psyche of struggling rural communities. "There are places in the United States where the recession never ended," she writes. "For them, it has been 2009 for 10 years. That does something to people, psychologically."[46]

Evangelical and fundamentalist Christianity unquestionably play a large role in the life of rural communities, as faith is a primary source of community and hope for so many. While Democrats enjoy the support of 68 percent of religiously unaffiliated voters, the GOP's popularity among white evangelical Protestants continues to grow, with 77 percent of these voters identifying or leaning Republican.[47] The church has long been a cornerstone of rural living. Despite the worries of aging congregations, it continues to have great influence today. Wuthnow describes Christianity's presence as such: "Faith wasn't a quick fix for their family's finances or the town's economy. An outsider would probably say its role was mostly therapeutic. It kept them from being as depressed as they would have been otherwise. When times were tough, it helped them take a longer-term perspective, sometimes steeling their resolve to stick with what they were doing. I came away thinking, too, that faith was perhaps more meaningful in small towns because few other options were available."[48]

Something that has all too often been missed is how much religion and the sense of shared values and smallness define the feeling of home and way of life for many people in rural communities. "Understanding rural America requires seeing the places in which its residents live as *moral communities*," argues Wuthnow. "I do not mean this in the vernacular sense of 'moral' as good, right, virtuous, or principled. I mean it rather in the more specialized sense of a place to which and in which people feel an obligation to one another and to uphold the local ways of being that govern their expectations about ordinary life and support their feelings of being at home and doing the right things."[49] In this sense, "small-town life" is people's experience of a culture that feels familiar to them, centered in shared values and community.

When we understand the extent to which rural voters' identity and sense of home is wrapped up in their experience of rural America as a way of life, it is much easier to understand how values-based voting is in their self-interest. Their way of life is significantly defined by being part of this "moral community" that is central to the values framework from which so many rural people act—itself often wrapped up deeply in religion. Rural Americans feel a fierce loyalty toward their communities and their way of life, with 94 percent saying that "small-town ways of life are worth fighting for."[50]

LEAVING RURAL AMERICA BEHIND

Intentionally or not, liberal academics and mainstream Democrats have talked down to rural Republican voters for years, telling them that their ignorance leads them to vote against their own self-interest. It's a counterproductive, condescending story that only serves to demonstrate how out of touch Democrats are with rural communities. The reality is that government has failed rural economies. When folks struggle, they turn to their communities to fill the void left by a politics of exclusion. It is not uncommon for people to find work or have medical bills paid by fundraising through the social network of their church and tight-knit community.

If Democrats had been more effective at turning campaign promises into policy, it would be easier to follow the argument that rural people who vote Republican are going against their economic self-interest.

But the truth is that both parties have failed to successfully address the economic woes of rural America. Bill Clinton's neoliberal policies of the 1990s decimated rural jobs in a way that is still felt today, and rural America fared worse under Obama than any other part of the country.

Political scientist Angie Maxwell says that, for rural people, "no matter what the government does it doesn't feel like it gets better. For some of those who are lowest income, in rural areas where there is not opportunity, they don't see [the government] changing that much in their life. So they become 'rational identity voters.'"[51] As people understandably lost faith in either party to directly improve their economic situation, the cultural and religious side of the equation gained greater prominence.

By 2016, it was clear that the economic recovery had failed rural America, as the populations of small towns found themselves trailing the populations of every other part of the country by every measure of economic well-being. As poor rural people's struggles grew ever greater over the past decade, they watched helplessly as more and more power and wealth were consolidated in the cities, the domain of Democrats who were reaping the urban-centric and techno-centric rewards of the economic recovery. Democrats bailed out Wall Street, padded the pockets of suburban elites, focused on identity politics that did little materially for the acute suffering of BIPOC communities, and failed to relieve the struggles of marginalized rural Americans who fell further and further behind. In some cases, this was due more to Republicans' intransigence than to Democrats' policies. Medicaid expansion powerfully illustrates this, as 72 percent of all rural hospital closures were in the states where Republicans blocked Medicaid expansion.[52] But policy details such as these are not a part of most people's consciousness, and for many struggling people it boiled down to the simple fact that the economic recovery overseen by the Obama administration failed to reach rural communities.

As we will detail in the next chapter, Democratic leaders were largely nowhere to be seen in rural America. They were not listening. They were not cultivating relationships of trust. They were not telling a story that spoke to the sharp pain of the struggling rural poor. James Davison Hunter, author of *Culture Wars*, observes that when Democrats spoke about the downtrodden, it was usually "in terms of race and ethnicity, immigration and the like . . . not about the poor, per se."[53] A void opened. Into this newly uncontested battlefield rushed right-wing activist groups and media personalities.

Republicans successfully sowed a divisive narrative of out-of-touch liberal elites waging a war on religion and small-town traditions and positioned themselves to win over voters whose churches and communities served as their final safety net. Tea Party and Rush Limbaugh messaging found a ready foothold in rural America, drumming up acrimony over the idea that small-town taxes were being used to bail out the rest of the economy as rural America was left behind. Although policies that created problems for rural America date back well into the twentieth century, it is clear that not enough was done to help rural people in the wake of the Great Recession. Fear was cultivated. Festering anger was inflamed.

And then Trump stormed onto the scene. In this context, he seized the attention of the nation by trading the dog-whistle for the megaphone, channeling these powerful emotions into stories of xenophobia that heaped blame onto immigrants and people of color—particularly Latino, Asian American, Muslim, and Black people. The roots of racist rhetoric run deep in the Republican Party, and Trump was ready to draw it all to the surface. Angie Maxwell illustrates how the groundwork for Trump's style of racism was subtly laid for years: "[Republicans] really adapted their coded racial language to fit the moment, which in the '80s became a pitch towards color blindness. Doesn't sound like a bad thing, but it's really a denial of structural racism. And then into fiscal conservatism, but not on everything—just on social programs that were aimed at leveling the racial playing field, so to speak, or welfare reform issues."[54]

Trump's message to rural white voters "forgotten no more" struck a deep chord, built on the dishonest racist narrative that the government disproportionately looks after people of color. He conjured images of rusting factories and boarded up Main Streets and spoke directly to people's painful discontent. "Trump turned to the old but effective strategy of lifting them up by pushing down others," observes Jon Tester, Democratic senator from Montana, "by stirring up race-based fears and by giving angry and scared white voters permission to distrust other religions, other cultures, and other people."[55] The unapologetic stirring up of racial resentments was clearly one driver of Trump's success in turning out rural voters who had previously been checked out of the electoral process. "He speaks louder and clearer to people for whom the dog whistle wouldn't work because they didn't quite hear it or didn't know what it meant," explains Maxwell. "But when he says it explicitly, it can draw in whole other crowds."[56]

Meanwhile, establishment Democrats were ill-positioned to prevent this narrative takeover or demonstrate what—if any—understanding they had for the problems faced by rural America. As a result, even many voters who were turned off by much of Trump's message saw him as the candidate more willing to do the necessary work of confronting the establishment. Rural organizer Bill Hogseth captured this dynamic in rural Wisconsin, noting the many Trump voters "who were well aware of his shortcomings or admitted to disliking his leadership style, but who nonetheless believed he was willing to stand up to 'elitist' Democrats and fight for citizens like them."[57] These are the types of voters Maxwell is describing when she talks about "rational identity voters." They ask, "Who do I feel gets me? Who do I feel like would fight for me?" Maxwell says. "It's irrational only if we look at bottom line and pocketbook policy issues. It's not necessarily irrational if we look at identity values and political emotions."[58]

People were fed up with the brokenness of a political system controlled by a technocratic elite with whom they did not identify and that they viewed as far removed from their troubles. Rural America has understandably wanted to see change in DC for decades and has a long-standing simmering distrust and resentment of Washington. Some of it echoes the famous Reaganism that the scariest phrase in the English language is "I'm from the government, and I'm here to help." Many rural people feel like the government has not helped them and so badly misunderstands their situation that it would be best if it would just leave them alone.

This deeply ingrained frustration with Washington helps explain the phenomenon of so many counties across the country, including Lincoln County, Maine, that voted for Obama in 2008 and 2012 and then for Trump in 2016. Obama and Trump both ran as outsiders intent on bringing change to a broken, out-of-touch Washington. "This year, change isn't coming *from* Washington, it's coming *to* Washington" was Obama's passionate refrain in 2008. Trump echoed this at his own rallies, with promises to "drain the swamp." Their rhetoric spoke to the anger that so many rural people feel at a national politics that has left them behind. Bernie Sanders too earned widespread support in rural communities, speaking to their pain, challenging the establishment, and promising transformational change to create a system to serve everyone—not just Wall Street and the 1 percent.

Obama, Trump, and Sanders all spoke compellingly to the acute suffering of rural Americans. Each of them promised to confront the political establishment and shake things up in Washington. The stories they told were very different, of course. Obama, promising a rural initiatives package in his first one hundred days, told Iowans, "What's good for rural America will be good for America. The values that are represented . . . are values that built America, and we've got to preserve them."[59] Trump wove threads of nativism and nationalism to tell a brazenly dishonest and racist story that built on a long tradition of pitting poor whites against poor immigrants and people of color. Sanders rightly pinned the blame on greedy corporations and the ultrarich top one-tenth of 1 percent, earning the passionate support of rural working-class voters all across America who were fed up with the economic elite. "Sanders was a living symbol of what the Democrats used to stand for, and party leaders didn't seem to appreciate being reminded of how far they had strayed," writes Thomas Frank in *Listen, Liberal, or, Whatever Happened to the Party of the People?*[60]

Hillary Clinton and Joe Biden were ineffective in their limited attempts to connect with rural folk, running on platforms of keeping things more or less the same. Clinton proudly proclaimed that "America never stopped being great."[61] Biden assured wealthy donors that under his administration "nothing would fundamentally change."[62] Both were seen by most rural voters as symbols of the elite Washington political establishment through and through.

The reality is that rural America is struggling enormously and is not getting enough support to meet its ever-growing challenges. Amid a changing economy and changing culture, many rural people fear that what they perceive as their once stable, familiar, "small-town way of life" is slipping away, never to be found again. "People who feel their rural communities are threatened have few options for taking action that will make them feel stronger," argues Wuthnow. "The kind of action in their wheelhouse is listening faithfully to Rush Limbaugh and voting to shut down Planned Parenthood. It is invigorating to imagine kicking the government out of one's farm business and even more energizing to imagine draining the swamp in Washington."[63]

Much of what animates Republican voters in rural areas are cultural battles against "the establishment" or "urban elites." But the Democratic Party has not offered a persuasive case for how their policies can reverse the economic damage that rural America continues to experience every day. To rediscover rural America, Democrats need to take a close look at their own past.

CHAPTER 2

HOW DEMOCRATS LEFT RURAL AMERICA IN THE REARVIEW

Rural America is vast and complex. Its story unfolds over decades. This history holds the experiences of families, businesses, and communities that were left behind—like so many in the US—to struggle, to fend for themselves, to compete for scant resources. Republicans capitalized on the profound frustration of rural citizens, capturing state legislatures, but the destructive policies that they propagated then intensified the misery. The election of Donald Trump was also in large part due to rural voters' response to their abandonment by Democrats.

Nevertheless, the Democratic Party is best poised to rebuild the political power necessary to reunite our country, best poised to fight for equal access and opportunity. But first, Democrats must win back the trust of rural communities. Targeted and effective solutions depend on first understanding how we messed up. In this chapter, we'll walk through some of the ways that the Democratic Party has failed rural Americans.

When we refer to "the Democratic Party," we refer to a conglomeration of party organizations that support candidates and campaigns across the country. At the national level, there's the Democratic National Committee (DNC) as the overarching umbrella organization, along with the affiliated Democratic Senatorial Campaign Committee (DSCC), Democratic Congressional Campaign Committee, and Democratic Legislative Campaign Committee.[1] Then there are state Democratic Party organizations, which in turn have subunits to support state races, and county

Democratic groups to support local organizing. Sometimes in this book we focus on a certain party entity, but the pitfalls that we're about to lay out for you are seen across these organizations.

IGNORING RURAL PLACES

One of the Democrats' biggest downfalls at the state and national levels has been a relentless focus on densely populated places. This may seem like an obvious point, and we have noted it already, but it is crucial: this is the primary reason for rural voters' abandonment of the Democratic Party. The party's constituency and strategy focus are almost entirely urban and suburban. In 2018, two editors from the *Daily Yonder* said it well: "Democrats don't have a rural problem. They've got an everywhere-but-the-nation's-largest-cities problem. None of this is exactly new."[2]

The result is that campaigns focus on urban and, increasingly, suburban turnout with policies built for white, wealthy, educated communities. Democratic politicians mostly come from the cities. The party has left behind rural perspectives—both within its own organization and with its outward messaging. Lamenting the lack of understanding of rural lifestyles, one shrimper told Chloe in 2020 about Democrats: "They're just gonna win in the cities, and all the rural places are going to vote for Trump." How did the Democrats end up so focused on urban spaces? There are many books written on this issue. We are not political scientists, but we will summarize the key highlights here.

The dynamic began to emerge in the mid-twentieth century, as Jonathan Rodden describes in *Why Cities Lose*. During the New Deal era, demographics began to reflect a relationship between population density and Democratic leanings. The correlation became ingrained by the 1940s in northern cities.[3] People were moving en masse to urban areas for better jobs and more opportunities. They joined unions, fought for their rights, and became a political voting bloc that formed the foundation of the modern Democratic Party.

As the Democratic constituency became more solidly urban, the party's platform and identity came to reflect those interests. As we will dig into later, there are some politicians—like Senator Bernie Sanders and Senator Jon Tester—who have resonated with rural voters. But, for the most part, Democrats' platforms aren't warmly received in rural places.

As Democrats lost themselves to the city lights, rural communities felt left behind. This feeling not only motivated rural people to vote Republican but also created an anti-urban sentiment that was essentially synonymous with being anti-Democrat. For some rural voters, "urban" does equal people of color, and racism is embedded in their anti-Democratic views. For others, "urban" means wealthy educated folks in tall apartment buildings. Katherine Cramer explores this anger at being left out in her 2016 opus, *The Politics of Resentment: Rural Consciousness in Wisconsin and the Rise of Scott Walker.* She writes that "many rural residents exhibit an intense resentment against their urban counterparts." This phenomenon has become what Cramer calls a "rural consciousness," which is "an identity as a rural person that . . . includes a sense that decision makers routinely ignore rural places and fail to give rural communities their fair share of resources, as well as a sense that rural folks are fundamentally different from urbanites."[4]

Cramer, during her field research in Wisconsin, dug into why rural communities felt so resentful of the cities. These feelings mostly revolved around rural communities feeling judged or overlooked entirely. There were perceptions that "city dwellers thought they [rural people] were just 'a bunch of rednecks'" and "uneducated."[5] Cramer also writes about how some of her conversations revealed that rural communities "perceive that the decision making or the exercise of power in the major cities victimizes people in small towns." Politicians get together in the urban state capital, often sending mandates and laws back to small towns that create a perceived or real burden to the community. Sometimes what works best in a city isn't best for a rural town.

The on-the-ground impacts of the urban-rural divide and how they've led to a corresponding Democratic-Republican schism also play out on the pages of Ross Benes's *Rural Rebellion: How Nebraska Became a Republican Stronghold.* A young man who grew up in rural red Nebraska and then moved to liberal New York City, Benes has a unique perspective on how rural communities feel left behind by city folks and, on the flip side, how city dwellers don't understand rural realities. He talks a lot about what rural citizens feel about urban Democrats, saying: "One reason the Democratic Party, and the national press for that matter, have become such a toxic brand in rural America is because people in small towns are tired of being told by liberals in big cities that their views are outdated, their concerns invalid, and that they need to vote for Democrats if they know what is good for them."[6]

A huge consequence of this rural disconnect is that Democratic ideas and policies land badly in small-town communities like ours. For instance, Cramer considers school funding. Rural folks want more funding for their schools. But, since so much of the funding relies on property taxes, they are sensitive to state mandates or changes because "decisions about funding for schools mean that small communities are the victims of distributive injustice."[7] Rural communities are worried that the distribution of funds will disproportionately impact their taxes in unfair ways because city folks don't understand rural towns' financial struggles. The Democratic policy staple of education funding is therefore a loaded topic in rural communities.

Jane Kleeb showcases another example in *Harvest the Vote*. She writes about how the Green New Deal, although loaded with good stuff for rural communities, was not favorably received in rural America. Kleeb was in DC at a breakfast with the Nebraska congressional delegation (all Republicans) when the Green New Deal hit the news. She writes: "The headlines were not good for rural America. Jokes were flying around the city about banning hamburgers and farting cows. . . . I felt compelled to stand up and apologize . . . for the way Democrats had rolled out this policy."[8]

LOSING STATE LEGISLATURES

One of the immediate consequences of the Democrats abandoning rural America is that we have a really hard time gaining ground in state legislatures. Democratic leaders and donors tend to focus on national politics to win the presidential race, relying heavily on urban and suburban turnout. Rodden's *Why Cities Lose* opens with the harsh truth: "The Democrats' problem with votes and seats is even more pronounced in state legislatures."[9]

Democrats have an abysmal track record at the state level. In 1978, the Democrats controlled both chambers in thirty-one state legislatures.[10] In 2009, that number was twenty-seven. By 2017, Democrats controlled both chambers in only thirteen state legislatures.[11] In 2010, Democrats controlled at least one chamber in sixty state legislatures. By 2016, that number had dropped to thirty.[12] The 2016 elections led Republicans to control more state legislatures than at any other point in history.[13] As we mentioned earlier, this means that Democrats lost nearly *a thousand* seats in legislatures over the course of Obama's presidency, the largest loss since Eisenhower was in office, from 1953 to 1961.

There are many reasons for these shifts. For example, Ross Benes describes how Obama's choice to bail out the banking and automotive industries alienated rural communities. In *Rural Rebellion*, he writes, "'All Obama cares about are those big wigs in big cities,' I'd hear from townies at Husker Bar and on Fox News."[14] Matthew Yglesias in *Vox* reflected on this trend, noting that Democrats had moments of great success in the 2006 and 2008 cycles, quickly gaining legislative seats that they were also quick to lose.[15]

We want to home in on one key reason for this massive loss in state-level political power: Democrats' obsession with federal races. David Axelrod, the former senior Obama administration advisor, said it best in 2016: "I wonder, sometimes, whether the Democratic Party has contributed to [a decline in local politics] by making the president and the federal government the fulcrum of so much, and suggesting that we can solve these problems from the top down. . . . Democrats have ceded a lot of statehouses and legislatures."[16] The founders of Run for Something, an organization that supports down-ballot young progressives, reinforced this message four years later, warning that "many Democratic donors are failing to meaningfully invest in state and local elections. To them, defeating Trump is the only point of 2020. That myopic focus on winning the White House is a critical failure of the Democratic party's strategy."[17]

This exclusive emphasis on national races ends up prioritizing Democrats' base in urban centers. If more people live in cities than all the rural places, then you can win a lot of votes just by getting urban citizens to vote. Obama's two elections illustrate this point. In 2008, as reported in the *Daily Yonder*, "John McCain built a 5 million-vote advantage in 2,553 rural and exurban counties. Obama wiped out that margin in just ten urban counties."[18] In 2012, the *Washington Post* reported: "He won a second term by dominating the nation's large urban areas—although mostly by smaller margins compared to his 2008 vote totals."[19] Resources are therefore sent to squeeze every last vote out of an urban center to ensure that a state goes blue.

Rural communities and state legislative races are the collateral consequences of this national strategy. Neither are built into the Democrats' campaign calculus. The shock of 2016 was that the rural vote retaliated against the Democratic playbook with enough force to elect Donald Trump. It was then that we truly realized how urgent it was for Democrats to reforge relationships in rural America.

State legislatures are important, and there are consequences for overlooking local races. Reid Wilson wrote in the *Washington Post* in 2020, "Initiatives such as welfare reform, health-care reform and criminal justice reform sometimes originate in state capitals."[20] State legislatures have a lot of power to influence policy in ways that have very real consequences on people's lives. Medicaid expansion is a key example. In

2012, the Supreme Court ruled that Medicaid expansion is a voluntary program to be approved by each state before enacted. Maine's governor at the time, a right-wing Trumper-before-Trump named Paul LePage, refused to implement the program. The legislature tried to pass it as a bill, but LePage vetoed it. To override a veto, two-thirds of the legislature needs to vote in favor of the override. The Maine legislature, too clogged with Republicans, failed to do so.[21] It took the election of a Democratic governor in 2018 for expansion to be enacted. To date, twelve states, all red, still have not enacted Medicaid expansion.[22] This is just one of many examples of how state legislatures have very real—and often overlooked—power.

There is another glaring reason why it's important for Democrats to have control of state legislatures: to stop gerrymandering, the art of drawing district lines every ten years in ways that heavily favor one party or the other. It is the state legislature that is responsible for this monumental task. Gerrymandering essentially ensures party control of certain seats for at least a decade. A recent study found that, from 2012 to 2016, Republicans gained thirty-nine seats in the US House of Representatives that they *would not* have won without gerrymandering.[23] As the adage goes: the voters should pick their legislators, rather than the legislators choosing their voters.

The Republicans understand the power of gerrymandering and have a thorough strategy to maintain power through state politics. Jay J. Chaudhuri, the North Carolina Senate minority whip, wrote in *The Hill*, "Compared to Democrats, Republicans have long better understood the importance of state legislative elections." He added: "A few years ago, the Republican State Leadership Committee, the group that led the RED-MAP project, created REDMAP 2020 that aims to keep State Houses red in key battleground states. REDMAP 2020 plans to raise $125 million. In comparison, the National Democratic Redistricting Committee plans to raise $30 million."[24] The Koch brothers also have spent hundreds of thousands of dollars to influence state level races toward the Republicans.[25] Meaghan Winter, who wrote *All Politics Is Local: Why Progressives Must Fight for the States*, summed it up in *The Guardian*: "There is no way for Democrats to execute a long-term proactive political project without winning in the states immediately. . . . Over the last several decades, Republican operatives and lawmakers found multiple ways to build self-perpetuating political power via state politics."[26]

By overlooking state politics, the Democratic Party has also missed the huge opportunity to cultivate authentic relationships with rural voters. In many states, State House and State Senate districts are small enough to build a campaign that is rooted in a community. Campaigns can take the time to reach beyond the choir to develop real relationships with voters. These campaigns can feel like they come from home and rebuild from a foundation of trust. Races in rural America are a powerful way to rebuild the bridges that have collapsed.

LOOKING DOWN ON RURAL AMERICA

As an urban-centric party that focuses on national races, forsaking rural and local politics, the Democratic Party is perceived as an elite establishment. Rural communities feel misunderstood and looked down on from the ivory tower of blue America. Benes reflects on how this theme has played out in his own life. For him, the sense of elitism was embodied in how liberals look down on places like his hometown. He writes, "As much as I'm irritated by my home state's unquestioning loyalty to the Republican Party, I'm also frustrated by how ignorant many liberals I've met on the East Coast are about places like Nebraska. Some liberals I've met view the Plains as a hopeless cause, populated by racist and backwards people. . . . These same liberals will insist that those who don't share their views are by default bigots, and they talk down to anyone who so dares to disagree with them."[27]

Cramer also describes this dynamic. In the midst of her field research in 2008, there was a "fascination that someone 'like Obama' could have appeal in small places." Cramer continues, "That fascination came crashing down a bit in April 2008 when a citizen journalist told the world something Obama had said at a San Francisco fundraiser. He had said that working-class voters in old industrial towns 'get bitter, they cling to guns or religion or antipathy to people who aren't like them.'" A few days later, she talked with some of the rural folks she had met throughout her studies: "They were mad . . . and any aura of affinity between Obama and folks like themselves seemed to have worn off."[28] Even though Obama still won a greater share of the rural vote in 2008 than John Kerry in 2004 and Al Gore in 2000, this example reflects how rural folks react to objectifying liberal language.[29]

Another infamous example is when Hillary Clinton said in 2016, "You know, to just be grossly generalistic, you could put half of Trump's supporters into what I call the basket of deplorables. Right?" A consultant for the Clinton campaign, Diane Hessan, wrote in a *Boston Globe* op-ed, "[This was the] one moment when I saw more undecided voters shift to Trump than any other, when it all changed. . . . All hell broke loose."[30] Jon Tester echoes the impact of this shift in his autobiography, *Grounded: A Senator's Lessons on Winning Back Rural America*, saying he is "not sure Secretary Clinton's campaign fully understood the irreversible damage [of that comment]."[31] It hit especially hard in places like Benes's home county, where 80 percent of voters supported Trump. CNN sent a crew out there to talk with folks to understand why. A Vietnam veteran who was interviewed said, "Well, they forgot about us deplorables here in the Midwest. They totally forgot about us."[32]

The Democratic Party has alienated rural voters with out-of-touch, elite messaging and verbal slips that communicate to many that they are unwanted and unwelcome. So, in 2016, it should not have been a big surprise that these folks went toward a man who seemed to talk more directly to rural working priorities. Senator Tester reflects, "Trump brought charisma to the politics of millions of ordinary people, making himself relatable, tough, and believable. . . . As Trump spoke directly to rural America, most Democrats ignored it."[33]

Chloe heard the same theme on the campaign trail in Maine. In 2018, she spoke with a woman who had been undecided (between Clinton and Trump) until Election Day and then voted for Trump. Why? Because, at the Republican Convention, he was talking about regular working American people and Clinton wasn't. In 2020, someone commented to Chloe, "[Democrats] don't care about us working people."

In addition to Tester, another politician who managed to defy the elitist narrative in the Democratic Party is Bernie Sanders. In Pennsylvania, which has sixty-seven counties, Sanders beat Clinton in thirty counties—mostly rural—during the 2016 primary. Trump went on to win all but one of those counties in the general election.[34] In Michigan, Sanders won nearly 60 percent of the rural vote.[35] Like Trump, he bucked establishment politics, calling for a presidency fueled by working people and not corporate donors. Over 10 percent of Bernie supporters, most of them non-Democrats, ended up voting for Trump.[36]

Jane Kleeb shares a story that showcases how Bernie connected with so many in communities that have been left behind:

> In a 2016 exchange with coal workers, Senator Bernie Sanders nailed the response to climate change. He made it clear he believed in climate change and acknowledged that jobs in the coal industry had been declining since the seventies. He then looked at a young coal miner and said: "I do not hold this gentleman and the coal workers responsible

for climate change. In fact, I think these guys are heroes. I grew up in a rent-controlled apartment, and I will never forget the piles of coal that kept my house warm."[37]

Democrats do have the capacity for profound storytelling that includes rural Americans. We need to reorient our policies and messages to include these values and these stories.

TALKING POLICY RATHER THAN VALUES

As Democrats became further and further estranged from rural communities, the way that the party talked about its policies and platforms fell even flatter in rural America. We touched on this briefly earlier. Rural voters are rooted in values of independence, common sense, tradition, frugality, self-reliance, community, and hard work. They vote around their identity, what's important to them, what they think is right and wrong in their hometown. But Democratic agendas revolve around specific policies, fiscal notes, political agendas, white papers, and wonky details—leaving out the focus on values that rural communities respond to. As a result, rural Americans haven't resonated with what Democratic campaigns put out there.

This is a well-documented phenomenon among the plethora of reasons why the Democrats have alienated rural voters. We return to sociologist Robert Wuthnow's insight of rural communities as "moral communities." He observes: "Talking to rural Americans, you learn quickly how deeply their identity is rooted in their town."[38] Rural communities, he adds, don't "make up their minds about issues and elections based on only individually held economic interests or personal anxieties" but rather the "moral fabric of what they consider to be right and good." When leaders in Washington talk highfalutin policy, all they see is "cultural distance from rural communities . . . without bothering to hear what ordinary people say or to understand local needs and differences."

Tester noticed the same pattern during his years campaigning as a Democrat in rural Montana. In the conclusion of his autobiography, he has a big section called "Don't Overthink the Message." He writes: "Democrats . . . overcomplicated things with wonky, abstract, or even impossible messages . . . [and] we are getting whupped in the messaging war." He used the 2009 American Recovery and Reinvestment Act as a prime example. The Democrats went around calling it the "stimulus bill," which Tester says is "a terrible phrase that suggests big government reigns over our economy." But when Republicans passed Trump's tax law in 2017, they called it "The Tax Cuts and Jobs Act." Tester concludes that the Republicans "sold their terrible policy to the public . . . with simplicity, with relatable values, and with *power and speed*."[39]

When Cramer discussed messaging with rural voters, she found that many voters agreed that wonky policies were falling flat compared to values-based messaging. She reinforces that rural folks vote on what rings true and personal to them, not necessarily policy. She writes: "Perhaps when people vote for a candidate their overarching calculator is not how closely does this person's stances match my own, but instead, is this person like me?"[40]

She uses an example from Wisconsin to illustrate this point. Former Democratic governor Jim Doyle initiated a process to build high-speed train service between Madison and Milwaukee, an important piece of infrastructure for CO_2 emissions control, air quality, and accessibility but also a policy geared toward city folks. When Scott Walker ran for governor in 2010, he turned this policy proposal into a war of values, saying, "This is a classic example of runaway government spending. . . . That's money that comes out of important highway and bridge projects all across the state."[41] And Walker specifically cited rural communities. Democrats tried to just focus on the merits of policy, but Republicans swooped in with values-based arguments instead. Walker won.

Another good case study of this gap between policy and rural voters' values is Maine's Susan Collins versus Sara Gideon US Senate showdown of 2020. Republican Collins has been in office as a US senator since first elected in 1996. Once beloved in Maine, she is now more infamous than anything else. In 2015, 78 percent of Mainers approved of her record. In 2020, that crashed to 42 percent.[42] Her bipartisan reputation disappeared as she aligned herself with Trump. She rarely is available to constituents, refusing to do even a town hall meeting. But she's also born and bred in real rural Maine, and that holds a lot of water with Mainers.

Running against Collins was Democrat Sara Gideon from southern Maine, the state's liberal stronghold. She had served eight years as a state representative, including four as a strong Speaker of the House. She ended her service in the State House and launched right into the fight to unseat Susan Collins. Collins raised $29,835,198, while Gideon raised $74,495,369.[43] And thus commenced the most brutal and nasty campaign that Mainers had ever seen.

This race exemplified the battle between policy and values. The *New York Times* reported that Maine voters did not respond well to the

Democrats' strategy: "The Gideon campaign, they said, was too focused on national politics. It was too negative, they complained. And it cost too much money, too much of it from outside the state." One Mainer reflected, "I'm not opposed to someone bringing their views here, but you can't shove it down our throat. You cannot force something down the throat of a Mainer. If we agree with it, we agree. If we don't, we don't."[44] The Democratic Senatorial Campaign Committee endorsed Gideon, creating a sense that she was the party's rising star. But there wasn't a single person from Maine on Gideon's communications team.[45] Collins, on the other hand, touted her bipartisan reputation and her rural Maine roots. Whether out of love for Collins or to reject Gideon, Collins won reelection in 2020.

We need communication and policies that are by and for rural communities. The gap between Democratic policy and rural values is far too wide. When we speak through values, we realize that we have a lot more in common than we might think. We can build common ground in rural conservative communities *without* sacrificing our values as citizens or as Democrats. When we speak through values, we can see that we all want affordable healthcare, broadband access, money out of politics, and a solid education for our children. We just disagree on *how* we get there. But right now, we can barely even have enough of a conversation to realize that maybe we could all get along more than we think.

ABANDONING MOVEMENT BUILDING

Democrats have also undermined their successes in rural America by avoiding long-term movement building. A key part of durable political power is using each campaign season to build movements that not only get people elected but can also sustain momentum between elections. The Democrats, for the most part, don't do this.

The most poignant example of this pattern occurred in 2008. Barack Obama's campaign built a massive groundswell, launching "Camp Obama" trainings, conferences, canvasses, rallies, and massive digitally mobilized armies across the nation. The campaign developed an email list of thirteen million Americans and three million donors. After the 2008 election, David Plouffe, Obama's campaign manager, emailed the list to better understand how people wanted to be involved. Over fifty thousand people said they wanted to run for office, and 68 percent wanted to support local candidates.[46] But the potential did not become reality. The organizing platform never became part of the DNC. In the words of Marshall Ganz, the famed organizer behind Obama's 2008 campaign model, Obama "demobilized the widest, deepest and most effective grassroots organization ever built to support a Democratic president."[47]

This pattern is especially clear from how Democrats have operated in rural communities. Kleeb writes, "The Democratic Party largely does not do any of this [organizing] nationwide and certainly does not engage rural communities in a deep and authentic way. Instead, what we see happen over and over again is if a race gets close in a rural district or rural state, they send in outside consultants and staffers to try and win the race."[48] She says, "Generations go by with no investments from the Democratic Party to win elections, and you get where we are at this moment . . . a place where rural people agree with us on major issues . . . but they are not yet voting for Democratic candidates." Tester powerfully reinforces this point. He says, "Showing up at the Iowa State Fair every four years doesn't count. Paying attention to only rural swing states doesn't count either." His conclusion is the same as ours: "We have—for the large part—just stopped talking with people outside our comfort zone. . . . Democrats have written off entire regions of our country."[49]

A 2021 poll from Rural Objective PAC, which works to support Democrats in rural communities, asked respondents whether they would vote for a candidate who "grew up in a rural area" and whose "main values are his Christian faith, his support for gun ownership in this country, and his support for the workers in his district who he says deserve higher wages and a safer workplace."[50] Over half—54 percent—said yes. They then asked whether respondents would vote for the same candidate if they knew that the candidate was a Democrat. Only 38 percent said yes.

What will bridge this gap? Organizing and movements. Joy Cushman, deputy field director for Obama's 2008 campaign, wrote in the *New York Times*, "We need to get back to the basics, before Republicans beat us at our own game. . . . If Democrats want to win in 2020, they must get back to investing in the power of everyday people through organizing. . . . The kind of politics that puts people first, invests in organizing and delivers material change in people's lives will always win."[51] It's time for the Democrats to organize—really organize—once again.

RUNNING BAD CAMPAIGNS IN RURAL AMERICA

We've talked about how the Democrats have—intentionally and not—created a party that is urban, focused on national politics, and elitist, forsaking rural messages and lacking a long-term vision. Collectively, these ingredients are the perfect recipe for bad campaigns that reinforce negative perceptions of the party and leave votes on the table.

Democratic campaigns are all about turning out the urban vote. The blunder of this strategy was fully felt in 2016 when we realized that squeezing as many votes as possible out of urban districts couldn't sustain the state or federal power that we need to enact transformative policies to improve Americans' lives. *Atlantic* staff writer Derek Thompson concludes, "If Democrats don't find a way to broaden their coalition into less populous states with smaller metro areas, it may be impossible to pass liberal laws for the next generation."[52]

Let this one sink in: "According to Politico's Helena Bottemiller Evich, the Clinton campaign intentionally decided not to spend resources on rural voters, apparently only assigning a single staff person to rural outreach in their Brooklyn office late in the campaign."[53] Here's another doozy: Tom Perez said in a 2018 interview, when he was chair of the DNC, "You can't door-knock in rural America."[54] As we'll show in the next chapter, you absolutely can door-knock in rural areas! In fact, door-knocking is central to the type of politics that builds trust and real relationships, so it's startling to think that Mr. Perez said that.

Matt Barron, a lead rural strategist, offers more damning insights in the *Daily Yonder*. After the 2010 midterms—when the Democrats lost the House of Representatives—Nancy Pelosi got rid of the House Democratic Rural Working Group. Senator Harry Reid then eliminated the Senate rural outreach group. Barron writes, "Over at the Democratic National Committee, the Rural Council is still stuck in second class status, unable to become a full-fledged caucus. Why? Because under party rules, the group must represent at least 2 percent of the DNC membership."[55] The DNC's membership barely represents rural communities.

There's an often undiscussed consequence to this pattern. At the state and federal levels, Democrats want to run for and stay in safe seats, so they run in urban districts. It's a nice deal. Easy to get elected. You more or less know where your community stands and how to best represent them. Everyone knows your name, and, once you're in, you're almost guaranteed to be reelected. Why would a Democrat want to campaign in a tough rural red district when safe urban seats are so enticing? The only way for Democrats to regain traction in rural places is by running campaigns in districts that usually go Republican. Even though it's hard work with no guaranteed outcome, it is necessary.

Many Democratic campaigns are also saddled with expensive, out-of-touch consultants. As Matt Hildreth, the executive director of the organization Rural Organizing, tweeted, "'Don't mistake your consultants for your constituents.' That's my number one tip for Democrats running in rural America."[56] This was a key finding of a 2018 report by Congresswoman Cheri Bustos and Robin Johnson, *Hope from the Heartland: How Democrats Can Better Serve the Midwest by Bringing Rural, Working Class Wisdom to Washington*. Bustos and Johnson interviewed seventy-two current and former Democratic elected officials running in rural red Midwestern states. They write, "One of the most important takeaways from our Heartland outreach is the dissatisfaction of most elected officials with how rural campaigns are approached by party officials, activists and consultants."[57] These outsiders bring "'cookie cutter' approaches that aren't effective" in rural communities, using the same messaging cycle after cycle and listening to the polls and data instead of conversations. This leads the candidates and the campaigns astray.

Let's take up Sara Gideon's 2020 Senate race against Susan Collins again. The *Mainer* reported: "A review of the Gideon campaign's finance filings reveals page after page of big payments to out-of-state consulting firms and media companies. DSCC executive director Mindy Myers personally received over $100,000 from Gideon's campaign for consulting services. Bully Pulpit Interactive, a Democratic ad agency that also worked for Biden this year, handled over $8 million. Aisle 518 Strategies, a D.C. digital fundraising outfit, managed over $6 million."[58] None of this expensive advice and strategy could win the most rural state in the country for Gideon.

Consider too the 2004 presidential election of George W. Bush over John Kerry. As Thomas Frank argues in *What's the Matter with Kansas?*, Bush was far from a champion of working-class people. It was an "illusion," Frank says.[59] Part of this facade was created because the Democratic campaign chose to side with "tired consultants, many of whom work as corporate lobbyists." They gave Kerry bad advice and led him to be silent on Wall Street and corporate abuses instead of speaking out for the people.

There's another pervasive problem in the campaign world that is not often discussed: campaign offices can be toxic workplaces. Staffers work many more hours than they are paid for. For example, Canyon was paid $3,600 per month to work for Bernie Sanders in South Carolina, but he was working over one hundred hours a week with no days off. What's more, the job ends abruptly on Election Day, and staff must find another job.

Working conditions can be so harsh that it led some staffers to form a union in 2017 called the Campaign Workers Guild. They wrote, "Until we founded our union, campaign workers routinely worked more than twice the standard workweek for less than minimum wage and no health-care benefits. . . . Working from one election cycle to the next should not mean working from paycheck to paycheck. It shouldn't mean having to put up with unsafe housing and abusive bosses. And it should never mean staying silent about sexual or racial harassment out of fear of being fired or blacklisted."[60]

Campaigning is rarely a sustainable line of work, even for passionate people. A Pew Research study analyzed data from 2001 to 2014, finding that the number of people working for some kind of political group during both presidential and midterms years "peaks in October (with 19,754 and 14,607 respectively employed on average)." During off years, only 6,839 people were employed in the field.[61] Many folks only last a cycle or two in this business, whether due to burnout or job security. And then a campaign needs to train a new generation of staffers. What results is little opportunity for long-term leadership training or development in the campaign world, which further disadvantages the good work that campaigns must achieve in election years and beyond.

This has been our tough-love letter to the Democratic Party. We critique because we care. We care about our rural hometowns that have experienced the Democrats' disdain. We care because it is time for the Democratic Party to show that our purported values of inclusivity and justice extend to the rural corners of our country. We're bound together in a fight for all that we hold dear, and we need to understand each other if we are to weather the years to come. We need, in short, a Democratic Party that can compete and win in rural America.

There is hope. But we need candidates who can translate that hope into tangible results for people who have been left behind. It *is* possible to forge real connections with rural America and win as a Democrat in districts considered safely red. We have done it, and now we'll show you how.

PART II

DIRT ROAD REVIVAL

*Our Campaigns in
the Most Rural
County in the Most
Rural State in America*

CHAPTER 3

HOUSE DISTRICT 88

There is a trailer at the end of a dirt road in one of the most rural counties in the most rural state in the nation. Chloe walks up to the door, noticing that all the curtains are drawn, and knocks. A man emerges in a cloud of cigarette smoke, appearing skeptical of the stranger on his doorstep.

"Hello, my name is Chloe Maxmin. I'm running for state representative. I was stopping by to say hello and listen to any issues that you're thinking about this year."

For a moment, there is only silence between them as the man takes stock of Chloe. Then he invites her inside. As a twenty-six-year-old woman canvassing alone in the middle of the woods, she's aware that she's vulnerable and perhaps disarming. For ten minutes, they simply talk. At the end of the conversation, he tells her: "You're the first person to listen to me. Everyone judges what my house looks like. They don't bother to knock. I'm grateful that you came. I'm going to vote for you. Thank you."

Encounters like these occurred on a daily basis as we campaigned for the Maine House of Representatives in 2018 and the Maine Senate in 2020 in deep-red rural parts of the state. While we set out to win elections, what we uncovered in the process was a world of inspiring organizing, seldom-listened-to stories, and political hope that needs our attention. We campaigned to confront the dynamics plaguing Democrats in rural America. Both our campaigns were in rural red state legislative districts that voted for Trump in 2016. We knew that Democrats focused heavily on consultants, elite messaging, and transactional relationships instead of movement building and long-term relationships. Our mission was to show that there is a way forward for Democrats in rural America.

This chapter and the next are a journey through our campaigns, their ups and downs, the excitement and anxiety, the confidence and doubts we felt as we fought—and won—two political races that we were told Democrats could not win.

THE PRIMARY CAMPAIGN

On February 20, 2018, Chloe filed to run for office. By March 2018, Canyon had piled his life into his battered little '98 Honda Civic and moved from North Carolina to Nobleboro, Chloe's picturesque Maine hometown of 1,600 people. And so we launched our campaign for state representative in District 88, a strongly conservative community made up of only 27 percent Democrats. When we filed to run, there was already a Democrat (whom we'll call Mr. Smith) who was running, as well as a Republican, Michael Lemelin (real name). Neither had held office before. That meant that we would first have to win the primary against Mr. Smith in order to challenge Mr. Lemelin in November's general election. The district had never been represented by a Democrat.

The story of District 88, which includes almost nine thousand residents in the towns of Chelsea, Whitefield, Jefferson, and part of Nobleboro, is the story of so many rural communities left behind by politics as usual. This part of the country uniquely represents the challenges and opportunities that we have described. Chelsea is a working-class town in Kennebec County with some of the highest property-tax rates in the state. The other towns are in Lincoln County, where 100 percent of the population is rural. Healthcare costs leave many people one emergency room visit away from financial disaster. Many areas lack high-speed internet access and cell coverage. Loved ones fall prey to opioids and substance abuse. Local schools struggle with shrinking budgets. Nearly 20 percent of the children live in poverty.

Lincoln County is demographically the oldest county in the state, and, in terms of its residents' ages, Maine is the oldest state in the country. The median age in Lincoln County today is fifty-one, over thirteen years older than it was in 1990. We knew that demographics weren't on our side, but we also saw that this district needed real change. While many Democrats would shy away from running on such uphill terrain, we got to work launching our campaign for a better kind of politics.

Our motto from day one: politics as unusual. Everything that we did was different—from messaging to campaign signs and volunteer trainings. We weren't jumping into the traditional mud-slinging of electoral politics. Instead, we viewed the campaign as an extension of the social movements that we had both been part of for years, built on relationships, trust, and conversation.

Usually, local candidates are provided support from the state party to help them navigate the necessities of campaigning, such as creating a canvassing universe, designing literature, and building a website. The Maine Democratic Party does not endorse in primaries, so resources were limited. However, the House Democratic Campaign Committee (HDCC) did contact campaigns regularly. We briefly considered taking them up on offers of outside support. They were intent on getting us to hire the consultants that they had hand-picked to create our mail program in particular. Canyon pored over their proposed budgets. We gawked at a straight-to-trashcan mailer mock-up that they provided. It looked like an Ikea ad for a new politician. So right from the start we knew that we would have to do it all ourselves.

Step number one: build the team. Canyon was the campaign manager. We also needed a treasurer. Chloe called another young woman in Maine politics, whom she had met while working on Bernie Sanders's 2016 campaign, and nervously asked if she would consider joining the team. The response was enthusiastic. Three other friends hopped on board to help with social media, letters to the editor, and volunteer coordination. We were all in our twenties and ready to go.

Like any self-respecting movement organizers, we acquired a gigantic flip chart to plot out our vision and make sure that our campaign would intentionally and methodically align with our values and goals. One sheet laid out "The Problem," where we scribbled down things like "burnout," "no investment in state politics," "Dems leave behind rural America," and all the other challenges described earlier. Another chart was labeled "Our Vision," and this was filled with exciting thoughts about youth-led political revivals in rural spaces, organizing that felt fun and rejuvenating, and building broad, inclusive movements. By the end of March, these huge sheets were plastered across the walls of our two-bedroom house in Nobleboro.

With our vision in place, we mapped out key community leaders and local organizations we could count on to help us win the Democratic primary. We needed support for things like getting on the ballot, fundraising, hosting house parties, and media outreach. We reached out to everyone that we knew in District 88 to tell them about our campaign. We also mapped out oppositional forces for the primary: Mr. Smith's connections, businesses that supported him, and organizations that might lean toward supporting him instead of us.

Most importantly, we began the crucial work of identifying the many folks on the sidelines who might lean toward either candidate. We attended the Lincoln County Democrats meeting to make the case for our campaign to local party folks. We also identified influential organizations that would endorse in the primary—potentially swaying hard-core Democratic voters. Also on our radar were Democrats who don't usually vote in primaries but could be persuaded to do so if we made the effort to talk with them while door-knocking. We drafted press releases to generate some early name recognition in local papers. We committed ourselves to a 100 percent positive campaign, never employing negative messaging or uttering a mean word about our opponents. At the time, Mr. Smith responded with a promise to do the same.

There were two more logistical hurdles to launching the campaign: raising money and getting on the ballot. In Maine, we are fortunate to have public campaign financing through the Clean Election Fund. Candidates for state-level races in the state can choose whether to run a "clean" race or a "traditional" one. Most choose clean, which we did too. For this, a candidate needs to raise a specific number of five-dollar contributions (called qualifying contributions or QCs) from registered voters in their district. For a Maine House of Representatives race, every fifteen QCs unlock a new tier of funding, maxing out at $15,000 total. For the State Senate, every forty-five QCs leads to a new level of funding, with a maximum of $63,000. In State House races, candidates are also allowed to raise $1,000 of "seed money" from donors to jump-start the campaign as they collect the five-dollar contributions. (You are right if you are thinking that this is not much money. We'll talk more about clean elections later on.)

To get on the ballot, our State House race needed twenty-five signatures from registered Democrats in the district. For State Senate, you need one hundred. These signatures can come from any town in the district, but each town has its own separate signature sheet for its residents. So we had four pages of signatures circulating to get Chloe on the ballot for District 88 state representative.

In the first fifteen days of our State House campaign, we collected all the signatures that we needed to place Chloe on the ballot, all of the seed money, and all the initial qualifying contributions necessary to receive public financing for the campaign. Chloe had also started to canvass. We hit these benchmarks before Mr. Smith or Mr. Lemelin did, even though they had entered the race weeks earlier.

Voters that we met started to take note of the energy behind our campaign. Within a month of launching, new supporters whom we met while door-knocking wrote about our campaign in the local papers. One woman wrote: "Racing around back country roads, I was continually impressed with her determination to talk to everyone she could possibly find—posting stickers when no one was at home and then making the effort to go back another day to make that contact." Another noted: "We never heard a critical statement about her opponent. How refreshing that is when it is so absent in most of today's political dialogue!"

That's not to say that everything went smoothly, but we embraced failure as an opportunity to learn. The first lesson was small but jarring and came in the form of a phone call one day in March. Canyon had not yet moved to Maine, but Chloe was already knocking on doors, learning to maneuver her car down all the winding, steep driveways. One day, an angry old man called to yell at her for driving on his lawn and leaving a tire mark. Chloe drove carefully, but the muddy spring ground could have betrayed her. It was the first time that a voter had shouted abusively at Chloe, and it left her in shock for a few days. (It was not to be the last time, and she has much thicker skin now.)

Another one of our favorite failures was born out of our effort to be different and hip. In April, somebody suggested that Chloe go on the internet forum Reddit to do an AMA—an "ask me anything" Q&A. We had some reservations but decided to go for it in the spirit of putting our cool new approach out there and embracing social media. Chloe posted the AMA with the subject line: "I'm a 25-year-old Democrat running a District that's never gone Blue—ask me anything!" Ready for an inspiring dialogue on running for office, the first comment popped up. We looked with excitement. It was an extremely aggressive question from a man about Chloe's position on guns, a tricky topic in a community that enjoys hunting. Another one followed on its heels in the same vein. We panicked. "This is a bad idea! We're not ready for this!" We deleted the AMA instantly. We learned that we had to put more thought into the pros and cons of different communications approaches going forward, and we did.

We brainstormed creative ideas that never quite made it out into the real world. We dreamed of hosting biking canvasses, where volunteers could bike from house to house instead of driving. But the curving backroads with no shoulder gave us pause. We also dreamed about doing a big town hall with Republicans, Democrats, independents, and everyone else taking time to talk through controversial issues, hoping that listening and kindness might help tear down some barriers. But it felt like it could just as easily go wrong as right.

Instead, we poured ourselves into reinventing the staples of campaign life. Chloe canvassed for several hours every day, en route to talk with every Democrat in the district before the June primary. That's right: every single Democrat. At first, she followed the traditional campaign advice and asked a volunteer to drive her. This usually allows the candidate to move more quickly from door to door. But Chloe was too emotionally exhausted from knocking on doors *and* conversing with a loyal volunteer, so she started to canvass solo. She quickly learned tricks and maneuvers—like creative ways of parking in driveways and choosing strategic canvassing routes—that allowed her to move faster alone than with a volunteer.

We worked hard to build relationships with voters. If Chloe had a conversation with someone, she went back once or twice to build rapport. If no one was home, she returned again and again until she connected with them. In total, Chloe did eight passes through our primary universe to build relationships with District 88 Democrats.

After each long day of door-knocking, Chloe came home to write "clincher cards." These are personal handwritten postcards to each of the people she met that day. By the night before the primary, her right hand was covered in blisters from writing fifty or more postcards every day.

We connected several sheets of flip chart paper together in our living room to mark progress toward our win number—the number of votes needed to win the primary. For every ten people who said they would vote for Chloe, we colored in a section with blue. We used purple and red markers to keep track of undecideds and Smith voters. The primary was June 12, but by early June the blue tracker column was spilling off the ends of the paper, soaring past our projected win number goal. We taped together extra sections of paper to extend the chart and mark our progress.

Canyon spent long days at home in front of his laptop figuring out by trial and error just exactly how one runs a campaign. He analyzed the data from canvassing, determined whom Chloe and volunteers should talk with and when, developed a budget, implemented a targeted social media strategy, designed our logo and campaign literature, priced out and ordered campaign materials, and made ad buys in local media. It was uncharted territory for both of us and incredibly time-consuming for Canyon. But politics as unusual meant pioneering these strategies on our own. While we had read books on organizing and politics, there was no playbook to reference. We learned as we went along.

On May 12, 2018, we held our first volunteer canvass to increase our voter contact ahead of the June 12 primary. Almost twenty folks gathered at the North Nobleboro Community Hall—from high school and college friends to neighbors Chloe had met while door-knocking. We created our own training that focused on listening. Chloe paired up a driver and can-vasser for each car, Canyon assigned each pair a route and list of doors to knock on, and off they went.

Our volunteers returned to the community center greeted by live music, food, and a debriefing of the day's experiences. We heard lots of positive stories of District 88 residents supporting Chloe. But we also heard some stories of voters' concerns about Chloe's age and experience (or lack thereof). Some canvassers ran into difficulties finding houses or felt like we gave them too many doors to knock on. All of this feedback— positive and negative—helped us fine-tune our messaging, trainings, and outreach.

Twice before the primary, we invited friends to Maine for a can-vass weekend. Familiar, friendly, and beloved faces drove our way and pounded the pavement with us during the daylight. When the work was done, we'd meet back at our Nobleboro home. With a keg on hand, we played capture the flag and flip cup until our energy was all used up. We proved to ourselves and to our friends that the campaign life can be legit-imately fun and bring people—especially young folks—together. Those oases of community energy were much needed amid the intense experi-ence of daily campaigning.

One of Chloe's friends, a local artist, volunteered to convene a group of painters to create campaign signs. Soon happy, colorful placards, with images of loons, canoes, trees, stars, flowers, Chloe's huge hair, and more dotted the countryside throughout the district, standing out at intersec-tions and in driveways crammed with traditional campaign signs. No one in the district had seen anything like these beautiful heartfelt demonstra-tions of support. People began to grasp the spirit of our campaign and to sense that it was truly different—politics as unusual.

A final key to our primary strategy: house parties. These were an opportunity for folks to learn about Chloe. More importantly, they were a chance to bring more neighbors into the campaign fold by explain-ing the importance of volunteering, letters to the editor, sign painting, canvassing, and anything else that they wanted to contribute. We hosted four house parties that spring in supporters' lovely homes, each with around two dozen guests. These gatherings built up a volunteer base that got us through the primary and all the way to the general election in November.

The saga of our first few months of campaigning would not be complete with a mention of our first debate with our primary opponent on May 24, 2018, at the Whitefield Grange Hall. Chloe was twenty-five years old at the time and going up against a fiftysomething man. She knew that she could handle the situation and take whatever came at her. She memorized six pages of facts and figures on issues ranging from gun control and marijuana legalization to healthcare and education funding. She spent countless hours practicing her opening and closing statements. A debate prep squad was assembled to ask complicated prep questions and critique answers. Chloe was prepared for the worst—"gotcha" questions, skeptical audience members, men talking over her . . . the works. Moderated by the editor of the largest local paper, the *Lincoln County News*, we knew that a misstep could be printed and sent out to hundreds of homes the next week.

As it turned out, the whole thing was simple and straightforward. Chloe walked into the Grange to see many familiar faces and supporters. Mr. Smith was kind and respectful. The candidates were asked about healthcare, the environment, minimum wage, and other standard topics. Chloe threw out her facts and figures and energized the room with her statements about a better politics. She asked: "By a show of hands, who thinks that politics as usual is failing our community?" Everyone raised their hands. Then: "By a show of hands, who here is ready to flip this district in November?" Again, everyone raised their hands. "Me too. That is why I'm running."

After the debate, only a few weeks remained before primary day. The pressure was on. This is when we started to notice negative rumors floating around. People started to say that Chloe had never held a job in her life and was living with her mom—both false. Supporters also reported being told that Chloe was too young and inexperienced to be able to win the general election in November. One elderly man told Chloe: "I don't know if I can vote for you. You're too young to fight for us seniors." At a local Democratic Party meeting, another senior told Chloe with a condescending sneer to "stay involved after the primary. We need your energy and we need your help figuring out how to get more young people involved." He assumed that we would lose.

In a small community, word travels fast. Someone called Chloe to say that Mr. Smith, who had just visited her house, was spreading these rumors about Chloe's background. He was also trying to convince folks that he would have a better shot than Chloe of winning in November. Despite his commitment to join us in a 100 percent positive campaign, our community was still injected with the old political poisons.

Chloe, Canyon, and their team talked it over and doubled down on the campaign's commitment to avoid negative campaigning. We called Smith and confronted him. He admitted to having said those things and promised to stop. But on June 9—just three days before the primary—Chloe texted Mr. Smith: "Mr. Smith, I still have multiple people telling me that you are saying negative remarks about me at the doors. Please stop. I have kept my word since the beginning and am disappointed to be hearing this from so many people." He responded: "Chloe, A friend who has been in politics for years said this. 'Message is the articulation of differences for the voter to have a choice in the voting booth.' Again, I'm articulating those differences to constituents with comments that I've heard from you, have verified facts from my campaign team, or have verified myself." Disappointingly, we heard the night before the primary from a frustrated supporter that Mr. Smith was calling voters to tell them that Chloe couldn't win in the fall. (We have to add here: Mr. Smith and Chloe are friends to this day. He helped volunteer for her general election campaigns in 2018 and 2020. This story is not to disparage his character but rather to highlight how intense and challenging the campaign life can be.)

The final hurdle before primary day was GOTV (get out the vote). A campaign essential, it is the sprint to the finish line to make sure that voters actually turn up to vote. We had volunteers canvassing all day, every day, in the five days leading up to the big day. There were so many folks joining our campaign that we were able to reach out to each Democratic voter *twice* by the time voting time came. Typically, GOTV efforts barely make it to each voter once.

Since the local and state Democrats did not endorse in primaries, it was up to us to make sure that voters not only came to the polls but also voted *for Chloe*. Based at the trusty North Nobleboro Community Hall, waves of volunteers drove down the dirt roads to GOTV and returned with reports of support. There were even some requests to stop visiting people's homes because we had been there so many times.

Again, that's not to say it all went smoothly. On the morning of the primary, we were getting ready to send volunteers out to distribute door hangers on front doors and porches. We opened the box of over a thousand hangers for the first time to find that Canyon had misspelled the word Democrat (D-E-M-O-C-R-A-C-T). We laughed hard and long and then went to hang them anyway. All was okay.

Even on primary day, we couldn't be certain that our methods were resonating. We had no idea whether we would win or lose. All the tactics that we had employed were so different and untested. Would they work? On the one hand, we felt good about the ways in which we had translated our organizing skills to build a true grassroots campaign. We were buoyed by the number of Democrats who had pledged to vote for Chloe. On the other hand, this was our first rodeo. Our opponent's bad-faith attacks had rattled us. There was zero polling to give us any clue about where we stood.

After wrapping up the final GOTV canvass and closing up the community center at 6:00 p.m. the night of the primary, Canyon reflected:

> I feel like no matter what happens we have totally actualized our vision for this campaign, making it something that is fun and inclusive and builds community and inspires people and really brings a focus back to rural politics and getting young people invested in it and really making it a positive thing that isn't centered around money, isn't centered around any kind of negativity. It is really grounded in love and building community.

Family and friends gathered around the kitchen table awaiting results. Multiple computers were used as we refreshed the pages of national and state newspapers to track primary results. Minutes turned into hours. Excitement buzzed, and the stress was palpable. Then, at 10:59 p.m., the *New York Times* results for Maine District 88 appeared. Our campaign won the primary with 80 percent of the vote.

The votes for Chloe alone were greater than the total turnout for any previous Democratic primary in the district's history, including presidential primaries. Voters showed up in droves, breaking record turnout by an astounding 40 percent. The turnout was so unprecedented that half of the precincts ran out of ballots. They needed special authorization from the secretary of state to make photocopies of the blank ballot so that everybody could vote.

Our gamble on a new kind of politics had paid off, but we didn't have much time to celebrate as we shifted gears. We steered our campaign toward the November election, as things got real, real fast.

ON TO THE GENERAL ELECTION

The sweetness of our primary win felt great. Really great. But the hard work was just beginning as we headed on to the general election. Canyon ran detailed analyses of registered voters. House District 88 had a negative-16-point score on the Democratic Performance Index created by the National Committee for an Effective Congress. This meant that over the past three elections, the Democratic candidates had lost by an average of 16 percentage points. Although we had solidified a formidable Democratic base during the primary, Canyon calculated that, if Chloe was to become the first Democrat ever to win District 88, we needed to win 60 percent of the votes of high-turnout moderate Republican and independent voters, as well as nearly 80 percent of Democratic voters.

We launched into the general election campaign with the same spirit and strategies that served us in the primary. We gathered at the North Nobleboro Community Hall for a primary celebration and general campaign launch. People showed up en masse. The Leopard Girls, a local band, wowed the crowd. We enjoyed a massive potluck feast together, heard from community members, and laid out the vision for our campaign. The crowd spilled out of the hall into the parking lot and across the grounds of the community center.

We continued to develop all our campaign tools and materials ourselves instead of relying on the HDCC and their consultants. As a result, it was a monumental amount of work for Canyon. He had to learn the ins and outs of designing and running an effective direct-mail campaign from scratch, planning our overarching strategy, developing the messaging, and determining how to invest our precious resources in the right voters. It was worth it. Our mailers stood out because they were authentic and beautiful. They didn't look anything like all the other consultant-created junk that floods every mailbox in the election season. And because it cost half as much to do it ourselves, we were able to stretch our limited state-funded budget in a way that no other campaign was able to achieve.

We began talking with Republicans and independents throughout the summer and into the fall. We decided to yet again create our own list of doors to knock on instead of using the Democrats' playbook, which would have doomed us to the same defeat suffered by all the Democratic candidates who preceded us. This is when our entire worldview began to change. We saw, up close and personal, the profound lack of investment in rural politics—and the huge opportunity to fill that space. Every single day, Chloe talked with people *who had never been contacted by a Democratic candidate or canvasser in their entire voting history.* There were also many who hadn't been contacted since Obama's campaign in 2008. We had a front-row seat to witness how the Democrats had simply ignored rural people in our district. It was heartbreaking and infuriating to recognize all the people who had been left behind and all the ground that had been conceded to Republicans. But we were also filled with hope and inspiration when we understood that these abandoned dirt roads were also a big space for a new politics to emerge

Learning how to navigate this new space was the challenge. A voice memo from Chloe in summer of 2018 captured her sense of treading on new ground and her determination to find the missing pieces of this new puzzle: "This round of canvassing is so not fun," Chloe said with a sigh after her first week talking to general election voters. "Talking to Democrats for the primary, 90 percent of the doors were fine. There were only a few here and there that were really mean. But now, you just really never know what each door is going to be like. Most of them say they're undecided though, and I think I can win a lot of them over if I go back and continue the conversation."

We knew before launching this campaign that Democrats face a complex political reality when it comes to rebuilding trust in rural America. The reality on the ground—going door-to-door, striking up conversations, listening carefully—reinforced the harshness of the situation. Chloe came home visibly distraught one Saturday in August, and she told Canyon, "I spent the past five hours canvassing to get ten people to say that they would vote for me. I knocked on eighty-two doors, which I believe is my record. Really frustrating day. Talked to a lot of people I've known my whole life, and they wouldn't commit to vote for me . . . including my own neighbor. Which to me just goes to show how well Republicans have eschewed Democrats. Even if you know I'm a good person, I'm not going to get your vote because I'm a Democrat. I've known these people my whole life. By saying they're not going to vote for me, it's like an inherent signal that they think I wouldn't do the best thing for our community. 'Democrat' is a bad word around here."

Part of what made this round of canvassing so different from the primary was the kinds of conversations that Chloe was having. During the primary, Mr. Smith and Chloe battled it out for who best represented the Democratic Party. Talking with voters felt natural. Most folks thought of the world and political issues similarly. During the general election canvassing, the dynamics were very different. Chloe talked with folks who shared viewpoints that were wildly different from her own. She had to learn how to have these conversations if there was to be any hope of winning, let alone collaborating with constituents to improve life in the district. A 2018 voice memo of Chloe's reflects this struggle:

> I was talking to a couple, and I agreed that people should be able to snowmobile and hunt and fish and ATV on protected lands. I consider myself to be extremely progressive, but there are some things that I think the Left is too rigid on. This couple was having a problem with that, so it's like okay, that frustration is understandable.
>
> But then they were saying that "illegal is illegal" and that "if you do something illegal in the U.S. and go to jail, you're separated from your kids, and so if you come across the border illegally then you should be separated from your kids too." And it's, like [deep sigh], I literally have no idea what to say to that besides just not getting into it. But is that being disingenuous? Is that not fighting the fight? But I'm not going to win them over in that argument anyways. But it makes me feel so gross and sleazy to listen to it.

Conversations like these were deeply challenging. Sometimes walking this line took a huge toll and left us feeling like we were betraying our core values. It made us want to scream in people's faces. It was also draining to show up and be present and earnest every day, trying to embody a new kind of politics, when you didn't know if your efforts would pay off or not. People don't know you or your intentions, so they see you as part of the political establishment that has let them down for so long.

The breakneck pace mixed with the exposure to anger every day at the doors was exhausting. We were also campaigning during the hearings to confirm Brett Kavanaugh to the Supreme Court. Chloe canvassed for hours alone, having disturbing conversations about sexual assault and the importance of believing survivors. One man, alone with Chloe in his backyard, told her: "I could pick you up and spank you right here and no one would ever know." There were moments when Chloe thought that she couldn't take any more, that the adversity of campaigning as a Democrat in these rural red places was too much to bear.

These challenges were exacerbated by our bitter Republican opponent, Michael Lemelin. He picked up where Mr. Smith left off. The whispered seeds of sexist and ageist narratives blossomed into full-on attacks from Lemelin as he went to extreme lengths to erode Chloe's support. Our campaign signs began disappearing all across the district. Without the funds to continue replacing them, we worried about our dwindling presence. Then Lemelin was caught red-handed ripping up a Chloe sign at the end of a supporter's driveway and replacing it with his own. This incident was reported to the local authorities, his car was identified, and Lemelin received a visit at his home from a state trooper informing him to stop this illegal activity. To everyone, he repeated the lie that Chloe had never held a job. He said he would never trust his daughter to be in office and so no one should trust Chloe. He insisted that Chloe was unfit to serve because she wasn't married and didn't own her own business. (He owns a Curves fitness franchise.) What's worse: many people believed it, repeated it to Chloe's face, and refused to support her candidacy.

But the more conversations that we had, the more we discovered the powerful act of listening. We heard some rough stuff, and we didn't tolerate hate. But simply by listening patiently, we were almost always able to glimpse common ground. As we told our canvassers, the purpose became to listen and build relationships. This is how we can slowly build the trust that changes minds and elects different kinds of representatives. Here is a stunning example of that from Chloe (*trigger warning*):

> I've been canvassing in Chelsea and been talking to these super-avid Trump supporters. They are pro-life even if the baby was a product of rape or incest because it should be God's will, they say. They think the border wall should be built, and they don't want immigrants to receive any kind of public support even if they've been fleeing war-torn countries, because "that's their problem." This guy told me he spanked (he "whipped their asses," to use his language) his children. Our conversation got a little heated at times. But we agreed on gun control, and most importantly we agreed that we need to have these kinds of conversations—that you can still be a good person and a good neighbor if you have different political views. We ended on a really nice note.

Faced with all of this, our mantra was: "Prepare for Mordor!" (This play on the land of evil from *The Lord of the Rings* translated to "more doors.") We had to keep going. We had to keep talking with folks. Amid these often demoralizing, confusing, challenging, and sometimes uplifting conversations, we launched a dirt road revival as summer turned to fall and fall turned to snow. Our campaign knocked on over ten thousand doors in a district with only nine thousand people. (This number includes multiple contacts with the same voters.) Both Chloe and volunteers visited homes two, three, and even four times to build real relationships instead of knocking once and asking "Will you vote for Chloe?"

Slowly but surely, we thought we might be able to turn things around. A young mom who opened her door to Chloe said that she couldn't afford to take her child to the ER. She had never voted Democrat, but she committed to vote for us. There was a man with a Trump bumper sticker on his truck who, after talking with Chloe, put her bumper sticker on his tailgate too. There was a preacher who had never put up a political sign in his life until our campaign. Arthur, an eighty-four-year-old man in District 88, said that Chloe was the first state representative that he was ever voting for and that she was the first politician to ever knock on his door. There was a widower who found hope, community, and fulfillment in volunteering with our campaign. Another voter wrote to Chloe:

> I am registered as a Republican. However . . . I do not vote across party lines, but rather, for the individual candidate. . . . Yours is the very first handwritten postcard/letter that I have ever received from any candidate in my life. This, in combination [with] your actually taking the time to visit the voters in your district speaks volumes for your efforts, sincerity and integrity in your running for election. Your efforts are unheard of by other candidates, who instead, opt for derogatory TV ads and junk mail. As such, you have most assuredly earned my vote.

Voters were not the only ones taking notice of our campaign. We were one of only eleven campaigns in Maine to be endorsed by Barack Obama. Karen Mills, the former administrator of the US Small Business Administration under Obama, also endorsed us. National organizations like MoveOn.org and Run for Something lent support. Maine's secretary of state, Matt Dunlap, and the Lincoln County sheriff, Todd Brackett, proudly stood by our side. Over ninety supportive letters to the editor flooded local papers.

There were now two more big hurdles before Election Day. The first was the debate. Gone were the comfortable days of Democratic debates at the Whitefield Grange. The *Lincoln County News* hosted our District 88 debate once more but lumped it together with two other local House races. At the Waldoboro Town Hall, six candidates debated. Five of them were men with gray hair. And then there was Chloe. Ready for this dynamic, Chloe stood up to give her speech about the need for a new kind of politics, as the men squirmed. None of the other candidates stood up to address the audience during the entire debate. Chloe emerged from the night having shown Mr. Lemelin and the community that she could manage herself just fine.

The second big hurdle: our second GOTV effort. From June to November, we had canvassed the roads of District 88 gathering support. It was now or never: all those folks needed to actually show up and vote for Chloe. Again, rather than be lumped in with the state party's one-size-fits-all efforts alongside every other campaign (including the gubernatorial race), we organized our own GOTV operation. We carefully trained volunteers on how to talk with the Republican and independent voters with whom we had worked so hard to build relationships. We had enough volunteers for our campaign to get the job done. Canyon launched canvasses from the North Nobleboro Community Hall as Chloe continued driving the dirt roads and talking with undecided voters until the last moment.

GOTV came with its own set of challenges. Back in August, we had begun trying to coordinate GOTV with the state party. We knew that there would be a massive Democratic GOTV effort for the US Congress and gubernatorial races. But we needed to run our own GOTV effort to sensitively handle conversations with the many Republicans and independents who had said that they would vote for Chloe. We feared that well-intentioned Democratic volunteers spouting the party line would ruin the relationships that we had so painstakingly built.

The party communicated in no uncertain terms that the statewide campaigns called all the shots on GOTV. They would not coordinate with us. Instead, the party insisted on sending its generically trained, clipboard-wielding volunteers to every single household that had indicated support for a Democrat. This included, in a woeful disregard of nuance, Republicans who had said they would vote for Chloe but not any other Democrat.

Imagine this: you're a Republican who has never had an in-depth conversation with a Democrat before. You say you'll take a chance on Chloe. But then the Democratic Party shows up at your door, reading a canned script and handing you a Democratic slate card. Will that get you to vote? Nope. We pushed back and told the party that they could only GOTV for Democrats and voters they had identified themselves, which would exclude Republicans from our campaign (since they only talk to Democrats). The party refused.

Fortunately, through our strong relationship with the Lincoln County Democrats, we were at least able to ensure that we would have advance notice of where their volunteers were headed each day. This meant that we could avoid aggravating voters with multiple visits in the same day. In the end, the party failed to recruit enough volunteers to execute their GOTV plan and never even made it out to District 88. We dodged a bullet.

The whole ordeal was a major distraction that ate up precious hours that we did not have to spare in the final days.

November 6, 2018—Election Day—finally arrived. Chloe stood outside the polls from 8:00 a.m. to 8:00 p.m. True to form for a campaign that had endured its share of difficulties and rolling with the punches, Chloe spilled coffee all over her pants on the way to the polls in the morning. Luckily for her, a freezing cold rain produced the need for a long raincoat that covered the evidence. Looking back on it, the day was a blur. Chloe spent three hours at each town's polling place, ending the day in Jefferson. Canyon joined her there with hot drinks. We slogged through, huddling for warmth, shaking hands, and praying that our hard work had been worth it. At the polls, the vibe was positive. There were a lot of friendly faces, excited hugs, and thumbs up. Someone yelled to Chloe: "You're the first Democrat that I've voted for in twenty years!"

We were exhausted by the end of the day. Canyon stood loyally by Chloe for the last few hours as she greeted voters on their way home from work. "Have fun in there," Chloe would say. Canyon ultimately got up the nerve to tell Chloe that "have fun in there" was perhaps not the best phrase to use. Chloe's tired brain agreed. The next time a voter walked by, all that came out of her mouth was "Super-duper!" It sounded idiotic the moment it was spoken, but in our giddily tired state, it made us laugh.

At 8:00 p.m., we headed home to change into dry clothes and join family and friends around a table of food and beer. We first got the results from Chelsea, Lemelin's hometown and a Republican stronghold. We managed our expectations. We lost the town by a large margin: 679 to 526. Then the Nobleboro results: we won, 317–226. Whitefield: we won, 695–500. With three out of four towns reporting, we led by just over a hundred votes. All our hopes rested on Jefferson, a town that always votes Republican. Would we get enough votes to win, even if Mr. Lemelin carried the town, as we expected?

We waited and waited, but the Jefferson results never came. We asked a volunteer to drive down to the Jefferson town office to try to find a clerk. The building was empty, lights off, doors locked, results nowhere to be found. We stayed up until 4:00 a.m. waiting for a miracle. None came. Canyon fell asleep on his laptop.

We slept for a few hours. Canyon set an alarm for 7:00 a.m., when he began a cycle of calling the town clerk's office and hitting the snooze button. At 7:57 a.m., the town clerk finally answered. "We're emailing you the results now," she said. Canyon ran up the stairs to Chloe's room. He opened the results, preparing his tired brain to calculate whether the vote deficit in Jefferson was small enough to win the election. To our utter surprise, we won the town of Jefferson, 727–648. That meant that we won the District with 52.4 percent of the vote. To say that we were elated would be an understatement. We had poured a year of our lives into something that had never been done—that experienced politicos said could not be done—and, against all odds, we had succeeded!

Observers across the state were shocked. Chloe was the first Democrat ever to win District 88. Some people chalked it up to the "Blue Wave" that swept the country that year. The results showed otherwise, as all other Democratic candidates struggled in District 88. In Jefferson, for example, Chloe was the only Democrat to win out of all local, state, and federal candidates. Democrat Janet Mills, who won the governorship in 2018, received only 45.5 percent of the District 88 vote, although she won by a comfortable margin of nearly 8 percentage points statewide. The Blue Wave had not reached the dirt roads of District 88. We won because of a campaign that focused on our shared humanity, real relationships, and a determination to listen our way to common ground.

Statewide and national media took note of the stunning upset in our most unlikely district. Reflecting on the election results, Bill Nemitz, a Maine Press Association Hall of Fame journalist and political columnist for the *Portland Press Herald*, said, "It struck me that this woman [Chloe] is the future of the Maine Democratic party." Reporting on the campaign in the *Washington Post*, Katrina vanden Heuvel wrote: "Maxmin is one of many progressive candidates who prevailed in this month's elections despite the long odds that Democrats traditionally face in their districts. Yet her victory stands out even more because of where she was able to win: in a district that contains the most rural county in America's most rural state."

Because our campaign was rooted in community, we couldn't truly celebrate without our people. A few nights after the election, we organized a party in Jefferson at the Damariscotta Lake Farm restaurant. In our state of utter fatigue, we barely did any outreach. With such short notice, we expected a couple dozen folks to attend. Instead, people arrived in droves. The parking was packed, the bar was three-deep, and more than one hundred community members crammed into the warm fairy-light-lit room to celebrate all that we had done together. There were no words to express the feelings of gratitude, support, and love that filled the room that evening. A couple of young musicians performed, local beer was served, people took turns at the mic spontaneously sharing stories from the campaign. It was perfect.

So many people want to know how we won in District 88 with a movement of Republicans, Democrats, and independents. The heart of our success is simple: we listened to everyone and respected all. Democrats are quick to judge anyone with an "R" next to their name, ignore anyone who voted for Donald Trump, and erupt at anti-welfare, gun rights, and immigration arguments. One of Chloe's constituents, a self-described "rock hard Republican," thanked her for taking time to converse because most liberals, "if they disagree with you, they ascribe bad character to you." We found that people from all across the political spectrum share one thing in common: a deep distrust of politics and a profound frustration with not having their voices heard in our government. We have more in common than we believe, but we can only discover the common ground when we take the time to show up, to listen, and to respect one another.

One volunteer summarized the feeling of our 2018 movement beautifully: "It's a connection with each other and with something bigger that each one of us craves."

DOUBLING DOWN ON THE DIRT ROAD REVIVAL

We pulled it off in November 2018, flipping a rural red district to blue. After holding our breath for months to win, we needed to exhale, and that sent each of us on different journeys. Canyon returned to his home mountains in North Carolina to be with family and friends, recharge after the exhausting intensity of campaign work, and put time back into his other passions. He rowed the Colorado River through the Grand Canyon on a three-week expedition with friends. He perfected his craft of making and selling pottery, thrown on the old potter's wheel handed down through his family. He trained for and ran a hundred-mile mountain race. He taught leadership and outdoor skills to young adults, working multi-week wilderness expeditions for the National Outdoor Leadership School. He brought lessons from the campaign trail back to his own district in North Carolina, where he was asked to serve as vice chair of the Eleventh Congressional District Democrats. He had big plans to coordinate a series of trainings across his home district to support the incubation of a real rural organizing movement in the mountains.

Chloe's hard work paid off as she was thrust into the life of a state representative, finally able to craft a real-life politics that was by and for District 88. From the second that we won, she was flooded with calls from excited legislators. As the saying goes, when you're newly elected, it's like drinking from a water hose. Chloe entered a Democratic Maine House of Representatives paired with a newly flipped Democratic Senate and Democratic governorship. For now, we offer a glimpse into this new world and how Chloe learned to translate a new rural politics from the campaign trail to actual governance.

The first step of being in the state legislature in Maine is to figure out what bills you're going to sponsor. Chloe wanted all her bills to come from constituent conversations or promises from the campaign trail, so she set out on a path to find the experts who could help turn ideas into policy. For example, transportation access was a key part of the vision on the campaign trail. But how does that get translated into policy? This work is also strictly time-bound. There is a deadline called "cloture," usually in December. That gives you less than a month and a half to figure out your bills. If you miss cloture, any bill that you propose has to be considered an emergency and be approved by leadership from both parties. So you effectively have to meet the cloture deadline.

Chloe carefully researched and crafted four bills: (1) to figure out a solution for rural transportation, (2) to develop well-paying green jobs, (3) to reform the Windfall Elimination Provision in Social Security payments for state employees and public school teachers, and (4) to ensure that sexual assault kits are stored for more than ninety days. Each of these bills became law, with the exception of the transportation bill, which died when COVID forced the legislature to adjourn suddenly.

Chloe worked to put the values of the campaign into practice. Promising accountability, she held "Coffee with Chloe" sessions each month at the diner in Jefferson, providing a forum for constituents of all backgrounds and persuasions to come together and talk about politics. Staying true to the community, she supported local organizing efforts that arose out of her campaign, including one called Revitalize Jefferson that works to rebuild the community through beautification projects, community events, and support for local businesses. Committed to listening, as problems and conflicts arose, she convened constituents on both sides of issues to understand the whole picture and seek constructive action.

The idea of what it meant to truly represent the people of her district consumed Chloe. She had once thought that it would be easy to tell where her community stood on different issues. She spent all those years looking at politicians and wondering why they weren't following "the will of the people." That "will" seemed so obvious to Chloe as a constituent, but it was more complicated to discern once in office, especially when representing a community of diverse values. There was rarely an issue where she could clearly tell that a majority of the district was on one side or the other. The upside of this is that it forced Chloe to solicit and listen carefully to all sides of an issue. The downside: you're always letting some people down, no matter what you do, and you have to learn to live with that.

Over time, these tensions found some resolution in Chloe's own sense of integrity. Vowing not to fall prey to party politics, she did her own research on bills rather than only voting the party line. This meant many late nights of intense study, reviewing upcoming bills, reading committee testimony, examining the legislation, pursuing discussions with experts and constituents, all of it to decide the course of action that was genuinely in the best interests of District 88. On some of the most controversial votes, Chloe worked to communicate to the district what she had learned from close study of an issue. Many constituents thanked her for her honesty, hard work, and transparency, even when they didn't agree with her vote. As the months went by, Chloe learned to balance all the input until she achieved a feeling of "doing the right thing." When she arrived at that sense of integrity, she felt that she was fulfilling her responsibilities to the district, the State of Maine, her party, and her own moral compass.

This inside experience of politics changed Chloe's perspective on the process. The state legislature is a slow-moving beast for a reason, at least in Maine. It gives ample space for public input, research, and debate. This is especially important in a citizen legislature where many members are not career policy makers but are in the position of creating lasting laws. Of course, many issues are urgent, but that clashes with the nature of the political beast, creating new challenges for democratic societies.

Maine's citizen legislature also means getting paid less than minimum wage for the time put in, making around $14,000 the first year and $10,000 the second—with a full-time workload during session. This leads to two categories of legislator. The first is composed of retired or independently wealthy people who can devote all their time to being a legislator. The second is composed of people who work at two or three jobs while in session, meaning that their attention—by necessity—cannot be completely focused on politics. Chloe fell into the second category, which meant for an unbelievably hectic life.

Newly elected lawmakers face a steep learning curve, but Chloe loved being in office. It was an honor to represent her hometown and contribute to her community, and she realized the deep importance of electing good people. Even if Chloe didn't vote with the Democratic leadership 100 percent of the time, her votes for reproductive rights and LGBTQIA+, climate, and immigrant justice are better than having a Republican vote against them every single time. She loved fighting for her neighbors' interests, understanding how policy can best reflect and serve the people who live down the dirt roads, and working across party lines to create a new kind of politics.

One day in the early spring of 2019, in the midst of her first year in the State House, Chloe received a call from State Senate president Troy Jackson. He asked if she would run for the State Senate in 2020 against Senate Minority Leader Dana Dow, an entrenched local businessman who had been in and out of office for almost twenty years and had never lost a general election. We had to decide by June 2019, just a couple of months away. If Chloe decided to run, she would have to forgo her House seat. It was a huge gamble. The Senate district is almost six times larger than District 88, which meant that Chloe would have to organize many new communities with many new people.

Chloe called Canyon. The idea was at once terrifying and motivating. We agonized over the decision for weeks as we embarked on a sober assessment of what we would be up against.

The first thing that we did was to review the facts. Senate District 13 is home to approximately thirty-eight thousand people compared to District 88's population of nine thousand. The entire district, with the exception of two towns, lies within Lincoln County, the oldest county (by age) in the oldest state in the country. It is also tied with Piscataquis County as the most rural county in the most rural state.

The southeastern border of the district traces the distinctive jigsaw puzzle pieces of peninsulas and small islands up the middle of Maine's coast before slicing north and west to cover a large swath of inland territory. House District 88 includes three towns and half of Nobleboro. Senate District 13 comprises twenty-seven small towns. The largest, Waldoboro, is Dow's hometown with just over five thousand residents. It takes over an hour to drive from one end of the Senate district to the other. The coast, from Wiscasset to Waldoboro, is home to world-class oyster farms, and the working waterfronts are populated by lobstermen, clammers, shrimpers, boat builders, and seaweed harvesters. The district's islands, small harbors, and large ports are characterized in part by summer tourists and winter solitude. Farms dot the countryside inland from Newcastle to Whitefield, with dozens of family-run operations providing fresh food for our community month after month, year after year. The vast network of Maine's central coastal watershed connects small rivers, brooks, and streams to hidden ponds and long lakes. There are oceanfront mansions occupied for a few short summer months and trailers without insulation whose residents struggle all winter long. It is a dynamic and complex district with diverse needs to represent.

US Route 1 is the major highway through District 13. It follows Maine's coastline, bringing visitors through some of the state's most picturesque towns. If you find yourself on Route 1 in Waldoboro, you can't miss Dow Furniture. Out front is one of the largest Adirondack chairs that you will ever see next to a large Dow Furniture sign. Directly across the street is the Midcoast Sports Hall of Fame and Dow's Discounts. Mr. Dow and his family have been business icons in the community for over sixty years. Dow's father, Wilmot, was a state senator for Lincoln County in the late fifties. Dana Dow grew up to become a teacher at the local high school and inherited the family business. He began a new chapter in the Dow political dynasty with his election to the Maine Senate in 2004, then served on and off for the next sixteen years, alternating between the Senate and the Maine House of Representatives. He was elected as the leader of the Republican Party in the Senate during his 2018 term. Everyone—and we mean everyone—knows of Dow Furniture and its owner, Dana Dow.

Next we did some quick political analysis, especially of the 2018 State Senate race in District 13. The district had voted for Obama in 2008 and 2012 and then Trump in 2016. Over the preceding three election cycles, the district had voted Republican by a margin of 3 percent overall compared to the 16 percent margin in District 88. The Democrat who ran against Dow in 2018, Laura Fortman, lost by less than four hundred votes. Her entire campaign team had knocked on eleven thousand doors. We had knocked on ten thousand doors to get elected in smaller District 88. If Fortman had attracted all the votes that we flipped in District 88, she would have won.

Our dramatic 2018 win was no fluke. We knew that it was the result of the systematic, relentless, and comprehensive application of a framework of theory and practice, strategies and tactics, values and principles. We shared a growing conviction that our ever deepening and more detailed system of politics as unusual could move the dial on one of the most critical political challenges of our time: the revival of Democratic politics in rural America. Troy Jackson's request now forced us to put this conviction to the test. For us, the choice was double or nothing. Should we go all in on our belief in the dirt road revival, knowing that we could lose everything that we had worked for?

Then we ran across an unusual article. Lincoln County was spotlighted nationally by political experts in *The Hill* who called it one of "the 10 counties that [would] decide the 2020 election."[1] One of the experts described the dynamics of Lincoln County as "a mix of working-class fishermen, deep-pocketed retirees (both liberal and conservative) and tourism-dependent workers and business owners, where partisan political contests are highly contested at almost every level." The article concluded, "If Trump keeps his blue-collar base, or if ancestral Republicans break against him and cost him the White House, Lincoln County will be the microcosm through which to view the 2020 outcome."

Analysis in *The Hill* said that if our dirt road revival could succeed in Lincoln County, then it could succeed in rural America, serving as a map and a model to candidates across the country. We grasped the significance of this opportunity to further scale, test, and refine our work, methodically recording our insights and practices as we moved through the many months of a new and more complex campaign. In the end, we reflected on our identity and purpose: we are movement builders, and we know that movements are built on the campaign trail. The opportunity to effect that kind of change on a larger scale was something that we could not pass up. Anything can happen on Election Day, but movements never fade. Running for the Senate felt true to the original purpose of running for office: to build true people power.

And so began our journey to win Senate District 13. The last time that any member of the State Senate leadership had been knocked out by either party in Maine was in 1992, the year that Chloe was born. The *Bangor Daily News,* one of the state's largest papers, would later compare our race to the boxing match between Buster Douglas and Mike Tyson with 42:1 odds. But we were prepared. We were ready to turn our vision into action once again, this time working to bring a new politics to every corner of Lucky District 13.

CHAPTER 4

LUCKY DISTRICT 13

On January 24, 2020, we launched our campaign for Maine State Senate District 13 with a community potluck scheduled for 6:00 p.m. at our familiar stomping ground, the North Nobleboro Community Hall. We had spread the word about the campaign launch through our networks, social media, and the local papers. But with our other jobs demanding most of our attention in the lead-up, we hadn't done the serious outreach that we had intended to ensure that people would come. We hoped that at least fifteen or so supporters would show up as we gathered cups, plates, napkins, a pot of soup, bread and cheese, a speaker system, and headed out to set up the hall. Chloe surprised Canyon by making a batch of chocolate chip cookies, a rare event for sure, which later received positive reviews and didn't cause a single fatality. We pulled into the gravel parking lot that icy cold January evening to begin setting up and were pleasantly surprised to find Senate President Troy Jackson already waiting for us. Troy helped us set up a few folding chairs, and we silently worried whether anybody beyond Chloe's family and a handful of close supporters would show up. Then everything changed.

We began to hear a din in the parking lot. Canyon went to the door and saw dozens of people parking their cars, standing around chatting, and a long line of cars heading up the road. Within minutes, Crock-Pot after Crock-Pot floated in out of the darkness, matched by fragrant pans of lasagna, roast chicken, fish cakes, fresh bread, muffins, cakes, and cookies. The aroma of home cooking filled the room to the rafters as a crowd of cheerful faces from across the district appeared. Volunteers sprang into action, setting up long tables and chairs as more than one hundred people packed the hall. The movement that we had built in 2018 had not stopped over the past year. Everyone was eager to spring into action again.

Chloe and Canyon were already working every minute. Once again Canyon had reoriented his life to Maine. In May 2019, he had accepted a climate organizing job in Boston, collaborating with fellow alums to ramp up pressure on Harvard to divest from fossil fuel companies. He negotiated to work thirty hours a week, including remote work, so that he could be in Maine planning the State Senate campaign. Too many mornings saw Canyon up at 4:00 a.m. in Nobleboro to arrive in Boston later that morning for work, then back to Nobleboro a few days later. Chloe was in Augusta, the capital, finishing her term as state representative, then home for campaign work and juggling the two other jobs that helped keep food on the table.

After the January launch, we hit the ground running and set to work crafting what we call our canvassing universe: the voters that we needed to talk with—mostly Republicans and independents—to win. Canyon needs certain data and modeling to create this list of voters, but the party had not supplied this information as of early 2020. Like failed Democratic campaigns before, we were stuck using the universe that the Senate Democratic Campaign Committee (SDCC) created. We could tell right off the bat that this universe was deeply flawed and would lead to a major loss if we stuck with it for the year. Chloe talked mostly with Democrats who already supported her. She was missing conservative households that she had canvassed in 2018. These essential votes were excluded from the Democratic Party's universe of voters. It was a mess. As Canyon worked with the SDCC to try and correct the universe, Chloe charged on because we knew that hitting some doors was better than no doors at all.

FROM CAMPAIGN TO COVID

Then March rolled around, and COVID hit. The legislative session abruptly ended, as it was no longer safe to gather almost two hundred legislators in the State House. Chloe and Canyon hunkered down in quarantine together. The beginning of COVID was stressful for everyone. The uncertainty around the disease, communication around "bubbles," finding masks, quarantining for two weeks . . . it was all so unprecedented and overwhelming. We knew that our entire community was feeling this stress. There was no question that we should stop campaigning indefinitely. No more doors. No more meetings with volunteers. No more social media or letters to the editor.

Pausing the campaign was undoubtedly the right thing to do, but a sober reality began to set in. Our strategy revolved around mass movement building—events, canvasses, parties, and so much more. Our success depended on knocking on thousands of doors with dozens of volunteers. It didn't take long to realize that the pandemic rendered this impossible. Everything that we had banked on quickly disappeared. We went quiet for a few days, pondering our huge gamble.

As we let go of our campaign vision, we quickly found ourselves discussing ways to help people in our community who were frightened and vulnerable, especially seniors suddenly isolated by the COVID lockdown. We realized that we already had access to the voter database with phone numbers for almost every household. We also had over one hundred campaign volunteers across District 13 who had been ready to organize for the election.

We put the pieces together and decided to transform the campaign into a COVID mutual aid effort for the district—offering support for seniors who needed it. We knew that this would be a huge undertaking, though. Chloe called our treasurer, Ellen Dickens, who also worked at the local food pantry, to get her take. Ellen said, "It's a good idea, but beware of the Pandora's box that you're about to open." That was good advice. We had no idea the scale and variety of assistance that people would need or our capacity to provide it amid such uncertain conditions. We decided to start on a small scale and test drive the idea in one town, Jefferson.

We called our friends from Revitalize Jefferson, the local group that grew out of our 2018 campaign. Chloe, Canyon, and two volunteers called every single senior living alone in Jefferson in just a couple of hours. We checked in to see how folks were doing, provided the latest information from the CDC and the state, and also offered rides, pharmacy pickups, connections to food banks, and a buddy to call them every day or week to check in. We found quite a few people who needed help. This included one woman who told us that she was running out of food. We connected her to the amazing volunteers at the Jefferson Food Bank that day, and she had food delivered later that night.

There was clearly a need, so we decided to launch this relief network to every senior in District 13, regardless of their political persuasion. We put out a call for additional volunteers and soon had two hundred neighbors joining the effort. We started organizing two phone banks a week.

And it took off. We found dozens and dozens of seniors who needed help. And we found even more who were grateful for the call. We gave each senior a phone number to call in case their situation or that of a loved one changed in the coming days or weeks.

The stories that emerged were beautiful. One volunteer connected with an elderly woman who depended on the library for large print books because of her eyesight, but the libraries were closed. We went through our network to find a bookstore that delivered some large-print books to her. Another volunteer talked with a gentleman who had no internet and therefore no access to the news. She bought him a subscription to the *New York Times*. "It's a real sense of neighbors looking out for neighbors," reflected one volunteer.

We live in a rural area with no public transportation options, and so a lot of our citizens' needs revolved around access to a car. We had volunteers pick up prescriptions for neighbors, deliver groceries, drop off toilet paper, and more. These seniors had relied on family members for rides, but elderly folks getting in a car with someone was now risky, and many didn't feel safe going into the grocery store. We also developed a trusted network of drivers. Although the world had shut down, the need to get to the doctor or get chemotherapy did not. We also had a number of people who got an ambulance ride to the ER and then had no way to get home. We had our drivers sign waivers and connected them with patients in our community to give them rides.

Within a few weeks, we had created an intricate system to bring on additional volunteers, organize phone banks, identify people who needed help, and get them help quickly. We developed a partnership with a COVID food relief network, sending volunteers their way for food bank information or meal deliveries. We attended coordinating calls multiple times a week with local organizations to make sure that we were all on the same page about the services to provide for our community.

Other legislators heard about the effort, and we shared our model with them to replicate for their own constituents. We told the SDCC what we were doing. The next day, they sent out an email to every candidate encouraging them to make similar calls. But there were problems. In most cases, campaigns didn't have robust volunteer networks in place to meet the needs of their community that would emerge from the calls. And, most disturbingly, the SDCC instructed candidates to only call people within their "persuasion universe"—people whose votes they thought that they could win. We read this email in horror and immediately wrote back imploring them to not limit the scope of their calls to what was politically expedient during such an acute crisis. They curtly brushed us off and held the course, so we continued to focus on our own efforts.

Overall, our 200-plus volunteers made just over 13,500 phone calls in the span of three months. It was a mighty effort. We saw the neighborliness and caring of rural communities. As inspiring as this was, it also took an extraordinary amount of work. Chloe was on call 24/7, as urgent requests for help or a ride came in consistently. The computer time was off the charts, causing Chloe to one day literally lose her sight. She then had to get glasses for the first time in her life. Canyon was making sure that we were keeping track of whom we called and organizing all our phone banks. It was a heavy lift for us and for our volunteers.

The network has continued to this very day. Any given week, we send half a dozen volunteers to deliver groceries to elderly neighbors in our community. As of 2021, we are still organizing rides for seniors. We did two rides the week of this writing. Our model has been adopted by town leaders to call seniors with information about free local organic meals and vaccine availability.

Early in April, with COVID in full swing, the prospects of being able to resume the grassroots neighbor-to-neighbor campaign necessary to unseat a longtime incumbent seemed extremely slim. But we were at peace and believed that the mutual aid work was just as important for the community. After all, we weren't running the campaign just to win a State Senate seat—we were doing it to transform our community for the better and show that a different type of politics was possible. Chloe reflected in a voice memo the first week of April: "The phone banking we're doing and the good work we're doing is worth it. And even if it's just for a couple months—we started a movement with this phone banking and you know. . . . It's so important and so in line with our thinking, and we never would have had the opportunity to do that. We probably won't win, and that's okay."

BACK TO THE CAMPAIGN TRAIL

Slowly but surely, the panic of the first wave of COVID began to subside in late May. People could go outside. Summer was coming. We knew more about the virus and how to manage it. Our phone calls were still appreciated, but we were finding fewer and fewer folks who needed help. So we started to pivot back to campaigning. We had ground to make up, as Dow had not stepped out of the public spotlight for a moment. While we were quietly coordinating the massive mutual aid effort, Dow had been a steady fixture of the news cycle with political stunts and aggressive calls to reopen the economy and strip the governor of her emergency powers.

Our transition back to campaign life was slow and careful. We didn't want to alienate the community with political talk when the world felt so raw. We had also called upon a massive amount of volunteer capacity for the mutual aid network and wanted to give people a break.

We eased back in a few ways. First, we scheduled weekly check-ins for every Monday. Canyon and Chloe would sit down with a methodical checklist. This system had been perfected after several fights that resulted from poor communication, bad note-taking, and shortsighted practices. We checked in about the week's needs, items that would come up in the next two weeks, and long-term items that we needed to keep an eye on. We also did emotional check-ins and set aside time to exchange positive and constructive feedback.

Second, two interns came to work with us for the summer. Both had planned to join us before COVID hit, expecting a summer of building a vibrant local movement and hanging out. They chose to come anyway at the critical moment of transition back toward campaigning. Both were young folks looking to work on rural environmental issues and bravely adapted to socially distanced outdoor working. One was Jasper, a student at Bates College in Lewiston, Maine, who was excited to dig into campaign work. The other was Claire, a recent college graduate and science teacher who farmed and lived in a yurt while she worked with us.

Jasper and Claire took on the job of recruiting volunteers to start "soft" campaign activities—such as writing letters to the editor—for the coming weeks. We held virtual house parties on Zoom to introduce people to Chloe and the campaign. Jasper and Claire made hundreds of calls each week to spread the word about these events. We organized socially distanced phone banks at a local brewery and other locations across the district. Jasper worked with a local artist to set up a sign-painting party and re-create our handmade road signs. Slowly but surely, the building blocks of the campaign started to come together again. The movement was springing back to life.

Chloe discreetly began to knock on doors again in June, despite the party instructing candidates not to. As far as we know, Chloe was the only Democrat in the state who was out canvassing. Some independents and Republicans were pounding the pavement, but no Democrats. This was a very tough decision for us. We didn't want to make anyone feel unsafe during a pandemic. But we also didn't want people to feel left out and further ignored by politics because of the pandemic.

Chloe eased into this process. The first day, in the high heat of summer, she did a "lit drop," which meant simply leaving our palm card (flier) at each door—no knocking or face-to-face communication. She ran into a few people who were outside working, and people seemed to welcome her presence. The next day, she tried real door knocking, staying well over six feet apart, outside always, not touching any doorknobs or door handles, with mask on or visible. Everyone was okay with it! So we kept going.

Our canvassing territory for 2020 was different than 2018, but the same themes applied. We did not use the SDCC's universe. With requisite data in hand by early summer, Canyon spent days meticulously crafting the universe. We cast a wide net, knowing that we would need to persuade an unprecedented number of voters in order to unseat Dow. Canyon's persuasion universe was more than four times the size of the one originally created for Chloe by the SDCC.

The SDCC director straight up told us that they didn't believe in talking to Republicans. In 2018, Chloe had spoken with a ton of hard-core Republicans to win. The dynamic was different in 2020 because we were running in a more moderate district. But we still talked with mostly Republicans and independents who had never been contacted by a Democrat (or at least not in a very long time). We also knew, thanks to Canyon's analysis, that there was a large chunk of Democrats who had voted for Mr. Dow. So we went to talk to them too.

Canvassing is key to winning rural districts. It's part of our secret. But it was just as brutal in 2020 as it was in 2018. Most people Chloe talked with still had deep prejudice against anyone with a D next to their name. A candidate's responsibility is not only to muster the courage to drive down dirt roads but also to disarm the hatred that frequently comes your way—or to deal with it if all else fails.

Once we discovered that the canvassing was viable, Chloe went at it. We didn't feel comfortable sending our volunteers to the doors during COVID to talk to Trump voters, so the burden was on Chloe to make those connections. In 2018, Chloe knocked three hours a day. Since she had a smaller universe, she could knock on thirty to forty doors in those three hours. In 2020, we had more people to reach and less time. That meant five to seven hours of intense canvassing daily, five or six days a week, from June to November, averaging over one hundred doors per day. This was unlike 2018 or anything else Chloe had faced. Canvassing consumed her life. By Election Day, Chloe had knocked on 13,314 doors.

It was a chaotic year to campaign in Maine. We saw the most expensive and fraught election in Maine's history as Sara Gideon took on incumbent US senator Susan Collins. The airwaves and mailboxes were flooded with attack ads. No one was enjoying it. Distaste for Democrats was high after fallout from Trump's impeachment. Trump flags, banners, lawn signs, bumper stickers, and other paraphernalia greeted Chloe at many of the doors that she visited. Sometimes these Trump flags were accompanied by a sign featuring a gun and the words "Prayer is the best way to meet the Lord. Trespassing is faster." All this was heightened by the Right's anti-mask vitriol that ran deep and strong.

Chloe canvassed by herself again in 2020, finding it faster and less draining. Similar to 2018, many days led to uncomfortable and rude encounters. Once, as she canvassed in Jefferson, someone opened a second-story window before Chloe had even knocked and yelled out, "Are you a Republican or a Democrat?" With a disarming smile, Chloe replied, "I'm a Democrat! I'd love to talk." This woman slammed her window shut. Through the thin walls Chloe heard the husband ask, "Who was that?" The woman responded with deep anger, "It was a Democrat." At almost every door, Chloe was asked whether she was a Republican or Democrat. She always answered honestly, prepared for yelling or a door slammed in her face. People frequently told her to get off their property or simply shut their front door on her, mid-sentence.

Perhaps the best and worst story from canvassing: It was the end of a long day of knocking doors along the coast. Chloe was down a long dirt road that had quite a few upscale homes on it. She knocked on a door. A woman came, took one look at Chloe, and slammed the door. Chloe yelled, "How could you be so mean? You don't even know who I am!" But then she heard the woman snarl to her husband inside, "It was Chloe Maxmin."

Despite these harsh encounters, the canvassing magic of 2018 made a reappearance in 2020. There was the staunch Republican who first told Chloe to go away but softened up and allowed a long, in-depth conversation. He told Chloe that he would vote for her and later sent her a picture of his ballot to prove it. She was the only Democrat that he voted for that year. There was the gentleman who was going to vote for Chloe but no other candidate on the ballot. And there was the man Chloe met through our volunteer transportation network who registered to vote just for Chloe. And there were the many people voting for Trump and for Chloe who proudly displayed both lawn signs at the ends of their driveways. The stories of tenderness, hope, and connection are there, but Chloe had to fight hard for them.

One big surprise came in the form of a phone call from Les Fossel, the former chair of the Lincoln County Republicans and former Republican legislator, following a long day of canvassing in the summer. Chloe had spoken with Fossel's wife that afternoon at the door, and Les was impressed by what he overheard of the exchange and read about the campaign. Les told Chloe that he would support her. Shortly thereafter, he made good on his word with a letter in our biggest local newspaper: "To Chloe, this work is not about a party. It is about service through shared values, through listening, and through mutual respect. Please join me in voting for Chloe Maxmin on November 3rd."

Another unexpected boost came in the form of the annual award from the nonpartisan Maine Council on Aging (MCOA), which in September recognized Chloe as the 2020 legislator of the year. This statewide honor was given to Chloe for her "outspoken passion for her older residents" and in recognition of the innovative ways she "worked through the COVID-19 crisis collaboratively with communities, institutions, governments, and businesses to develop and implement solutions that have improved the health and safety of older Mainers." As a first-term legislator, this was a big surprise and gave us crucial added credibility on the campaign trail going up against one of the most experienced legislators in the state. "Chloe Maxmin may be a new face in the Maine legislature," said Jess Maurer, executive director of MCOA, "but she is already a strong voice for Maine's older adults."[1]

Meanwhile, Canyon slogged away at his computer at home all day long. In 2018, a flow of family and friends would visit from near and far to keep us afloat. But with COVID, 2020 was largely a solitary affair. While Chloe was canvassing, Canyon did everything else, at home, alone. He built up our mailer program, designing and writing content for the mailers that we sent out across the district. He worked with the local newspaper's printer to get them sent out instead of using the SDCC's expensive campaign consultants.

Canyon worked with a local video producer to write and shoot a campaign video. The SDCC wanted us to use their video consultants, whose videos were canned with the world's most boring scripts. Canyon drafted a script for Chloe and worked with our producer to set up the perfect scenes for shooting. At one point, one of the SDCC staffers saw our script and accidentally sent us a response meant for someone else: "Yikes." Our video received almost 23,000 views—a massive number for our district.

We did our best to tackle the challenge of reimagining our grassroots campaign under the shadow of COVID. Canyon began organizing volunteers for remote voter-contact phone banks in the summer. He used social media to recruit dozens of friends and acquaintances who were eager to support. A lot of local folks who had participated in the mutual aid calls also joined. Twice a week, volunteers hung out together on Zoom for two hours while making calls to voters to identify support for Chloe. This allowed us to get our message out on a wide scale and further hone our mailing and canvassing lists.

As the summer began to fade, our interns went back to school, the weather got colder, and we braced ourselves for the last few months of a hard run toward the finish line. It was "all hands on deck" time. We needed our volunteers to get locked in and committed to the end. We decided to organize four volunteer launches across the district. Since the region is so big, we divided it into four hubs and started volunteer teams in each hub. Gathering outside by the ocean, in a farmer's field, at a disc golf course, and outside Chloe's middle school, we recruited dozens of volunteers to get us through the finish line in each region. In just one weekend, we had enough capacity to hit all of our volunteer goals to finish the race.

We identified five priorities. First, we focused on letters to the editor (LTEs). We wanted to make sure that each of the local papers had at least one LTE per week, if not more, leading up to the election. In our neck of the woods, people still read the local papers. From our launches, we had enough folks to fill those slots.

Next, we geared up for massive sign distribution. Per state law, we couldn't put our road signs up until mid-September. So we readied volunteers for that fated day to erect signs across the district. We also assigned regional sign captains so that, if someone requested a sign for their road or lawn, it would be delivered right to their doorstep.

For those who wanted to volunteer from home, we continued to organize two phone banks a week dedicated to voter outreach. By the end of the summer, we had made over fifty thousand phone calls. By calling each person up to five times over the course of a couple months until we made contact, we pretty much reached every voter who was willing to answer their phone. While most other campaigns were just ramping up their phone-banking efforts as the election approached, we had already maxed out our efforts and were positioned to transition our volunteer energy into other areas.

Another COVID-safe tactic that we used to reach voters directly was postcard writing. Over five thousand personal postcards, handwritten by our volunteers and addressed to neighbors in their own community, were mailed or delivered to voters' doorsteps. These cards were striking, joyful, and authentic, shining through the muck of political smear that clogged our mailboxes in Maine.

Finally, we asked volunteers to do lit drops—dropping off our campaign literature on stoops and porches across the district. We still didn't feel comfortable with mass canvassing, though our volunteers ended up running into many residents in their yards or on their front porches and having good conversations. It became the perfect way to maintain a strong grassroots ground game, manage the risk of COVID, and make sure that our volunteers didn't have to step outside of their comfort zones.

This much activity across four regions in a rural community was a lot to coordinate. We built an amazing volunteer leadership team that picked up where Jasper and Claire left off and took us all the way to the finish line. From a part-time farmer to a college student working remotely for the semester, our team met every single Monday throughout the fall to make sure that our campaign was running smoothly. In moments of uncertainty, we would also rely on the wisdom of elders in our inner circle for additional perspective. Whether responding to attacks or preparing for a debate, we had both experienced and fresh voices on our side the whole way.

Another key to our success in the home stretch was our dear friend and fellow divestment organizer from college, Henney Sullivan, who moved to Nobleboro in early September to run our field program. "Field" includes anything "out in the field," like lit drops, canvassing, postcards, sign distribution, and phone banks. Henney had been a field organizer for Bernie Sanders in 2016 back in his rural New Hampshire hometown. He knew how to run a successful field campaign. We were able to reimburse Henney for *some* of his work with the money that we saved by eschewing the SDCC's consultants.

We built a mighty movement despite the pandemic, but we always knew that an ominous cloud was poised to soak us at any moment: Republican attacks. The sky opened in September with an ugly mailer. On the front, a huge picture of Chloe's face featured a thought bubble attached to a bunch of dollar signs. Next to it were the words "Chloe Maxmin is using taxpayer dollars for personal profit." On the back: "She's using taxpayer-funded Maine Clean Election Act dollars to write a book for her own personal profit." Their source? Canyon's personal website.

On one level, we were relieved. This was such a weak attack! The best that the Maine GOP could come up with was that Chloe was writing a book and the lie that taxpayer money was funding it? We could live with that. Then they took it to another level, releasing a video that spouted the same message but this time claiming that Chloe was paying her "boyfriend" to manage her campaign and write a book with her. The GOP sexualized our relationship and used it as a weapon to discredit Chloe simply for being young, female and unmarried. The video received tens of thousands of views on Facebook.

More mailers followed. One said, "Chloe Maxmin is not a moderate. She votes right beside Democrats in Augusta who would dismantle police departments." We had anticipated this line of attack long before it materialized and preempted it with mailers and video ads highlighting the Lincoln County sheriff's enthusiastic endorsement of our campaign.

One afternoon in September, a constituent alerted us to a disinformation-based attack from a fake "poll" making the rounds by telephone and email in our beloved District 13. This kind of fake opinion poll is called a "push poll," defined by the American Association for Public Opinion Research as "a form of negative campaigning disguised as a political poll . . . that aims to persuade large numbers of voters and affect election outcomes."[2] The push poll in District 13 used disinformation, inflammatory language, and extremely biased statements to praise Dow as a defender of small business and frame Chloe "in lockstep" with "New York and California radicals."

This is when Canyon became a lawyer. He worked with the Lincoln County Democrats to file a complaint with the Maine Ethics Commission and investigate the origin of this shady push poll. Ethics heard the case, and the bipartisan commission voted unanimously to launch an investigation. But they weren't hopeful that they could find the people behind it. The *Portland Press Herald* and *Bangor Daily New*—the two biggest papers in Maine—both covered this development, and the *Press Herald* published a scathing rebuke of this kind of dirty campaigning.[3]

We were just as surprised as the Ethics Commission when, only a couple of weeks later as their investigation began, the Maine Senate Republicans admitted to sponsoring the illegal push poll.[4] Their PAC was responsible for paying a hardcore Republican attack agency called Red Maverick to conduct the poll. Digging through online records, Canyon discovered that the "principal officer" of the GOP PAC—by definition the person responsible for all decisions—was none other than our opponent, Dana Dow. Canyon joined multiple calls with the Ethics Commission to try to hold Dow accountable. Dow pleaded innocent and ignorant of what was happening. The commission decided it needed more time to investigate the matter and was unable to make a finding before the election.

We had been braced for Republican attacks, but that didn't make it any easier. It was heartbreaking that the same disinformation campaigns destroying political discourse at the national level had infiltrated our community. Our political values of positive campaigning were unwavering, but we also knew that many a good candidate had fallen to the onslaught of Republican disinformation attacks. Did we have a responsibility to call out the lies for the sake of our community? Or would that just pump more oxygen into the disinformation effort and mire us in an endless rhetorical arms race? We talked a lot about how to respond and gathered family and mentors on Zoom for more discussion. We also did our research. Chloe found that the blatantly baseless attacks did not seem to be getting much traction at the doors. Hardly anyone mentioned them or asked questions about those negative claims. If they did refer to them, it was usually to say how quickly they had thrown the mailer into the trash. Canyon came to the same conclusion as he analyzed social media.

We talked often about how to respond to the barrage of attacks. We decided to do what we had always done, each time with deeper conviction and certainty. We would double down on the values that we learned on the dirt roads, the values that had brought us home. We would choose love, choose community, choose mutual respect. "We reject disinformation and attacks of all kinds in Senate District 13," Chloe wrote in the local papers. "It's not who we are. Our community deserves better. We are disappointed to see this kind of negative campaigning enter this district." We stood up for what the people of District 13 deserve, for what we all deserve. Dana Dow never condemned the negative attacks as they came out.

Our campaign charged along, true to our movement values. Our volunteers connected with voters. Chloe knocked on doors. Henney directed the field program. Canyon coordinated our mailers, literature, media buys, and general activities. Before we knew it, Election Day was right around the corner.

THE FINAL SPRINT

GOTV was odd in 2020. Due to the pandemic, many residents had begun to mail in their ballots by early October. By the time we launched our GOTV effort in the last week of October, many had already voted. This allowed us to continue reaching out to persuadable voters to the very end, rather than spending our final days exclusively reaching out to ensure supporters made it to the polls. Henney had teams head out every day from all corners of the district. We had so many contacts that, by the end of GOTV, people had either already voted or had told us exactly how they would vote on November 3, Election Day. That is quite rare in the GOTV world, and it was proof that our efforts had genuinely reached our persuasion universe.

Between our phone calls and canvassing, we ultimately made over eighty thousand voter contact attempts over the course of the entire campaign. These eighty thousand calls and knocks were in a district of thirty-eight thousand and a canvassing universe of about five thousand. This means that, despite the unique challenges of 2020, we were able to reach voters multiple times to build real relationships and offer continuous opportunities for engagement.

November 3, 2020, dawned cold and sunny, with a dusting of snow on the frozen ground. All the work was done. The hay was in the barn, as they say. Now all that was left was to stand outside the polls from 8:00 a.m. to 8:00 p.m. as Henney sent the final GOTV canvassers on their way. Canyon created a methodical schedule for Chloe, getting her to key polls at key times. Our first stop was Waldoboro, Dana Dow's hometown. We pulled up to the town office to find a huge line of people waiting to vote. Standing outside in the snow, we enthusiastically greeted voters as they filed in—including Mr. Dow. We then went to Jefferson, Windsor, Whitefield, Wiscasset, and back to Waldoboro.

The day was long, and a frigid wind bit at every piece of exposed skin. We ate a lot of food to keep ourselves warm. There was some nastiness. One man in Jefferson yelled, "Booooo you! Go Dana!" in Chloe's face at the polls. In Wiscasset, someone called the police on Chloe for greeting voters, which is legal. But there were many more words of encouragement, familiar faces, and thumbs up, all of it lighting up our hopes at the end of a dark year. One woman said, "I don't know if you remember, but I live at the end of a long dirt road, and you came to my house twice. It meant so much!"

The polls closed at 8:00 p.m. An enormous yellow moon rose above the tree line as we drove home for a bonfire with our family and a couple of friends. It was twenty degrees outside. The COVID life. We were consumed by stress and anxiety. Results slowly began to trickle in. With frozen fingers, Canyon typed them into his tabulating spreadsheet. Right away, we could tell that it was going to be close. Sometimes we were behind by a hundred votes. At other times, we were ahead by less than fifty. Between 10 and 10:30 p.m., the results from Waldoboro and Jefferson, two of the biggest towns in the district, came in. "That's not good," Canyon whispered as he put the results into his spreadsheet. We lost both towns by margins that left us with an excruciatingly narrow path to victory. The heavy reality of that began to sink in, and we struggled to keep it together. There were still a lot of votes to count, but now we would need to punch above our weight class in several of the remaining towns in order to have a chance.

The flow of results came to a halt for what seemed like forever. A biting wind blew, and temperatures dropped into the teens, causing Canyon's laptop to shut down. We drove a car into the field, next to the bonfire, to warm it back up so that we could continue tabulating results when they once again began to trickle in.

Ever so slowly, the picture evened out. Windsor's numbers came in and put us back on track to win by four votes based on Canyon's initial modeling that estimated the remaining votes in each town. Bit by bit, things continued to tip our way. As midnight neared, we knew that our fate rested upon the good people of Wiscasset and Boothbay. If we could keep it close and hit our respective targets of 43 percent and 48 percent of the votes for Chloe in those two towns, we would win. Wiscasset came in first: 48.58 percent—almost 5.5 percent more for Chloe than expected! Our razor-thin lead increased. All eyes turned to Boothbay, the last big battleground outstanding.

Boothbay always votes Republican, so it was a question of margins. If the vote for Chloe in Boothbay was close to the 48.69 percent for the Democratic candidate in 2016, we would win. But if Boothbay voted the way it did in the 2018 election, when only 44.88 percent went to the Democrat, then Dow would win. We braced ourselves and waited. And waited . . . Radio silence from Boothbay. We got a volunteer to drive down to see what they could find out at the polling place. They reported that it was dark and locked up. We let out a collective groan, bracing ourselves for another night of uncertainty as we had experienced in 2018.

The clock slowly ticked off minutes in the early-morning hours, and then Canyon's phone rang. It was the SDCC executive director. She had the results from Boothbay. Canyon asked what the margin was, preparing for the worst. "You won Boothbay," the director said. "Holy shit" was all Canyon could muster in response as he took down the exact numbers. We won.

Canyon kept his cool for a little while, still strung out by the stress of the night. Chloe burst into tears. To this day, she can't remember the next fifteen minutes of her life. She is told that she ran out into the field and collapsed weeping, while worried family tried to get through to her. Then it sunk in: we had done it. The pain and slog and uncertainty were over. Faith and companionship and our positive politics-as-unusual had pushed us over the top.

We celebrated without restraint, largely insulated for the moment from the somber reality of the historically bad night that Democrats were having across the country. Shockingly, Democrats didn't flip a single state legislative chamber in 2020. While we danced off the heaviest anxiety of our lives, the majority of the country watched in stunned horror as national results slowly trickled in. Having won Florida and racked up enormous double-digit leads in key battleground states, Trump declared victory. Republicans flipped US House of Representatives seats in congressional battlegrounds all across the country. Republicans held on to Senate seats in North Carolina, Maine, Montana, Alaska, and Iowa, which (at the time) appeared to all but guarantee that the Republicans would retain control of the Senate.

In Maine, the story was much the same. It was already clear that Susan Collins had won handily statewide, including by a double-digit margin in District 13. Republicans gained twelve seats in the Maine House of Representatives. Democrats only flipped one seat in the Maine State Senate—ours. Our campaign was the glaring anomaly in an otherwise terrible night for Maine Democrats.

Dow's shocking defeat was on the front page of the *Bangor Daily News*. "Maine Democrats oust top GOP lawmaker as Republicans erode House majority in mixed election," read the headline. "In Democrats' biggest pick up of the night," wrote the reporter, "progressive Rep. Chloe Maxmin knocked off Senate Minority Leader Dana Dow." Tweeting about Chloe's victory, veteran political commentator Michael Shepherd wrote, "This story, more than most, shows why it has been A Weird One tonight." Analyzing election results on NPR's *All Things Considered* the day after, Mal Leary told the host, "Nora, there are always surprises every election year. I would say the biggest one this year was Republican Leader Dana Dow being defeated by a freshman state representative, Chloe Maxmin."

The absurd thing about running for office in districts like ours is that you really don't know if you will win or lose. The journey has to be as meaningful as the outcome. But you also can't deny that you want to win because you want to fight for your home, for your community, for your family and friends. You give your heart and soul to a pure cause, a cause that is truly different, a cause that is trying to respond to the pain of your people. Winning is not everything. Our movement lives on whether we win or not. But winning still feels pretty damn good.

PART III

AS THE
DUST SETTLES

A New Way Forward

CHAPTER 5

STRATEGIC PRINCIPLES

Through true grassroots campaigns, communities can transform, take power, feel empowered, and make change. Every campaign is an opportunity to rebuild and transform our politics and our communities. The Democratic Party has forsaken rural America, relinquishing a tremendous amount of political power that has left our fight for social justice on the brink of despair. Yet we managed to win two campaigns in Republican-leaning districts. How do we account for these victories despite the odds? And, more importantly, how can we translate this vision beyond our districts—to rural communities and campaigns across the country?

We need a new way forward that goes beyond the tired traditional campaign playbook. One of the primary lessons of how we won—and one of the key ways that we can rebuild power in rural America—is through a new type of campaigning. It is on the campaign trail that we can and will build movements that shift our culture toward a more respectful, inclusive, and just path.

Our hope is that the lessons we have distilled from our experiences will be useful for you and your work, whether you're a first-time candidate or campaign manager—as we were when we began—or a veteran political organizer or a door-knocking volunteer. These lessons are for *all* of rural America, not just Maine. We try to frame our lessons in ways that are applicable to races in different parts of the country. That said, we understand that every rural community and every campaign are different. Some of the lessons in the coming chapters might be universally applicable, and others may be more specific to place, time, candidate, or context. You know your community best, what will work, and what won't. Here are a few disclaimers to start with:

- Every state has a different Democratic Party structure and therefore a different way of supporting campaigns and candidates. You may have much more support and flexibility than we did to cater your campaign to your community. Or you may have drastically less freedom. We understand that dynamic and tried to build this into our presentation of these lessons.
- Compared to many states, Maine has small state legislative districts. Our House districts consist of approximately nine thousand people each. State Senate districts average about thirty-eight thousand voters. The size of these districts impacted how we campaigned. For example, it was feasible to talk with persuadable voters more than once, even on the State Senate level. Chloe could often create real relationships with folks instead of showing up to a house once, asking for a vote, and never making contact again. Our smaller districts also enabled us to create a sense of community and camaraderie. Everyone is essentially a neighbor. We go to the same grocery store, walk on the same beaches, and are bonded in ways that can be amplified on the campaign trail. Another feature of small districts: word spreads fast, gossip flies, and reputations are quickly built or destroyed. You can't lie or say mean things about your opponent without the news spreading like wildfire. On the flip side, kindness and compassion become widely known. In smaller districts it is also easier to build name recognition and build a buzz around your candidacy. Finally, to state the obvious, smaller districts mean smaller budgets. You don't need as much money or as many staff members to campaign effectively.
- One of the biggest barriers to running for office and working on local races is the question of how to make a living. In places like Maine, you can't pay yourself to campaign. Maine also, like many states, pays legislators far less than a living wage. For both of us, we could make this lifestyle work because we are young, have no families to take care of, don't mind eating lots of mac and cheese, and have flexible jobs that allow us to campaign by day and Zoom at night. This was a special privilege. We recognize that many people are not in a position to take on this kind of lifestyle. We want to highlight the privilege and flexibility that allowed us

to charge down this path and acknowledge that this path is not possible for everyone.

- Both of us had prior organizing and campaigning experience before launching our campaign. We had spent years doing climate justice organizing together before we began working in electoral politics. We had both worked on other campaigns, getting a close-up view to the inner workings of those machines, their strategies, canvassing approaches, relationships with consultants, finances, communication structures, and more. We had volunteered for multiple candidates and understood how extractive and exhausting it can be to canvass by yourself for hours in the rain for a candidate you only *kind of* believe in. And we had both been through campaign and candidate trainings. Chloe went through Emerge Maine, a program that trains Democratic women to run for office. Canyon went through a campaign-manager training program sponsored by Lillian's List, an organization that trains staff to support progressive women to run for office. These experiences were invaluable for two reasons. First, they showed us the major flaws and pitfalls of traditional campaigns—where they leave people behind and turn people away and how there is space to create campaigns that look and feel wildly different. Second, they gave us basic foundational skills and enough confidence to march forth on our own. We couldn't have done what we did without those years of learning, observing, and analyzing. That's not to say that you absolutely have to have the experience or training that we did—for a state or local race especially, you don't. But having people in your network with some organizing and campaign experience can certainly help.
- Maine has a public-financing system for candidates called Clean Elections, which we described earlier. It's an incredible program for many reasons. Primarily, it makes running for office accessible to anyone. You don't need to know wealthy donors to have a successful campaign. What's more, candidates can spend most of their time talking with voters instead of constantly fundraising. This kind of program only exists in a few states so far, although we wish that more would adopt it. Clean Elections created the space that we needed to connect with voters in creative ways instead of dialing for dollars every day, which is the traditional hallmark of campaigning. If you don't have a public-financing system in your state, you might need to adapt and focus more effort on small-dollar fundraising.

In this chapter, we will dig into the strategic principles that grounded our campaigns. What does this mean? To go a little nerdy for a moment, "strategy" comes from the Greek word "strategos," which means military general. The two roots of the word are the verbs "to spread" and "to lead." Strategoi—or generals—were always centered on high ground where they could get the best bird's-eye view of the battle as it played out, and were thus able to react nimbly and deploy situationally effective tactics derived from a real-time understanding of the big picture.

In much the same way, it is crucial that campaigns be grounded in coherent strategies that stay constant amid the rapidly changing environment of electoral politics. Strategic principles make up the big-picture core from which tactics are formulated and deployed according to the changing context on the ground. Through our many years of organizing, we've distilled the following big-picture principles. Building these principles into the DNA of campaigns at every level is foundational for Democrats to correct course from the failures that we examined earlier.

COMMIT

In the days and weeks after Trump was elected in 2016, we received an outpouring of calls and Facebook messages from friends and acquaintances lamenting their lack of involvement and asking for advice on how to become more politically active. We attended meetings for upstart community organizing groups like Indivisible and Our Revolution that November and December with hundreds of attendees spilling into the hallways. People were more motivated to get involved with politics and organizing than we had ever seen after witnessing the profound failures of the Democratic establishment and the devastating consequences.

Despite this encouraging outpouring of energy, we felt frustration. Where were all these people in the months prior when we and so many other organizers were pulling teeth to get volunteers to canvass, phone bank, and get out the vote for Clinton and other candidates? Where were all these folks when movements for Black lives, indigenous rights, fair wages, climate justice, and all fights for human dignity were actively resisting the rise of Trumpism?

All too often it takes massive injustice—the election of a demagogue or the broad-daylight murder of a Black man while jogging—to motivate people to engage in political movements. Our task as organizers, therefore, is to tend to that fire after it starts to die down and nurture the embers so they don't merely turn into ash and blow away. The ultimate goal is to connect people with a political home warmed by the sustainably burning embers of commitment.

Commitment must be one of the primary principles of our political movement. It is the necessary ingredient for long-term social change. Motivation ebbs and flows, but commitment carries the day. It's okay that many people will only show up in those stark moments of upheaval. We need them too. The key is that more and more of us must commit to the long-distance organizing work so we can effectively harness the energy of those big moments to make sustained progress in between.

This strategic principle was important to us because we knew that our work was long-term, not just a reaction to the 2016 elections. It was that kind of commitment that allowed us to jump into the unknown, committing to bold, wild ideas, and letting everything else unfold from there. This commitment—to ourselves, to each other, and to the cause—is what enables us to put in the hard work day in and day out. Whatever your commitment—whether knocking on doors once a month or giving your all in a run for office—be clear about what it is. Hold that commitment sacred.

BE AUTHENTIC

We met so many voters who liked both Sanders and Trump and who supported both Trump and Chloe. Head-scratcher, right? Usually, we expect people to vote for the candidates with whom they align most closely with on policies. But, as far as policy goes, Sanders and Chloe could not be more different than Trump. So why would voters mark down both names on a ballot?

There are many reasons, but one that we heard throughout our conversations with voters was "authenticity." While we don't view Trump as a remotely authentic figure, many do. This is because, as they told us, they like candidates who say what they think, even when—or especially when—it goes against the grain of the political elite. Our communities do not resonate with regurgitated poll-tested messaging fed to candidates by party consultants. In fact, they are profoundly frustrated with the political establishment. They seek candidates who say what they believe, with conviction and emotion, even when they know the listener won't agree. In the case of Chloe and Sanders, this authenticity is further backed by ironclad integrity that leaves little doubt that they will walk their talk.

Over and over again, we heard voters express a desire for candidates who are not cut from the same cloth and don't represent politics as usual.

One of our campaign advisors, John deVille, joked that he's convinced the Democrats must have a candidate factory somewhere that churns out a consistent supply of processed, white-bread, moderate candidates with charming fake smiles. Election cycle after election cycle, it seems we get the same type of candidates saying the same things. They take their cues from the same party consultants and inundate voters with the same canned advertisements. People are sick of it, they see through it, and they distrust it.

We took a different route, and voters across the political spectrum liked what they saw. We looked at the scripts that we were sent by party consultants, read the binder of poll-tested messaging at the statewide training, picked out a couple of applicable bits of data, and then set them aside to collect dust. With every piece of campaign literature, every video and radio advertisement, every conversation we had, we strove to be authentic and speak from the heart. When you show up as your authentic self and your actions line up with your words, voters begin to trust you. People are much more inclined to vote for someone they trust, even if they don't agree with their entire platform.

Here is one of the most powerful examples of this lesson from our campaign experience. In 2018, as we campaigned for state representative, our current governor, Janet Mills, launched her first gubernatorial bid. Medicaid expansion was a huge topic during the campaign season. In 2017, Mainers had passed a citizen referendum to expand Medicaid to seventy thousand residents. Then-governor Paul LePage refused to implement the will of the voters, but Janet Mills promised that she would honor this mandate from the people if elected.

One day, Chloe was out door-knocking in Jefferson, and she came across a house with a detached garage. She found everyone in the garage working on snowmobiles and went in to say hi. The owner came out and asked Chloe, "Do you believe in Medicaid expansion?" Chloe answered honestly, "Yes." The man told Chloe, with a big finger pointing toward the road, "You can leave now." Baffled by the short conversation and directive to leave, Chloe thought that he agreed with her and that she could count on his support. It took a couple seconds of confusion to read his body language to realize that he was actually quite angry, that he disagreed with Chloe and wanted her to get off his property.

Genuinely taken aback, Chloe asked, "Hold on a second—what just happened? Can you tell me what you're thinking? I'm honestly just interested to hear your perspective. I'd love to have a conversation if you're willing." This gentleman told Chloe that he grew up on that very property without any electricity or running water. He had worked hard to build a life for himself and his family, which included buying his own healthcare. This was his way of life and what he believed in.

Chloe thanked him for sharing his story, telling how she could completely understand that perspective and frustration. She said that her support of Medicaid was not to take anything away from his hard work but to support those who need it in our state. They had an authentic conversation that was based in honesty. At the end of their talk, this man told Chloe that he would vote for her. In 2020, she went back to his house, told him that she had thought of him every day in Augusta and asked if he would support her again. He said yes. Even when there are policy differences, people resonate with candidates who say what they believe and say it respectfully but without apology.

BE CREATIVE

We both agree that one of the biggest lessons we learned was embracing the opportunity to get creative at any time. Too many candidates and campaigns seek to replicate what has been done before. While we certainly carried forward lessons and tactics from prior campaigns, our guiding philosophy was to do things differently, not to do something just because it was "the way it's done." Even when the old guard balked and insisted we would lose, we pushed forward and found our own way.

As noted, our campaign signs were a shining example of creativity paying dividends. All the other signs looked the same—as if they were spit out into the world alongside their candidate from the candidate factory. We recycled old campaign signs by painting over them, scavenged wood pallets and plywood, and painted Chloe signs ourselves with volunteers. It was a fun way to build community early on in the campaigns, it saved money, and—most importantly—the signs stood out as embodiments of the grassroots nature of our campaign. Perhaps our favorite sign was a pallet painted with fireflies that said "Glowy for Chloe," draped with fairy lights to illuminate at night. There were no other hand-painted political signs around, so they sparked people's curiosity. It made people think, "Wow, people actually took the time to make a sign for this candidate and put it in their yard?" Everybody noticed them, so much so that when we ran in 2020, candidates from each party were all painting signs by hand.

Mailers to voters and video advertisements are also a good example of putting creativity into practice. If we were following the well-trodden path of those who came before, we simply would have hired the same consultants to create the same tired mail and canned video ads. Instead, we applied ourselves to the task of creating something new. We learned new skills and leaned on the expertise of people in our volunteer network to create things that looked and felt authentic and unique to our campaign.

In turn, volunteers became increasingly motivated and invested in the cause as they got to apply their unique skills to make a discernible impact on the campaign. People are smart, and they can spot phoniness from a mile away. Genuine creativity in campaigning is an excellent way to cut through the noise and signal that real people really care about a candidate. More than that, we have no choice but to be creative if we want to win this uphill race.

BE RESOURCEFUL

When fighting to change entrenched systems of power, the cards are always stacked against the changemakers. We will almost inevitably be less resourced than those who are fighting to keep the system as it is. They are wealthy from reaping the benefits of a lopsided world. Therefore, in order to win, we must be more resourceful in making the most of what we have. This means being scrappy and stretching limited budgets as far as they can possibly go. There were so many things that we didn't know how to do when we launched our campaigns, but we put our heads and hands to it and figured it out in order to do a lot with a little.

One of the resources that always feels scarce, yet gives us a huge advantage, is time. If we fully commit to giving it our all and are clear about the urgency and importance of what we're doing, we will make sacrifices and live on very little in order to fully devote our time to the task at hand. That is what enabled Chloe to knock on almost twenty thousand doors in two campaigns and Canyon to take on so many pieces of the campaign that are typically outsourced to overpriced consultants. Reporting on Chloe's upset victory in 2020, Maine Public Radio analysts observed that she "basically outworked Dow." For all that political pundits typically get wrong, they hit that one on the head.

Canyon became a graphic designer on the fly, negotiated a good price with a local printer in the district, and coordinated all of the direct mail pieces that we sent to voters. We managed to do our own direct mail program for half the price of what the party consultants charged while reaching 20 percent more voters. Same story with most of the other things that consultants typically handle, from campaign literature for canvassing to newspaper, video, social media, and radio advertisements. Everything that we could possibly do in-house was done in-house—either by ourselves, as with the mail program, or by volunteers, as with photography, video production, and sign painting. Often it was our campaign staff and volunteers that enabled us to be resourceful and do a lot with a little.

No unjustified expense slipped by us. We were scrappy as hell. A dollar per metal wicket for each campaign sign? We thrifted them from former candidates across the state instead. When hundreds of the wickets needed modification to fit our signs, one of our team got a handful of farmer friends together and had a wire-cutting party to make them functional.

Being resourceful with our limited budget also allowed us to hire the staff necessary to maximize our work. Canyon only had to work part-time outside of the campaign thanks to a small salary. Henney was employed for the homestretch. Their support meant that we could organize volunteer leaders and mobilize our hundreds of volunteers to make the tens of thousands of voter contacts. You never know what the campaign trail will throw at you, but resourcefulness is the Swiss Army knife that can turn challenges into opportunities.

NOT ME, US!

Leadership, as defined by our Harvard mentor Marshall Ganz, is "accepting responsibility to enable others to achieve shared purpose under conditions of uncertainty."[1] We embrace this wholeheartedly. On the campaign trail, it is never about Chloe. Outside of telling her personal story, you'd be hard-pressed to find many instances of Chloe using "I" or "me." Instead, it is "us" and "we." This isn't just semantic nitpicking. It reflects the very core of our theory of change. Politics is about organizing communities to create the best society that we can for all people. Campaigns are about bringing people together to articulate their values and put them into action together.

When we view electing a candidate as the goal of politics, we all lose. The goal of politics is to make our reality align with our values so that everyone can thrive. This is what got us so excited about Bernie's campaign. As a longtime organizer, he understood this better than most. He insisted, "It is not enough to elect a president. We must create a political revolution." One of his slogans was, of course, "Not me. Us!"

We have a long way to go to get this message through to the media and mainstream political culture. People love the individualistic hero narrative and are used to checking out after performing the civic duty of casting a ballot. It is vitally important that we use the platform of campaigns to tell compelling stories of "us" that speak to our shared problems and shared responsibility to work toward solutions. By articulating a shared vision, we make progress—win or lose—and give our fellow citizens a glimpse of a different, more community-focused kind of politics.

YOUTH LEAD

With our future under attack, it is critical that young people continue to engage in politics with the intensity necessary to overcome the strength of our opposition. We are still at the very beginning. But our generation is standing up in huge numbers to build power on the scale that we need.

Young people across the country are running for office, engaging vigorously with politics, organizing for candidates and the issues of our time, and inspiring peers to do the same. In 2016 and 2018, younger generations—those ages eighteen to fifty-three—outvoted baby boomers and all older generations.[2] The number of millennials in the US House increased fivefold after the 2018 election, and Alexandria Ocasio-Cortez (AOC) became the youngest woman ever elected to Congress. Sixteen-year-old Greta Thunberg inspired millions to mobilize for climate justice. Youth-led organizations such as Run for Something and the Sunrise Movement have achieved important electoral and legislative victories.

Yet the growing engagement of young—and overwhelmingly progressive—people in politics is a defining challenge for the Democratic Party. Party operatives demonstrated this during a candidates' training that Chloe attended in 2018. The communications director for Sara Gideon, the Maine Speaker of the House at the time, was talking to local candidates about their relatability. Chloe wrote down what happened: "There were a few candidates in the room, and she was trying to relate to us. She was like: 'Jason, you're a small business owner and a dad. Holly, you work as the opioid outreach coordinator for the police department. And Chloe, you got a lot of energy.' It was just that ageist thing of a young person not being worthy of a substantive comment."

The political establishment, including much of the older Democratic Party leadership at the national level, is having difficulty adjusting to the new voices at the table. The satirical newspaper *The Onion* ran this headline in July 2019 making light of the struggle: "Pelosi Concerned Outspoken Progressive Flank of Party Could Harm Democrats' as Ineffectual Cowards."[3] This waggish take captures the real frustration felt by many young people who are trying to push the party forward and to the left. Speaker Pelosi and Representative Ocasio-Cortez met behind closed doors to discuss what CNN reported as "deep divides in a caucus fractured along ideological and generational lines."[4] The roots of this fracture lie in the unique context that is pushing so many young people to engage with politics.

Millennials are keenly aware that politics as usual is failing every American except the richest and most powerful. We came of age in the Great Recession, 40 percent of us saddled with student debt, all looking toward a future of climate chaos.[5] While the income of other generations rebounded from low points during the recession to back above projected levels, millennial families were left behind as the only group to see their earnings not only fail to rebound but even continue to fall.[6] Almost two-thirds of us "have more fear than hope" about our democratic future, and 77 percent of us blame politicians.[7] We saw firsthand how running and electing young leaders can turn this feeling around for young people in the region. "Politics in this area can so often feel entrenched and demoralizing," one woman wrote us, "it's inspiring to see another young person move back home and work for these communities and places we care so much about."

In 2019, millennials surpassed baby boomers to become the largest living generation and the largest voting bloc in America.[8] Yet even after the gains of 2018, we are grossly underrepresented in American politics, as only about 6 percent of lawmakers are millennials at both the national and state levels. Approximately 55 percent of lawmakers at both levels are baby boomers.[9] The average age of the Maine legislature is fifty-four, and chances are that number is similar in your state. Chloe was the youngest woman in the Maine State House. Canyon was the youngest campaign manager in the state. As we have mentioned, Chloe is the youngest woman senator in Maine history. Still, both parties keep running the same candidates who bring the same unchanging perspectives to a broken process. We need to inject politics with fresh points of view, creative energy, and passion.

In our districts and beyond, everyone is fed up with the current political climate.[10] It is time for something new. "I'm thankful for the leadership of previous generations," wrote a young farmer in District 88, "and I see a need for fresh perspectives. The old systems are not working for the majority of Mainers. I think people like Chloe who believe in investing in our people and communities are integral to the success of our state."[11] Some might claim that, because we are young, we are unsophisticated and inexperienced. But our generation sees through the fog of this way of thinking and understands what justice looks like. We are not afraid to demand what is needed and fight for what we love. We have the courage to turn disillusionment into hope and to fight for *everyone*.

Too often we listen to our elected officials talk about the limitations of what can be accomplished, stuck in the inertia of the world as it is. The leadership of youth brings a missing perspective that is desperately needed to counterbalance the entrenched mindsets of so many politicians. Young people have a remarkable ability to look at the world as it is, envision the world as it could be, and fight to bring our vision for a better world into action.

RESPECT WISDOM

While youth certainly has its own expertise, we recognize the vast stores of wisdom that our elders hold, hard-earned through decades of experience. We are incredibly fortunate to have tremendous friends, family, and mentors from whom we learned the art of organizing and leaned on for advice to make difficult decisions.

When Canyon was trying to decide whether to move to Maine in 2018 to manage Chloe's campaign or stay in North Carolina with a higher-paying, higher-profile job, he called up one of his mentors, Julia Buckner. Julia is a political force in North Carolina, and she helped get Canyon into a campaign manager training program to support North Carolina's legislative races in 2018. Canyon fully expected her to lay out the case for why he should stay in North Carolina to work on helping flip the State Senate there. He was taken aback by the certainty of her immediate response: "Go and work with your friend, Canyon." It was such a tough decision at the time. In retrospect, it was indeed a big decision, and choosing the path of friendship and belief in the possibility of the improbable over money, prestige, and certainty was without a doubt the right choice. These are the kinds of things mentors are for.

Throughout our campaign, we actively sought the wisdom of our elders. We gathered in person in 2018 and over Zoom in 2020 for debate prep, chuckling and taking notes as our mentors recalled memorable debate moments from the 1980s and '90s. The first thing we did before launching our mutual aid network was call up our treasurer. Her advice to pilot it on a small scale first allowed us to iron out some important wrinkles and confirm that there was a need for it in the community and that folks were willing to step up to volunteer and make it happen. Cultivate mentors in your community and learn from their experience and wisdom.

ALWAYS BE LEARNING

Campaigns are incredibly fast-paced, so it is imperative to have structures in place to ensure that active learning and reflection don't get swept to the side. You need to look critically at what you're doing and innovate, evolve, and change constantly. Cultivate a growth mindset in your campaign so that folks can comfortably make mistakes and use them as an opportunity for the whole team to learn. Accept and encourage the feedback cycle.

In our team, we encouraged on-the-fly feedback and also created structured space for it every two weeks. This was a space to reflect and give positive and constructive feedback for ourselves as well as for each other. "Canyon, I'm super-grateful for the increased texting communication, it makes me feel so much better," said Chloe in one such check-in, following up on constructive feedback from the week before. "I *must* leave earlier for doors," she reflected another time during self-feedback. "Really screws me up when I think it'll take four hours but it takes five or six and I'm out there knocking in the dark."

Much can be said about feedback and how to provide it, but a good starting point for us was the following set of principles that Canyon brought with him from instructing with NOLS (formerly the National Outdoor Leadership School):

- *Be timely.*
- *Be growth-oriented.*
- *Be specific about your observations.*
- *Acknowledge your share of any problem.*
- *Be clear about what you will do next.*
- *Be as open to receiving feedback as giving it.*

In addition to giving and receiving feedback among our team, we also sought consistent feedback from volunteers following phone banks and canvassing days. Feedback from volunteers led to changes big and small. Sometimes it was as small as a word choice in our talking points. Sometimes it was as large as deciding to stop making phone calls altogether, as in summer 2020 when volunteers reported that value was drying up as we had already attempted everyone multiple times and most of the folks who were willing to talk had already spoken with us. Without this feedback loop, it could have been easy to keep on pushing through, chasing the next milestone of number of calls made.

Turn your vision into action. Actively reflect on your action to evaluate what went well, what didn't, and why. Use this information to create a new vision and put it into action. Vision. Action. Reflection. Repeat.

STAY CONNECTED TO THE PEOPLE, NOT BIG DONORS OR PARTY ELITES

The people that you surround yourself with inevitably influence the ways in which you see the world. That's one of the many reasons why we distrust any politician who spends the majority of their time talking with the richest donors they can find. Our campaigns are all about grassroots organizing. People are the heart and soul of this approach. We benefit from a great public campaign finance system in Maine that makes this easy for us, but the same principle applies no matter where you're running or what you're running for: you have to stay grounded and connected with the people. No matter what your fundraising approach is, remember that the most important people to talk with are the folks on the ground.

When we talk with voters, we don't show up and simply preach our gospel. We listen to people to learn where they are, and we make sure that our campaign is reflecting that reality. People influence our campaigns as much as the other way around. This isn't usually the case. Most politicians become disconnected from the people, interacting with and surrounding themselves with uber-wealthy elite donors, pollsters, consultants, lobbyists, and party leaders. Or they're only talking to Democrats while they campaign. The inevitable result is that campaigns do not reflect the lived experiences of the people, causing more and more of a disconnect and feeling of alienation.

Chuck Schumer reportedly had a call with Jeff Jackson, a prospective 2020 US Senate candidate for North Carolina, in which Jackson said that he would launch his campaign with a hundred town halls, visiting every single county in the state. According to Jackson, Schumer replied, "Wrong answer—we want you to spend the next 16 months in a windowless basement raising money, and then we're going to spend 80% of it on negative ads about Tillis."[12] Whether a purely factual recounting of the interaction or not, this story illustrates the backwardness of the Democratic establishment's approach to campaigning.

A young woman wrote to us in 2018 with an interesting story about how these dynamics play out on the ground:

> I was arranging a rural field program in Northern Minnesota and the article you wrote in *The Nation*, "What a Rural Maine House Race Can Teach the Left" really resonated with me. I read it when I was leading a canvass in Ely, MN (population 3,387). With 8 volunteers, we knocked on 200 doors that day, and I was so very proud of my work. My boss called me to yell at me for going to a rural area, bitched me out in front of my coworkers and host, and ordered me back to Duluth (population 86,000). I said NO. . . . Honestly, it felt like the Democrats were trying to suppress the rural vote. The myth "there are no democrats in rural areas" HAS to end and I think your work (and mine!) will be instrumental in that.

In much the same way that focusing on extracting the most votes possible for statewide races leads Democrats to abandon rural communities in favor of cities and suburbs, the singular focus on extracting the biggest checks possible causes party leaders and candidates to lose touch with working-class people. We are not advocating for the party to abandon the urban and suburban vote but rather insisting that it must be complemented by a vigorous new focus on the rural. By the same token, we're not advocating that Democrats give up going after big checks but are pointing to the importance of also centering grassroots organizing and small-dollar fundraising. An unwavering commitment to stay connected to the working class and rural people is a must in order to achieve long-term success.

RESPECT EVERYONE

Our campaign movements are made up of people from all walks of life. We respect the intelligence of the people whose votes we are trying to earn and who we are campaigning with. We respect diverse perspectives and viewpoints, even if we disagree. This is more important than ever in these divisive times. We move backward when interactions devolve into arguments with each person putting up walls and digging deeper into their opinions. There is something to be learned from every person. Everybody has their own story and is a product of their experiences.

This is how we see people and how we train our volunteers to approach conversations at the doors. Take the time to truly listen to why somebody believes the things they do, and you'll begin to understand why they think the way that they do. You may not agree with them, but when understanding—rather than anger or judgment—is the starting point, the conditions for worthwhile dialogue are created.

People have great intuition about how you view them. It doesn't take an unforced error that is the magnitude of referring to people as "deplorables" to make people turn away. They pick up subtle clues everywhere to connect the dots. Sending a clickbait email with an all-caps subject line might work a few times and rake in some extra donations, but it erodes trust over time. It cheapens you, and it cheapens those you are trying to reach. It betrays a disrespect for the recipient's intelligence and their time.

The final piece of mail that we sent out in 2018 is a good example of how we deliberately demonstrated respect in our communications. We sent a small card to conservative voters who were highly likely to turn out to vote. It was a photo of one of the hand-painted pallet signs leaning against Chloe's barn with the text "Chloe Maxmin is a trusted leader. Don't take our word for it, do your own research," followed by Chloe's and her opponent's name and the URL for their campaign pages. It was elegantly simple and demonstrated a respect for the voters' intelligence, as well as a self-respect that Chloe was confident to stand on her two feet in an unbiased side-by-side comparison with her opponent.

Similarly, most of our mail in 2020 looked wildly different from the glossy candidate-factory pieces other candidates sent. The backside of each of our first three mailers was entirely text. In the style of handwritten letters, we laid out Chloe's story and the story of the campaign and how they aligned with the story of the community and the urgency of the moment. Most mail consultants would have been dismayed by the amount of text we used. "People need to be able to read this in five to ten seconds" they would say. Sure, not everyone took the time to read these letters, but we heard from so many voters who did and who appreciated them. The folks who throw political mail straight in the trashcan were going to do so either way. And, who knows, maybe some of them even noticed that one piece was not like the rest as they sent Chloe careening into the garbage along with the others.

LISTEN

People always ask us how we won. Our biggest answer is listening. We cannot emphasize this enough. We see listening as an act of liberation,

resistance, and revival. We live in a democracy that is woefully disconnected from and unrepresentative of the people it is supposed to serve.
Public opinion has little bearing on whether legislation is passed, and
citizens' referenda are routinely ignored or altered. Meanwhile, an unfettered flood of corporate money and lobbyists work to ensure that the
monied elite—and no one else—have the ear of legislators. Politicians
rarely show their faces in rural communities and show little interest in
understanding the needs of the people who live there. In this oligarchical
society, and in this digital century, it is a radical act simply to show up,
meet a person face-to-face, look them in the eye, and listen. As it turns
out, people have a lot to say.

So many candidates and campaigns are all about output. They clog
people's mailboxes, televisions, social media feeds, and radios with their
message. Their canvassers show up at people's doors or on their phones
and see how much of their script they can read off before the voter gets
fed up and ends the conversation. We did our fair share of pushing our
story by traditional means too, of course, but we balanced it by seeking
heaping portions of input and conversation. We spent the majority of our
time working to connect directly with voters to have authentic conversations and gain genuine understanding.

Every time we trained new canvassers, we told them that the most
important thing they could do was to listen. If they found themselves in
an argument over policy, then they had already lost.

To skirt around a controversial word or topic in favor of finding areas of mutual agreements is not to cede that ground. You don't change
a worldview in a conversation. If that's your theory of change, you're
going to be discouraged real quickly. Human and political change is a
slow process. It is the long-distance grind of decades. One foot in front of
the other, one step at a time. You have to lay the foundation first, before
anything else can happen.

When you're campaigning, see people as humans, and focus on areas
of agreement. What are our common hopes, dreams, fears, and frustra-
tions? When we listen, thin tendrils of trust begin to sprout out of fallow
ground. The possibility of a relationship grows. Even if we don't convince
the other person, we become a little bit more open to each other's ideas,
interested in each other's experiences. Remember, it is not our responsibility to do everything all at once.

Listening also informed our decisions and the way we campaigned. As
we've discussed, listening to feedback from volunteers who were running

into diminishing returns on the phones in summer 2020 led us to pivot our direct voter-contact tactics. The single most common piece of positive feedback that the campaign received from voters was that they appreciated our commitment to staying 100 percent positive in our messaging. As the opposition attacked us, this feedback from listening to people at the doors bolstered our confidence in staying the course and not trading blow for blow.

Just as we all have our share of flaws as people, our political parties and our ideologies are inevitably flawed. Love means accepting one another, flaws and all, and seeking to understand and support. Love in public mirrors this. We spend too much of our energy trying to cut the other side down in politics and paint their views in the most uncharitable light possible. We create stories about "the other" with very little factual basis. As the artist Anne Truitt put it, "Unless we are very, very careful, we doom each other by holding onto images of one another based on preconceptions that are in turn based on indifference to what is other than ourselves."[13] If we spent half as much time trying to listen and genuinely understand the other side as we do trying to prove ourselves right and others wrong, we could really get somewhere. We need a whole lot less judgment and a lot more empathy in our politics.

TRANSLATE TO RURAL AMERICA

There is a dynamic at play in too many liberal and leftist spaces whereby people's tremendous empathy stops cold when it comes to people who support Trump. They create the most uncharitable picture of the imagined people who voted for him. Ironically, this inability (or outright refusal) to empathize is one of the same character flaws that the Left tends to ascribe to Trump voters.

Many people in rural America have been bombarded by the deliberate, twisted words of Fox News, conservative talk radio, web forums, and YouTube, Facebook and other social media channels to the point that there are certain phrases or ideas that are nonstarters in many rural communities. For example, Dolly Parton, when asked in a *Radio Lab* podcast whether she considers herself a feminist, flatly rejected the label. The hosts then talked with a Dolly Parton scholar and asked if it bothered her that Parton doesn't identify as a feminist. There was a pause, and then she replied that it bothered the part of her that went to college. What the scholar was suggesting is that over time a word or idea can be manipulated to the point that it comes to mean radically different things from one person to the next. Further, such words have a political charge powerful enough to electrocute a cow. We try to have a discussion about feminism but end up heatedly talking past each other because we ascribe radically different meanings to the words that we're using.

What we find in campaigning is that it is usually more productive to avoid charged labels and discuss ideas instead. For example, we could often reach someone who might be up in arms over the term "feminism" but agrees with the need to eliminate the wage gap and ensure equal pay and opportunity. Many people in our community want affordable healthcare, but they don't want to talk about Medicare for All because relentless right-wing messaging has made these words toxic. So many of the values and ideas that we talk about can resonate in rural America if we can translate them into a rural context.

Here's another example. When Chloe was door-knocking in 2018, she rarely heard folks talk about climate change. But she did hear people talk about the need for sustainable industry, good jobs, ice fishing on the lakes in the winter, rain for the farms in the summer. So, when elected, Chloe wanted to work on a climate bill but one rooted in the rural working-class heritage of District 88. She sponsored the Green New Deal for Maine, and that label drew a lot of attention, as intended. Her Green New Deal was very different from the one at the national level that was growing infamous for its idealism and price tag. The national AFL-CIO refused to endorse AOC's Green New Deal (GND), but Chloe worked with the labor unions in Maine to craft the first state GND to be endorsed by an AFL-CIO affiliate. The result was a climate bill that was starting a conversation about climate change through the lens of labor. This is a very rare sort of conversation. Chloe's explicit goal was to translate the values of the Green New Deal into a rural context, among other things writing into law requirements for apprenticeships to create career op-portunities for young people. She also worked very hard with reporters and with other legislators to carefully explain the purpose and intent of her bill and differentiate it from the national GND. Through TV, radio, and newspaper op-eds, Mainers began to see that this was not so scary after all.

One of Chloe's constituents, a local business owner, saw that she had sponsored "An Act to Establish a Green New Deal for Maine." He told her that at first he had been shocked and upset but that he had taken the time to read the bill and find that it was all about job creation. In the end, he commended Chloe for the work on the bill, and the Maine Green New Deal is now law.

The reality is that people must be given an on-ramp before we can have any hope of moving them. In this case, what we had to first demonstrate was a clear understanding of the fear and oppression of poor and middle-class rural Americans. That challenging work must be done in conversation and dialogue, such that interactions are generative and have the potential to result in a mutual revealing of truth in conversation together. Only once their struggle has been illuminated can you begin to move people, to help them see how their oppression is connected to the oppression of others: the oppression of BIPOC people, immigrants, disabled people, trans people, and so on. All of that work is only possible if built on a foundation of relationship. If you don't have that relationship of trust and mutual understanding and you try to skip straight into opinions about these other issues that you disagree on, you'll find nothing but an impasse. So, conversation by conversation, we strived to move beyond our heated divisions and search for areas of common ground and mutual understanding.

VALUES, NOT PARTY

In our districts, as across the country, the number of independent voters is greater than the number of folks who do identify with one of the two major parties. Campaigns should certainly be up front about their party affiliation. Beyond that, we've found it best to avoid getting too tangled up in party identity. To focus on party at this moment in history is to zero in on what divides us. When we focus on values, we open up space to connect over what we have in common. We all want affordable healthcare and a decent quality of life, though we might have different policy solutions. Of course, sometimes it is impossible when the door is slammed in your face before you get a word out because they've already seen that you're a Democrat. But if people stood there long enough to tell us "God, I'm angry at the Democrats!," that was just the opening for us to respond, "I am too!" Then we could share our mutual frustration and dig into the values that we share.

Research shows that liberals and conservatives are both terrible at accurately judging the moral foundations of their own groups, let alone the other group. We overestimate the extremism of people who identify the same as us, and we do the same on the other side. According to moral foundations theory, as described by Jonathan Haidt, moral virtues can be largely lumped into five psychological "foundations." These are "Harm/care" (connected to sympathy and compassion); "Fairness/reciprocity" (dealing with justice and fundamental rights); "In-group/loyalty" (underlying us vs. them divisions and patriotism); "Authority/respect" (concerning traditions and ingrained social orders); and "Purity/sanctity" (relating to moral disgust and the sacred).[14] Research has shown that liberals are moved significantly by the Harm and Fairness foundations, while conservatives are moved by all five of them.[15]

This kind of research is a useful entry point to understanding disconnects in language when talking about issues. We incorporated it into our campaign messaging, for example by appealing to the In-group foundation by translating Chloe's deep commitment and love for home as "loyal representation" and prominently centering the fact that she was raised in Lincoln County. We appealed to the Authority foundation by framing Chloe's vision for the future as the key to protecting the traditions and culture of the past. "I'm running for State Senate knowing that if we fail in the future, we are certain to lose what we cherish of the past," read the first mail piece of the campaign. "Together we can ensure that District 13 is a resilient community. That means the strength to protect our past, feel safe in the present, and stay strong in the future. It's about withstanding new challenges while holding on to what makes our community special."

Chloe also noticed something about the Republican Party. In the community, she really doesn't care what party people are from. There are good people and valid opinions on both sides. But something happens when Republicans are elected and their ethic gets concentrated into a few so-called leaders who express loud opinions in political spaces. Republicans in Augusta supported white supremacy overtly on the House floor, called transgender folks "aliens," and so much more. Most people don't vote for racism or bigotry. They vote Republican. Mainly it's the leaders who have distorted thinking.

An email from one of Chloe's constituents further demonstrated how our community responded to our approach. An eighty-year-old who has a 22.90 DNC Democratic Party support score (meaning there is a 22 percent chance that he will vote Democrat), wrote to Chloe in April 2021, "I know you are a Democrat, but you always weigh out the alternatives and vote your conscience, in a similar fashion of Senator Collins." The point is: he valued our commitment to values and thoughtfulness over party.

100 PERCENT POSITIVE CAMPAIGN

We knew from the beginning that we wanted to run a positive campaign. Both of us grew up observing politics as a negative, mud-slinging fight. Our vision was to create a brighter and better politics. What's more, so many people in our community expressed the desire for a positive political vision, and our commitment to a positive campaign resonated across lines. During both campaigns, we pledged to focus on issues, shared values, and uncovering our common ground from beneath the scorched earth of inhuman attacks. Our mailers, videos, digital and print advertisements, and volunteer trainings emphasized and embodied the fact that our campaign was completely positive.

We were cautioned that sticking to this principle was a strategic blunder. Traditional campaign theory posits that, although voters universally say that they don't like negative campaigning, attacks are still effective. While that may be true, it is not in line with our values and our vision for a politics that strengthens and serves communities rather than tears them apart. We showed that it is possible to run a completely positive campaign and win.

It was challenging to hold the line and not hit back as acrimonious attacks riddled with lies began to flood the district. Our opponents spread falsehoods about us. We stood up for ourselves, but we refused to say anything negative about them. Both the Democrats and Republicans sent out nasty negative mailers with blatant lies, which landed in thousands of mailboxes. We refused to indulge in that game and decried the role of negative campaigning in today's politics. Ugly Facebook attacks circulated, but we doubled down on positive politics. Volunteers heard voters talk negatively about Chloe or other candidates, but they knew to stay true to our positive vision and turn the conversation around.

People took note of our choices, sending us feedback that deeply reinforced our approach.

> I have been meaning to write to you for weeks, ever since I took note of the relentlessly positive tone of your campaign mailings
>
> —*October 26, 2020, email from a voter*

> I went and cast a ballot for Chloe and nobody else because I am fed up with how everyone else is campaigning.
>
> —*October 30, 2020, statement by a Republican voter*

Please tell Chloe that I talked a woman in Waldoboro into voting for her yesterday! She's known Dow for a long time and was planning to vote for him, even though she's not happy with all of his votes. It was the message about Chloe's positive campaign, her effort to reach every voter regardless of party affiliation, and her track record of always making time for constituents that sold her.

—*November 2, 2020 email from a volunteer*

Our commitment to a 100 percent positive campaign was critical in 2020, an especially vitriolic cycle in Maine when the presidential race had everyone on edge, as did the highly fraught US Senate race between Sara Gideon and Susan Collins. The latter was the most expensive political race in Maine's history, and one of its defining characteristics was "incessant negative advertising."[16]

Despite our persistent public messaging about our commitment to positive campaigning, we found sometimes that our values still could not permeate. A voice memo from Chloe after a long day of campaigning in 2020 captures this: "Just talked to someone who wouldn't vote for me because she didn't think I could make a difference. She's fed up with the negative campaigning. I said that we weren't doing any negative campaigning. And she just couldn't hear it." Your message may not win everyone over, but you still need to be bold and strong about presenting a new way forward.

The long-lasting change that we envisioned started with the culture of the campaigns and politics that are built to achieve that change. We had seen politics turn so negative and divisive that it tore at the very fabric of our communities. So a priority on our campaign was to center our positive vision, never employing negative messaging or uttering a mean word about our opponents. Politics needs to be grounded in the many values that we share by focusing on face-to-face relationships to rebuild trust and rekindle the public imagination of what we can create together.

BUILD COMMUNITY

One of the most beautiful and powerful aspects of grassroots organizing is the relationships that grow between us as we do this work. For us, campaigning is all about building community. This is an end in itself that makes the entire experience worthwhile, win or lose. It's about getting to know our neighbors and offering a space for people to connect around a vision that is positive and of our own making.

Too often campaigns are extractive. From volunteers and campaign staff, they take time and energy. They are stretched to their limits for a campaign cycle, maybe two, and then burn out. From voters, they take demographic information and votes, which turn into data, which turns humans into statistics.

After seeing and experiencing this firsthand, we wanted to model a better way. This motivation was one of the things that led us to take the leap into launching our own campaign in the first place. To us, fostering real mutual relationships is the bedrock of organizing.

In 2018, we would bookend most of our campaign activities with a space for people to share stories, listen to music, eat, drink, and play games. Strangers whom Chloe met knocking on doors became friends. Old friends from New York City and Boston drove hours to reconnect and be part of the campaign.

Things looked a little bit different in 2020, of course, due to COVID. But it was precisely these relationships that allowed us to spring into action and launch the enormous mutual-aid effort to help our community through the pandemic. We reached out to every single senior in the district and made sure that they knew the community was there for them if their existing support structures fell through. We navigated Zoom together, creating memories and new connections through our screens. We gathered with masks outdoors on a much smaller scale when the risk was manageable enough to be together again. No matter where you live, we guarantee you're surrounded by a community that can benefit from your engagement.

TAKE CARE OF YOURSELF AND EACH OTHER

Care is one of the touchstones of everything that we do. Care for others and the world that we inhabit is the driving motivation behind most of our work. It is what led us into climate organizing and into electoral organizing. Too often, though, in fast-paced organizing spaces, care is not centered on the individual. Campaign culture can be exhausting, grueling, and fatal to the development of young organizers, as we saw in our initial years of organizing for climate justice. Experiencing it in electoral campaigns is one of the things that spurred us to build a new culture that prioritizes self-care for ourselves and our team.

In the campaign, we strived to build fun, regenerative spaces defined by love, community, and fulfillment of the whole individual. We prioritized care for ourselves and our team. Self-care and community care are so easy to neglect in favor of things that feel more urgent and critical in the moment. But, bit by bit, that attending to the urgent at the expense of the self adds up, and, if left unchecked, the candle burning from both ends will quickly burn out. That is why it is so important to understand it as a long-term strategic principle as well as an end in itself.

During a May 2020 check-in, Chloe said: "I'm bored. I love the work that we're doing and wouldn't change a thing, but I hate everything about every day." Uh-oh, alarm bells. "You just described burnout," Canyon replied. We then took steps to create space for care.

Self-care looks different for everybody, and it is important to have an awareness of yourself and others to know what is needed and how to get support making it happen. Putting on our running shoes and going for a run is a salve for both of us. We feel so much better after we get up and move. It's a time to think and process the rapid pace of the campaign. Sometimes it's a space to clear the head. Often the kinetic energy feeds off itself, and we come back to work with so much more forward momentum. Trips to the city to be around more young people, dance, and go to concerts were a staple that kept us going pre-COVID. In the morning, before Chloe would leave for the day canvassing, we often made time to play catch in the yard or slug baseballs into the field. In 2020, we went through three bats—a metal one and two wooden ones—all broken into splinters. For Chloe, long skates on the lake, water skiing, and her favorite TV shows are a touchstone. For Canyon, it's blocking off time to go on river trips, make pottery, or take his kayak out.

It is best if self-care is not left solely in the hands of each individual to look after for themselves. In the nonstop environment of campaigns, it's easy to completely forget to slow down and do things for yourself. When you care about the work so much, you can get lost in it completely unless you have others looking out for you. We found that it was indispensable to check in and support each other and folks on our team to ensure that self-care happened.

PASS IT ON

In a culture that teaches us to covet resources and compete for money and recognition, it is easy to be possessive of your work, ideas, funding, and time. But we believe—as the saying goes—that a rising tide floats all the boats. We are forever indebted to the mentors, friends, and elders who helped us find our way. We see it as one of our most sacred responsibilities to pass the torch to others as we go. One of our greatest hopes for this book is that we can pass on our experiences to you so that you may run wild and free with them in your community.

We spent hours weekly on the phone with rural organizing groups, rural Democratic county committees, and anyone who reached out to share our work and offer support for folks struggling to build Democratic power in rural communities. Chloe never turns down a request to speak to students. We are both generous with our time with others who are exploring running for office or getting involved with campaign work.

A favorite story that Henney often recounts is of a Divest Harvard candlelight vigil we held outside the university president's office. As we sang songs together arm in arm, a stout breeze blew through Harvard Yard. Every minute or two some candles would flicker out. Each time one did, a neighbor turned and held their flame out, creating a wind shelter with their hand, to relight the candle.

One of the most important things that can be accomplished with this work is to be the spark for other people, especially youth, to become engaged or relight their flame. We have to look out for each other in this work. There aren't enough of us doing it to get lost in the sauce. Sometimes we burn out for a time and need others to reignite our flame.

IT'S ALL A SOCIAL MOVEMENT

This is a long lesson but an important one! One of the patterns that we have seen repeated in organizing is the separation of electoral politics and social movements. What does this mean? Electoral politics is all about Election Day, squeezing as much capacity out of money, volunteers, and other resources as possible, sprinting at breakneck pace toward one day. Then the whole apparatus is dismantled after the election. About a year later, it starts back up again. It's erratic, and it's unsustainable.

Social movements, on the other hand, are geared toward long-term cultural and policy change. Ganz defines them as "a result of the efforts of purposeful actors (individual, organization) to assert new public values, form new relationships rooted in those values, and . . . translate these values into action."[17] Social movements center around relationships that build trust and people power, change minds, and influence decisions.

Social movements can, of course, encompass political campaigns, but these two forces largely exist in separate worlds. The consequence is that electoral power comes in the form of getting someone elected but without long-term movement support behind that candidate. Social movement power is manifested through public organizing, but that does not necessarily translate into political outcomes. Neither electoral politics nor social movements alone can create long-lasting *political* change.

The climate movement offers an example of this. It has spent decades building up grassroots people power to demonstrate public support for climate action. Countless strategies and tactics have been used—from DC lobbying to mobilizing college students through fossil-fuel divestment to direct action shutting down fossil-fuel infrastructure projects. These efforts culminated in demonstrations like the People's Climate March in 2014, the largest climate protest to date, with hundreds of thousands of people marching in the streets. The grassroots momentum was palpable and exciting.

Despite all this movement organizing, the climate movement still lacked political power. In 2014, Republicans won control of the US Senate. In 2016, Donald Trump was elected president. Each election showcased a country getting redder and redder, and revealed a country uncommitted to serious climate action. How could there be such a huge gap between on-the-ground energy and the political representation required to tackle the climate crisis?

There are many answers, but one is that electoral politics is treated very differently than social movement organizing. American politics does not integrate the relational and community organizing that defines social movements. It treats voters as commodities and data points. Campaigns extract capacity and resources from volunteers instead of building out a new base and including more voices. Movements, though, embrace people in relationships that are deep and meaningful.

So what happens when we think of campaigns as social movements? It can transform our thinking on how we build power for change. When we do this, we can build political power that is sustainable, politically effective, and culturally influential during and beyond an election year. Policy can be achieved with a robust movement to back it up, reelect good people, and ramp up pressure to hold other elected officials accountable.

This way of thinking about political organizing also reframes how we think of power. When electoral politics is in its own sphere, the questions are: Are you on the inside or the outside of the system? Do you have access or not? But when you have a social movement paired with political strategy, the question isn't about access. It's about influence. Are you with the movement or not? Power isn't based in places like the State House but rather with communities and the strong coalitions that advocate for long-term change.

It was also crystal clear to Chloe as she entered office just how important movements are on the outside. On the inside, you get your bill passed by organizing—building relationships, talking about values, working toward a common goal. But there is also so much space for this organizing to happen on the outside too—getting constituents to pressure their elected officials, building bridges with movements that might not have access to political spaces, and calling out elected officials when they don't do the right thing. Yet, most of the time, the inside strategy is so inwardly focused that it leaves everyone else out.

For Chloe—as a candidate and legislator—it has been very important to stay rooted in the movements of politics and not get consumed by the internal games of the Maine State House. Part of the purpose of running for office is getting the voice of your community at the table through your representation. You're on the outside, and you're trying to get inside, where decisions and conversations happen that you only have access to if you are elected. But, once you're inside, it's really easy to get sucked into internal dynamics and forget where you come from and the movements that you are committed to.

There are so many examples of how we dealt with this in practice. It was a structure, a mentality, and an ethic that permeated our work and thinking. Perhaps the best example was our COVID mutual-aid phone-banking effort. We launched into action calling seniors to offer help at the height of COVID because we saw our campaign as a social good. We wanted relationships to fuel our way forward. We didn't do this to win on Election Day. It wasn't intended to help us get votes. It was done because we cared about our community and wanted to reach out to everyone, regardless of our campaign. It was fundamentally about creating a better life for people and creating resilient communities for years to come. One of our volunteers reflected, "In rural communities there really is a sense of neighbors looking after neighbors."

This work continued to build relationships going forward. People heard of our efforts and were drawn to our campaign because of our focus on community and a caring kind of politics.

Every month since Chloe was elected in 2018, she has hosted "Coffee with Chloe." Whether in person or virtual, this has been a consistent space for constituents of all backgrounds and political identities to come together, ask questions, and discuss politics in a kind, open, safe, and respectful way. This has continued our relationships, and even strengthened them, beyond the door visits of an election year.

In another example: a group of folks who found community and pur-pose in our 2018 campaign went on to create Revitalize Jefferson in 2019. After the local diner shut down for lack of revenue, it had left the town of Jefferson with no place to eat, nowhere to get gas, and no market. This group of citizens, born out of our campaign, started an initiative to change that. They are in the process of creating a community enter, of-fering discounted meals to Jefferson residents, and also calling neighbors to check in on them, a direct inspiration from our COVID relief effort.

In 2019, two women approached Chloe when she was a state repre-sentative with a new idea: to amend the Maine Constitution to include a right to clean air, clean water, and a healthy environment. Chloe was immediately intrigued by this idea. It was too late to submit a bill for such an amendment in that session, but it might be something she could work on if she were elected to the State Senate. Both of these women lived in Senate District 13, and so we started to plot out a path for this amendment. They also got involved in the campaign and helped get Chloe elected.

Once Chloe was elected, she introduced the draft bill language, and they all started building a movement. Dozens of folks from Chloe's cam-paign as well as people across the state came together in the effort to make this amendment a reality. Constitutional amendments require a two-thirds majority of the legislature, meaning that Chloe would need to get a significant number of Republicans (more than twenty) to support the amendment for it to pass. She spent hours connecting with Republi-can colleagues, sharing her vision, listening to their concerns, and craft-ing language to make the idea a reality that people could support. Chloe was successful in earning Republican votes for it and was also able to get Republicans to cosponsor the bill.

Elections tend to be boom-and-bust cycles for staffers, with momen-tum ebbing and flowing. But that doesn't build long-term power to not only elect candidates but also support their good policies, hold them ac-countable, and then get them reelected. We need to start thinking about campaigning as a process that is continual and consistent, with highs (elections years) and lows (in-between cycles).

Right now, we pour all of the resources into building a movement that gets someone elected. We don't continue to nurture and grow the election-year relationships until it's time to start campaigning again two or four years later. As Naomi Klein said in a 2020 tweet: "If we honestly believe we are building a movement, not just an electoral campaign, then the relationships we forge, and the political education we do along the way, is never wasted. It's all part of building power, which we badly need no matter what happens. Nothing is wasted."[18]

Taken together, these strategic principles formed the foundation of our campaigns as we strived to build a better politics in our rural districts. They guided our actions and enabled us to be clear about our shared vision and values. In times of uncertainty, they gave us confidence that our work was worthwhile, no matter the outcome of the elections. We don't have it all figured out. Nobody does. What we do know is that these principles gave us purpose and direction, and they enabled us to create successful campaigns in the face of great odds. We hope that they will serve you well as you carry them forward and develop additional ones of your own.

CHAPTER 6

CAMPAIGN BUILD

It is one thing to establish the strategies, ideas, and visions that you want to build on. It is another thing to put them into practice. Where does one even begin? This chapter offers a road map. We'll lay out some of the key pieces that need to be put in place early on before launching into full-on crazy campaign mode. The heat of campaigning is overwhelming. You need a working engine before you can drive the car. Our goal here is to demystify the process, provide some starting points, and highlight the links between our strategic principles and the actual campaign.

As early as possible, a campaign-to-be must assess the lay of the land, create a specific yet big-picture game plan from that assessment, and then cultivate the relationships and assemble the team that will execute that game plan. This process, "the campaign build," is what sets a good campaign apart and prepares it to move proactively—rather than reactively—through the complicated mayhem of campaign season.

DETERMINE YOUR WIN NUMBER

Your win number is the minimum number of votes that you need to win the election. This simple number is the ultimate goal of your campaign that everything revolves around. In a typical two-candidate race, you need to win a majority of the votes—50 percent plus one. The most straightforward way to determine your win number is to find the average of turnout of the past three similar elections, divide that number in half, and add one vote. For a midterm election, look at the results of the past three midterms. For a presidential year, look at the results of the past three presidential elections. This data is publicly available, usually via the website for the secretary of state in each state.

Here's our 2020 calculation, for example, using the Maine State Senate vote totals in District 13 from 2008, 2012, and 2016 to calculate our baseline: $((22,240+21,084+23,040)/3)/2 = 11,060$. We added an additional 10 percent, putting our win number at 12,167, to account for population growth and our expectation that 2020 would be a very high turnout year. We updated this number as new data came in from conversations with voters and especially from early voting data once it began. By late October, the models that Canyon built using historical voter data, canvassing and phone banking results, and early voting data indicated that total turnout would be likely be higher than even the 10 percent we added to our original win number. Those models predicted a total turnout between 24,827 and 25,011 for the district. Our final updated win number target was 12,506 (half of 25,011, plus one vote). The actual turnout was 24,879. Chloe won with 12,806 votes.

Determining your win number is an inexact process, but it must be done. A quick review: Expected turnout equals total votes cast in election 1, election 2, and election 3, divided by three. Divide this number by two and add one vote to get your baseline win number. Once you have established this baseline, look at voter data to determine the percentage growth (or decline) in registered voters for your district and adjust your number accordingly. This is only a formulaic guess, so add some margin of error. In a typical year, we would add at least an additional 5 percent to this number to land on our final win number target.

CHART OUT YOUR YEAR

We began each campaign with a big-picture but detailed plan. It's one of the first things that should be done. We planned the Senate campaign in January 2020 and continually revisited it. The vision was mapped out on huge flip charts, along with a careful timeline so that we knew what we were working toward and how we would get there. This way, we could ensure that our day-to-day work was in line with the larger vision that we had for ourselves, our strategy, our health, our campaign practices, and our volunteers. These maps papered our walls to ensure accountability and inspire us to put in the work to turn our dreams into reality.

There is still a piece of flip-chart paper hanging on the wall from our 2020 campaign. We made it back in March 2020. We had launched our campaign, then paused to unleash a massive COVID mutual-aid effort. By late March, we needed to chart out the transition back to campaigning. Our map lays out the action plans along three horizontal rows labeled April, May, and June. Then there are two vertical columns dividing up the tasks for each month into "urgent tasks" and "not urgent but important." In each box we wrote things such as target numbers for LTEs, "organize three phone banks," and "finalize budget," along with specific dates. That's how we charted our path forward. And we stuck to it. No matter the size or context of your campaign, take the time to sketch out your game plan from start to finish and continually refine it and reference it to ensure you stay on track, channeling your time and resources into the right things at the right time.

POWER MAP YOUR DISTRICT

Another important tool that we brought with us from social movement organizing was "power mapping." This is the process of laying out and categorizing all the constituencies and key players in the district. Power mapping, like charting the year ahead, is an ongoing process that should begin on day one. You can structure this however you like, but the way we learned was to create the following categories: (1) active supporters, (2) passive supporters, (3) neutral parties, (4) passive opposition, and (5) active opposition. Under each category we wrote down names of individuals, general constituencies, and organizations. For example, our active supporters included the Lincoln County Democrats, other Democratic candidates, and a number of local organizers with whom Chloe had pre-existing relationships. Passive supporters included all Democratic-leaning voters, volunteers of past candidates, and the Lincoln County sheriff. Neutral parties included non-voters, voters who didn't have a discernible partisan leaning, and local newspapers, churches, businesses, food pantries, and other community organizations. Passive opposition included core GOP voters and the former chair of the Lincoln County Republicans. Active opposition included Dana Dow, his staff and volunteers, conservative PACs, and other Republican candidates in the area.

Once you have filled each category as comprehensively as possible, the goal is to use this map to chart out the most strategic course based on moving as many people as possible from less supportive categories to more supportive categories: from passively supportive to actively supportive, from neutral to passively supportive, from passively opposed to neutral or undecided.

For each of your active supporters, for instance, how can you maximize the value of their support? Move them into a volunteer leadership role? Advertise their endorsement? Ask them to donate money or make an in-kind contribution? Activate their organization's network of volunteers?

Think about how you can connect with passive supporters in ways that move them into active support of the campaign. Which community leaders are ideologically aligned with your campaign? How can you engage them in the campaign early on? We turned dozens of passive supporters into committed volunteers through one-on-one meetings at the outset of each campaign—often before even filing to run. House parties were another key activity that helped to expand our volunteer base through community building and personal relationships.

Persuadable voters are the most obvious neutral party. You will spend most of your campaign resources working to move them from neutral to passive supporters. We did this primarily by going door to door to earn their vote. What other key neutral parties require your attention? Some examples include local media and community organizations. Create a game plan to get newspapers, radio stations, and TV stations to cover your campaign. Get active supporters to write letters to the editor or get their church to invite you to speak with the congregation.

For the passive opposition, look for ways to move them to a neutral position. An example of this in 2018 was the postcard that we sent to core GOP voters right before the election, urging them to compare Chloe and Mr. Lemelin, including web addresses for each of them. In 2020, we heavily advertised the endorsement of the former Lincoln County GOP chair to try to move some conservative folks out of the passive opposition category.

And for the active opposition, plot out their strengths and prepare tactics to neutralize them. Mr. Dow and Mr. Lemelin were both small business owners, so we put work into securing and then advertising the endorsement of the former head of the US Small Business Administration. One of Mr. Dow's big strengths was that he was one of the most experienced legislators in the state. We tried to neutralize this by drawing the distinction between experience and effectiveness, highlighting Chloe's accomplishments as a first-term legislator and her recognition as legislator of the year in 2020.

Finally, don't treat anybody as a lost cause. One of the great surprises of our campaign was Chloe knocking on the door of the aforementioned former GOP chair and ultimately earning his endorsement. Chloe's willingness to visit houses with Trump flags and backwoods trailers that others had passed over enabled her to win critical votes at the margins that other Democrats had not even competed for. Politics is a game of inches, and every single conversation has the potential to make a difference. Knowing where, when, and how to invest your limited resources begins with forming a coherent understanding of your district and the powers that be through in-depth power mapping.

CREATE YOUR BUDGET AND FUNDRAISING PLAN

With the notable exceptions of the uber-wealthy and the CEOs of mega-corporations, we all hate the deeply problematic role that money plays in politics. The nearly unfettered influence of money in our political campaigns is profoundly antidemocratic and requires massive reform on many levels. In the meantime, money is an important consideration that every campaign must address realistically from the beginning—before the beginning, really. Be clear-eyed about how much it is going to cost to run a successful campaign for your district and plot out whether you can realistically expect to raise that amount.

Creating a high-level budget for the campaign should be one of the first things you do as you chart the course for your campaign. The budget should reflect the values and strategy of your campaign, prioritize genuine connections through direct voter contact, and avoid unnecessary expenses. Creating the budget takes significant time from the outset and requires tackling big-picture questions about the direction of the campaign, as well as what is and what is not financially possible for the campaign to do.

The finances of past campaigns are all in the public record. Websites like Ballotpedia make it easy to get a bird's-eye view of how much campaigns have spent in recent cycles. As you home in on creating your own plan, more detailed records from every reporting deadline can be pulled from the state or federal oversight body for every campaign. It isn't necessarily a good idea to replicate what past campaigns have done, but it is important to study their finances and have a solid grasp on how much they spent and where they spent it. From there, you can begin to create a rough sketch of your overall budget based on how much you expect to spend on staff salaries, direct mail, campaign materials, events, rent, advertisements (TV, newspaper, digital, and radio), and any other needs you foresee. Each category should have a range of alternatives to account for best-case and worst-case fundraising scenarios.

Bring an ambitiously resourceful mindset to this process. Rather than rent a campaign headquarters, can you find donated space or share with the local Democrats? We were able to run our campaigns mostly from home, using donated co-working space for our interns, paying a nominal fee to rent our community hall for bigger events, and launching canvasses out of the county Democrats' office or library parking lots. Can you get a professional photographer to donate their time for the cause? We were fortunate to have local photographers and videographers volunteer their considerable talents to save us the expense of hiring these.

With the macro budget in hand, the next step is to sketch out a plan for doing the fundraising necessary to powerfully supply the campaign's resources. Here again it can be useful to examine the financial data of past campaigns to see who and where their money came from (and when). There are plenty of resources out there on the topic of campaign fundraising. We suggest using these and following a few basic principles.

First, create a fundraising timeline, informed by the needs and timeline of your budget, with concrete targets: how much you need to raise each month throughout the campaign. From there you can begin to sketch out your methods for fundraising. Direct calls from the candidate are one of the most tried-and-true methods, especially for state-level campaigns. In-person events, mail solicitation, volunteer calls, social media, emails, and calls to donors of allied organizations and past candidates are other important methods. Start as early as possible and be prepared to go back again and again to your strongest supporters. Bernie Sanders's presidential campaigns were a terrific example of the power of small donations adding up to huge sums over the long haul of a campaign cycle.

No matter your approach to fundraising, we want to emphasize how important it is to know from the outset how much you want to pay your staff. The boom-and-bust cycles of campaigning can be brutal for staff members' job security and financial planning. This may seem like an obvious point, but it's a big one to think about as you set up your campaign. How much will your core staff get paid? Can you provide stipends to volunteers? Can you reimburse for gas after a long day of canvassing? We were very constrained with our small, publicly funded budget, but we still asked these questions and then planned our lives and campaigns around the answers.

We planned our lives around running for office, especially for the 2020 campaign. In 2018, Canyon and Chloe worked part-time on environmental advocacy and lived off savings as they campaigned. In 2020, Canyon commuted between Boston and Nobleboro, working part-time to support himself outside of the campaign. Chloe worked her part-time job while also working in the State House and campaigning in 2020. We were able to give stipends of $1,500–$2,000 per month to both Canyon and Henney with our 2020 budget using the tens of thousands we saved by not using the party's consultants.

In both campaigns, we found ourselves constantly moving from meeting to meeting and job to job. There were times when Canyon would be on Zoom for his second job all evening, after doing campaign work all day; then he would shift gears back into pressing campaign work. "It feels like things are just on overdrive right now keeping up the part-time organizing work and the mutual aid effort," Canyon reflected in April 2020. "It feels like almost every hour in every day is called for, and as Chloe said today 'the work is endless.' We set out this vision of making organizing and campaign work a regenerative space that doesn't burn people out, but right now I feel like we're burning the candle at both ends. And that's okay if it's here and there, but it's feeling like it's persistent right now. It feels like we're overextended, and I'm worried about that because it's only April 15, and in a sense it's only the beginning."

Despite our lofty visions and best efforts, we often found ourselves overworked and exhausted as our passion for the urgent work at hand exceeded our desire to lead a balanced life on the campaign trail. Hopefully one day there will be structures that can better support people campaigning. For now, it requires thought and preparation to make it accessible for average people to run for office and constant vigilance to prevent burnout.

Below we have provided the budget that the SDCC suggested for 2020 along with our actual budget.

SDCC SAMPLE BUDGET	
EXPENDITURES	TOTAL COST
Direct Mail	39,000
Clincher Cards	975
Postage for Postcards	2,625
Palm Cards	1,350
Campaign Signs	1,740
Photography	500
Facebook Boosts	510
Clean Elections Contribution Solicitation Mailings	1,000

(continues)

EXPENDITURES	TOTAL COST
Digital Video Production	2,000
Digital Ads	13,000
Radio/TV	5,000
Miscellaneous Expenditures	1,000
TOTAL	$68,700

Our 2020 State Senate budget:

MAXMIN/WOODWARD BUDGET	
EXPENDITURES	**TOTAL COST**
Direct Mail	19,711
Clincher Cards	646
Postage for Postcards	2,600
Palm Cards	1,860
Campaign Signs	1,950
Photography	0 (volunteer photography)
Clean Elections Contribution Solicitation Mailings	0 (collected door-to-door)
Digital Video Production	0 (volunteer video production)
Digital Ads	0
Local Newspaper Ads	8,845
Facebook Boosts and Online Newspaper Advertising	5,378
Staff	20,000
Predictive Dialer Minutes	400
Radio/TV	7,010
Miscellaneous Expenditures	300
TOTAL	$68,700

BUILD A TEAM

One of the first things many candidates are told when they run for office is to build a "kitchen cabinet." We were certainly told to do this for both of our campaigns. A kitchen cabinet is a group of community leaders and trusted advisors—usually elders—to give advice and guidance throughout the campaign season. The idea is to make sure that the campaign doesn't run amok and that it has consistent input from folks who know the pulse of the community.

We took a different approach. We had a few key allies we sought sage advice from in pivotal moments. But we focused our energies on building an actual team with discrete roles and responsibilities instead of just an advisory council. We built up a group of committed leaders from the community who helped the campaign from start to finish. We relied on the experience of those who came before, but we also knew that we needed fresh perspectives to figure out a new way to campaign. We spent a lot of time building up our team so that we could have the capacity to actualize a new vision. We never met without a purpose. We also knew that the best feedback and input would come from actually doing the work. The more folks doing the work, the more feedback we would get.

Another important facet of approaching this process intentionally is to be selective about who is at the table. The span of a campaign is long, and its foundation is laid early. Congressional campaigns will be underway nearly two years before the election, state legislative campaigns generally begin the winter before an election, and small local races usually start several months ahead of a municipal or county election. Thus, the Democratic establishment often recruits candidates, staff, and advisors. This creates a cycle of the same voices influencing and crafting campaigns over and over, perpetuating the same brokenness that we are trying to repair. As our mentor Julia Buckner put it, "A team trusts each other, has each other's backs, and works like hell together. . . . A team is *not* a group of consultants on a weekly or monthly call." Part of breaking this cycle is intentionally bringing in new and different voices to push back against the status quo and get creative about new ways forward.

We put this lesson into practice in 2018 and 2020 with the ways that we set up our team. In 2018, Chloe remembers lying on her floor in her Portland apartment to call friends to ask them to join the campaign before we officially launched. We had an event coordinator, field manager, and letters to the editor coordinator. The entire team was young folks in their twenties—including both of us. In 2020, we went into the summer months with two interns working on the campaign. In the fall, we phased in a team that organized volunteers, coordinated letters to the editor, scheduled phone banks, and did everything else that we needed. For the whole year, our core team was almost all twentysomethings. Whether your team includes respected elders or hungry young changemakers, it's important to assemble your team early, make sure people have clear roles, and keep them meaningfully engaged.

CONNECT WITH LOCAL DEMOCRATS

Why is it so important to connect with local Democrats? First, there is the unguarded kindness and support that you get from like-minded Democrats that you won't find at the doors when you're talking with Republicans and independents all day. That kind of community is special and kept us energized through countless weeks of campaign slogging. It's important to stay rooted in the places that are kind to you and your message, no matter what.

If you're lucky, local Democrats will be well-positioned to focus on Democratic turnout during the election. They will help recruit volunteers, organize phone banks, canvass, and run GOTV for likely Democratic voters. That is so important because, when you are running in a red or purple district, you still need all of your Democrats to get out and vote for you. If your local Democratic organization can focus on Democratic turnout, that frees you up to focus on independents and Republicans. We were able to continue connecting with undecided voters right up to Election Day because the Lincoln County Democrats and the organizers from the state party had developed enough capacity to implement a thorough GOTV program.

In our case, we were fortunate for the help provided by the Lincoln County Democratic Committee (LCDC). In non-COVID times, this intrepid group of political volunteers meets monthly at the Newcastle fire station. Dozens of folks pack into the room to hear local speakers, connect around politics, and get ready for the next election cycle. They are always organizing, always engaging, and always working for a better community. The local Democrats also helped facilitate communication and coordination between all the different campaigns. The cochair initiated weekly Zoom meetings so that all the campaigns and staffers in the area would stay on the same page. Chloe had a relationship with the LCDC for many years prior to deciding to run. She knew their people from other local organizing efforts. They were also the first people that she informed of her decision in February 2018 to run for the Maine House of Representatives. Anything political starts with the Lincoln County Dems. That's just how it works around here.

The Lincoln County Democrats also provided invaluable support to our campaign during our 2020 State Senate campaign. We met with the cochairs during the summer of 2019. We kept in touch regularly, and when we were alerted to the fraudulent push polling against our campaign in 2020, they were quick to respond to our request for support. Canyon did some quick research and knew that we had to file a complaint with the Maine Ethics Commission. We needed to investigate the push polling, ideally identify who was behind it, and stand up for ourselves and our communities' right to a free and fair election. We didn't think it was good strategy to file the complaint ourselves without outside support. It might look like we were whining or lacked the backing to legitimate our claim. So we worked with Chris Johnson, also a cochair of the Lincoln County Democrats, to file a complaint.

Even if you live in a place where the Democratic Party's local infrastructure has atrophied to nothing, there are sure to be like-minded people around who would be willing to help your campaign. You might find them through nonpartisan community groups focused on the environment, for example, through word of mouth, or through calling the frequent voters in your community who are registered as Democrats.

MAINTAIN A STRONG RELATIONSHIP WITH THE STATE COMMITTEE

The central players for state legislative races are the campaign committees for the House (the House Democratic Campaign Committee for our 2018 race, the HDCC) and Senate (the Senate Democratic Campaign Committee in 2020, or SDCC). These committees are typically overseen by the elected Democratic leaders of the respective chamber and run by full-time staff. Their goal is to reelect their Democratic legislators and support Democratic candidates challenging Republican incumbents. These committees often recruit candidates, provide trainings for candidates and staff, facilitate connections to consultants, advocate on behalf of candidates for independent expenditures from PACs, and provide direct funding for campaigns.

There are two important realities to keep in mind when it comes to these committees. First, they often perpetuate many of the failings of the Democratic Party writ large that we laid out in part 1. They're not always the most forward-looking or rural-conscious, and their advice, in our experience, is best taken with a grain of salt. Second, they also wield a wealth of resources and experience that can be very valuable to any campaign. They are generally run by passionate staff who work tirelessly for what they believe in and are trying to do the best they can to support every campaign. The HDCC oversees 151 races every two years, and the SDCC coordinates 35 races, which means that staff do the best that they can but often can't provide individualized support given the number of candidates that they oversee.

Many candidates could not run without this support and all the resources that come with it. We have a citizen legislature in Maine. Most folks running for office are average Mainers who don't know how to create a canvassing universe or design a mailer, and don't have the time or willingness to learn.

In every state in the country, these committees are tasked with overseeing the success of Democratic campaigns in legislative races that are perennially short of resources. These committees are important players, and they can have an outsized impact on which campaigns get the resources to succeed and which ones don't. If you're trying to do things differently, it's likely you'll run into resistance in the party establishment that controls the committees. Therefore, navigating the relationship between your campaign and the state committee can be a tricky process that requires substantial attention. Relationship-building with the state Democratic Party required time and careful thought before and during each of our campaigns. One way that we attempted to head off tension over our new approach was to touch base very early on with the HDCC and the SDCC in the spring of 2018 and the summer of 2019 respectively to communicate our priorities and visions.

In 2018, as first-time candidate and campaign manager, we took the time to learn about the HDCC's campaign resources. We listened to their consultants and their plans for mailers, palm cards, and canvassing. We went to their candidate trainings so that we could understand their approach. Based on the very urban-focused cookie-cutter structure that they presented, we decided not to use many of their resources. They were going to target mainly Democrats in the canvassing universe. The messaging strategies were boilerplate and uninspiring. In our view, their literature was boring, and there was no room for substantial changes. We told them—honestly and kindly—that we were going to take matters into our own hands.

This decision was only validated as the campaign season progressed. Chloe attended a training from a woman who worked with the HDCC on communications and also ran communications for Sara Gideon, the Speaker of the House at the time. She told the local candidates, "Don't customize your message based on who you talk to." She advised having one message that you repeat to everyone you meet. Chloe wrote in her journal, "Probably that's why the Democratic Party is failing so hard, if that's the way that they're approaching things." The parts of your platform that resonate most with a Democrat who voted for Clinton are often not the same ones that appeal most to a voter with a Trump flag on the lawn.

Compared to 2018, we had more time and experience to focus on these relationships as we prepared for our 2020 State Senate run. We began communicating with the SDCC in the spring of 2019, while still deciding whether to run for the Senate seat. In the fall of 2019, we met with the executive director of the SDCC in our home in Nobleboro. We told her that we did not want to run a negative campaign and didn't want to see anything negative coming from the party. We also said that we wanted to design our own materials and, more likely than not, run our own mailer program. The SDCC did not honor our wishes to avoid negative attacks, and they gave us endless grief about our do-it-ourselves approach. But at least we could say that we had informed them months before so that they were not surprised. When we did make our final decision not to use their consultants for our mail program, the SDCC threatened to withdraw support for our campaign, as if our credibility depended on party consultants who had lost races in our district countless times.

Despite the friction, we were ultimately able to work through this impasse, given our long history of relationship and communication with the SDCC. And it was worth it. SDCC staff was always a phone call away to offer whatever support they could as attacks rained down or unforeseen challenges arose. The SDCC spent money on mail, radio, and digital advertisements in support of our campaign and undoubtedly helped mobilize additional expenditures from other PACs and political entities. The SDCC also provided access to the voter database, modeling of voter data, and historical voter and volunteer data from past campaigns.

WHEREVER POSSIBLE, BE YOUR OWN CONSULTANTS

A lot of the support that the state party offers is through connections to consultants. This is because, as we mentioned before, they are supporting dozens and dozens of candidates. They don't have the money or staff to provide customized support to each of the candidates. And so they partner with consultants who provide these services, and candidates pay these folks through their campaign budgets. Consultants can help with designing palm cards, postcards, mailers, digital communications, radio and TV ads, and more.

These services can be a good thing because they provide support that every campaign needs, but this also reinforces the status quo. Consultants are paid a lot of money to produce largely generic materials and advice based on data that might not reflect the nuances and realities of our communities. This is why it's important to develop a clear vision of how you'll respond to consultants whose ideas you disagree with or are unsure about.

We only dabbled with Maine party consultants in 2018. A consultant sent out a form for candidates to fill out asking about their vision, campaign colors, and slogan. They ran that through their corporate calculator and produced a draft palm card (the thing that you give to someone at the door that explains who you are). It looked like every other piece of political junk that we'd seen, and we felt that it didn't even come close to expressing the vibrancy or creativity of our campaign. So, we told the HDCC that we would not be using their consultants and that we would be doing all the design and mailing on our own. They understood that and granted us that latitude.

In 2018 and 2020, we figured out that we would save thousands of dollars by doing the work ourselves instead of paying the consultants with their inflated prices. Yes, it was more work for us. But we saved a lot of money and gained the freedom and flexibility to create literature that truly reflected our campaign. Figure out early on what, if any, consultant services you will need. This will inform many aspects of your campaign, from your budget to your team composition. Do you need to find a graphic designer in your volunteer network instead of using a paid consultant? Can your staff negotiate rates with radio and television stations and buy ad spots directly?

Far too often, especially in a rural context, consultants drain resources while failing to meaningfully move the needle in a positive direction for your campaign. Yet election cycle after election cycle they continue to be an appealing option for campaigns that don't know any better than to continue following the pattern of how things have been done before. The consultant habit of Democratic campaigns hearkens the old adage, "Don't blame a clown for acting like a clown. Ask yourself why you keep going to the circus." One of our mentors, John deVille, put it this way: "Consultants are like, 'Let me send you this car.' Then it blows up, and it doesn't get you anywhere. It drains resources. But candidates say, 'Oh yeah, I'll take three!'" We have found that as much as possible it is best to be your own consultant in rural America. Lean into your own experience and bring in diverse people from within your community who actually know the pulse of your district. Go out there door to door and listen, get your ego out of the way, empathize, and let those conversations inform your strategy.

TARGET VOTERS STRATEGICALLY

The most precious resource in any campaign is the candidate's and volunteers' time. When you go knock on doors, you can't knock on every single door. You must develop a strategic list of addresses. Even if you have the best candidate and all the resources and volunteers in the world, unless you can direct them toward the right voters, all will be for naught. Determining precisely the voters in which to invest your precious budget, candidate time, and volunteer hours to reach is therefore crucial.

A universe, again, is the group of people that you contact during a campaign. Often the party provides the universe, because creating one requires some technical skill in VoteBuilder, the software used by Democratic campaigns. We created our own universe that included many of the Republican and more conservative independent voters that the party never touches. Of all the tactics that we employed, this was one of the most critical.

The majority of voters are going to vote a straight party ticket, no matter what, and virtually nothing you do will change their minds. These are the core Democrats and core Republicans. Generally, it doesn't make sense to spend your limited resources on these voters. Depending on where you live, you can also usually count on at least a third of registered voters not turning out to vote. Then there's the huge chunk of citizens who aren't even registered to vote. Those constituencies can be worth targeting if you have the resources and vision to make it happen, but they should not be your main focus.

We believe that the bulk of your resources should be directed to winning the support of "persuadables"—voters who have a track record of showing up to the polls in recent elections and who don't demonstrate strong partisan leaning in either direction. Unless your state or local Democrats are exceptionally well-organized, you will also need to devote significant resources down the homestretch to turn out Democrats who aren't consistent voters.

Targeting is a refined skill. If you don't have the experience to implement these tactics effectively, then this is one skill set for which it's worth seeking outside expertise. Who you choose to target depends so much on the make-up of your district, historical turnout, educated guesses, and constant data analysis. For example, in 2018, Chloe's House district had a 16-point Republican advantage, so we knew that we would have to win over the vast majority of voters without a partisan leaning, as well as make significant inroads among Republicans. In 2020, the Senate district only had a 3-point Republican advantage and had voted for Obama twice before going for Trump in 2016. This meant that we didn't need to win as high a percentage of Republicans as we did in 2018; instead, we needed to really focus on the middle and on voters who may have voted Democrat up until recently.

A big part of deciding how many voters to target is being realistic about the number of persuadables you will need to win over in order to reach your win number. Before Canyon was able to access voter data, the initial universe that the SDCC created for us in 2020 consisted of fewer than three thousand voters. We knew that in order to win against Mr. Dow in District 13 we would need to go after a much larger swath of persuadable voters than that. So we expanded the universe by nearly threefold to begin with, slowly tightening our focus as we collected more data throughout the cycle.

Just as your finance plan should have different options depending on your fundraising success, your targeting should have a clear order of priority and options depending on the size of the grassroots volunteer base that you are able to build. As we've discussed, building a formidable grassroots ground game was a significant focus of our campaigns. We built sufficient capacity to expand our universe beyond our primary targets to also talk with people that no other campaigns had reached, including low-turnout Democratic-leaning voters and medium-turnout moderate voters.

Most campaigns simply ignore voters who haven't voted in recent elections. Cycle after cycle, these low-turnout voters feel further ignored and forgotten by the political system. We found that, when we would show up at these doors, we often could really get through and have meaningful conversations. We found that many of these people—surprise!—actually appreciated not being ignored.

CREATE YOUR FIELD PLAN

A robust field operation is the beating heart of the type of grassroots campaign that Democrats need to run at every level across the country. The field is where the majority of your direct voter contact happens. This is where you have the opportunity to connect, listen, build trust, communicate your message, and form real relationships with voters through authentic conversations. In other words, the field is where the magic happens. A great field plan, especially for local and state level campaigns, should be the cornerstone of the campaign. This is where the energy to sustain the campaign and give it life within the community comes from. This is where you put your values into action and have the biggest opportunity to actualize a different kind of politics that is deeply rooted in the people.

The most important first step before you even think about beginning to canvass is to put significant thought and time into the strategic targeting that we just discussed. This enables you to precisely identify the voters in whom you plan to invest your precious candidate, staff, and volunteer time. Once you have a grasp on your targeting and the number of constituents you believe can be moved from neutral to active support, it is time to begin setting goals and laying out a timeline. You should begin knocking doors and making phone calls as early as you possibly can, starting with the candidate and then building out volunteer teams. In both 2018 and 2020 Chloe began knocking doors in February. For our June primary in 2018, we had volunteer teams knocking by early April. Depending on the size of your district, you may even need to start earlier. Persuadable voters often are less checked in to politics, especially at the local level, so the earlier and more frequently you can get their attention, the better. Go to their homes and begin the conversation early, follow it up with a handwritten postcard, and never let communications lapse thereafter.

We are huge believers in the power of face-to-face connections, and thus we are big proponents of door-to-door canvassing above all else. In the digital age, face-to-face conversations have an outsized effect on people. Phone calls still have a place, of course, especially early on in your direct voter contact strategy for "ID calls," in which you collect information on whether voters are supportive, neutral, or opposed. However, political phone calls have seen a dramatic decline in effectiveness over recent decades, since it is increasingly difficult to reach people. Response rates for telephone surveys have dropped precipitously over recent decades from over 30 percent in the late 1990s to about 5 percent in 2020, and political calls have seen a similar decline.[1]

Set ambitious but realistic goals for the number of times you want to attempt to contact each persuadable voter and work backward from there to determine how many canvassing shifts it will take and what kind of volunteer leadership will be required to make it happen. You will also need a game plan for supporting staff in allocating their time effectively to recruit and train volunteers. The goals need to be bold enough that they draw you toward the outer limits of your abilities without being out of reach and thus inevitably discouraging. Our campaign's direct voter contact accounted for over a quarter of all volunteer and candidate voter contact out of thirty-five Senate campaigns statewide. This ground game, born out of our movement-organizing experience and mindset, was the most important way that we connected with voters and earned the broad base of support necessary to flip two very improbable districts in 2018 and 2020.

PLATFORMS AND MESSAGING
BY AND FOR RURAL PLACES

Every campaign needs to focus carefully on its platform and the messages that it puts out into the world. These are often people's first impressions of the candidate and their purpose. You can't talk with everyone, so you need to rely on your campaign literature and advertisements to reflect your candidacy well. It requires a lot of thought, reflection, and updating as you receive input and feedback from your community.

Most campaigns have a pretty generic platform so as to not alienate any potential voters. They talk about good jobs and affordable healthcare. But everyone agrees with that. For our campaigns, we tried to craft a platform that was grounded in themes more unique to our community.

In 2018, our platform included five elements. First was a foundation for the future, focusing on how our rural communities must be able to support young folks and how we must fund our public schools, lower burdensome property taxes, and welcome small businesses. Second was support for our seniors—from ensuring healthcare and transportation access to increasing the wages for in-home care workers. Next was support for resilient communities, emphasizing the need to protect our natural resources as critical to our economy and our way of life. Healthcare was also part of our core platform, with an emphasis on how rural communities are often disadvantaged by lack of access. Last but not least was rural transportation, the critical connector for access to food, jobs, healthcare, childcare, and everything else that we need to survive and thrive.

In 2020, our message focused on four themes that built on 2018 but also reflected Chloe's legislative experience. Our healthcare plank included access to mental health services and support for those experiencing substance abuse. We focused on resilience for farms, fisheries, schools, and businesses, with a vision of strong local economies that can withstand any crisis. Our transportation plank emphasized that only 12 percent of transportation needs in Lincoln County were being met. Lastly, we called for essential access to broadband internet—for emergency information, education purposes, and more—which families and businesses need 24/7, 365 days a year.

We hope that this gives you a sense of how we developed our platform from the specifics of our community's needs. While not all of these will apply to your rural community, many of the problems we face in ours will be relevant to yours as well. And we believe that the way we messaged these issues will work for other rural campaigns. For example, we talked about resiliency instead of climate change to ground our messages in rural working-class Maine. We talked about healthcare access as well as affordability, as rural Mainers struggle most with how to physically get to a healthcare provider. Our focus on youth and seniors emphasized how we need to hold on to our past while building a foundation for those who want to move here. Our platforms were intentionally crafted out of our community's reality.

Only a handful of times did someone ask about our platform while we were knocking doors. But our platform was prominently placed on our website, printed on some of our mailers, and reflected in letters to the editor. It was the unifying vision and message that we could send out into the world, knowing that it reflected our values in a way that spoke to the concerns of our community. Here are examples of our platform pieces as they appeared on various mailers (italic formatting as it appeared on mailers):

RESILIENCE
- Resilience means strength in District 13 to protect our past, feel secure in the present, and stay strong in the future. Resilience is about withstanding any challenge while holding on to all that makes our community special. Resilience is more than a thought—it needs to be baked into our public policy.
- We have a challenging path ahead. We must do everything in our power to *support our businesses and create jobs for a resilient economy* while also protecting public health and ensuring *affordable healthcare*. We need to expand access to *rural transportation* and make sure that everyone in District 13 has access to *high-speed internet*. Finally, we need *loyal representation* at every level that is accountable and responsive to the people.

OUR LOCAL ECONOMY

- We need resilience in local *agriculture*, supporting farms across the region that take care of the land, feed our communities, and make sure no one goes hungry. *Small businesses* are also the core of a resilient community, building a local economy that can sustain itself. We also need a resilient *coastal economy* that supports our fishermen and our fisheries for years to come. Lastly, it's about a strong *education system* that can attract young families & support our children and teachers *without suffocating property taxes.*

BROADBAND

- Everyone in District 13 needs access to broadband. As COVID-19 has shown us, connection to the Internet is *essential to access emergency resources.* We also know that *education—for young folks and adults*—is more accessible when broadband is available. We've heard countless stories of Mainers trying to learn from home but struggle with lack of Internet. Broadband is also how we ensure that residents can *move to our community to build* their business and their life.

HEALTHCARE

- Accessible and affordable healthcare is more important now than ever. It must be a human right. Part of this is ensuring that our *health centers have the funding* that they need to keep their doors open and service the community. Healthcare access also includes resources for the devastating *opioid epidemic* in our community and support for *mental health.* These are parts of our community's health that touch all our lives but often receive the fewest resources. Our campaign has also coordinated rides to cancer treatments, doctor's appointments, and prescription pick-ups. *Transportation is part of healthcare in Maine.*

TRANSPORTATION

- Access to transportation is a critical need in our communities because *it determines access to food, jobs, healthcare, school, family, and social events.* We need transportation systems in place in order to both survive and thrive.
- Maine DOT's Strategic Transit Plan concluded that *transportation access is far below demand.* Only 12% of our need is met in

Lincoln County; 7% in Knox County; 15% in Kennebec. In the 2016 Shared Community Health Needs Assessment for Lincoln County, *transportation is among the most critical factors leading to poor health outcomes.*

- I sponsored a bill with bipartisan support to address the transportation needs of our communities. It passed out of Committee ready to be voted into law, when Covid hit. *I am eager to return to the legislature as your State Senator where my top priority is to turn this bill into law with the funding we need for real change in District 13.* Meanwhile, throughout the Covid crisis, my campaign has worked to fill the gaps, coordinating everything from food and medicine deliveries to rides to cancer treatments and doctor's appointments for anyone in need.

SOCIAL SECURITY

- Many of our neighbors are over the retirement age and struggling on fixed incomes. It's a significant problem, especially for retired state employees—our dedicated teachers, government workers, and law enforcement officials who have paid into Social Security in the private sector as well as into the Maine Public Employees Retirement System public pension fund. An outdated federal policy known as the Social Security Offsets unfairly diminishes their Social Security income. *I crafted a resolution that passed with bipartisan support through the House and Senate to urge the President and Congress to alter the policy and protect hard-earned Social Security benefits.*

ASSESS YOUR STRENGTHS
AND SHORE UP YOUR WEAKNESSES

As your campaign and your core team begin to take shape, it is important to do a self-assessment. What experiences and skill sets make your team unique and strong? Are there any obvious holes that you need to fill or skills that you need to acquire in order to be successful?

Perhaps you have a field person who brings a wealth of experience in community organizing and building volunteer teams but lacks experience working with voter data. Get them into a training or find someone with electoral data experience to show them the ins and outs of the VoteBuilder database. Maybe you have someone who loves to create short, engaging videos for social media. Think about how to amplify this by getting volunteers committed to sharing content and moving money around in the budget for boosting posts. Do you have someone with the time and vision to run the direct-mail program but lacks graphic design experience? Have them create a free account on Adobe or Canva.com and begin experimenting with templates. Maybe it will come easy, or maybe you'll see that you need to find someone else to team up with them to handle the design side of the process. You'll never know until you run this kind of detailed self-audit of your team's skills.

Do the same thing for your candidate. What makes them compelling, and what vulnerabilities will the opposition seek to exploit? One of the first tasks that needs to be done is a review of the candidate's public profile, scrubbing social media accounts all the way back to the beginning for anything that could be twisted against them. Then begin anticipating likely lines of attack from the other side and do everything possible to fill in the cracks and buttress potential weaknesses before they're attacked.

For example, in 2020 we anticipated that Republicans would sow fear through the suggestion that if Chloe were to be elected then she would immediately abolish the local police departments. We believe in the need to envision and work toward a just society with a humane and anti-racist system of restorative justice, but we knew our opponents would erase all nuance and paint us as anti-police. So, to inoculate against this attack, before Republicans could sow their deceitful seeds of fear in the public consciousness, we made moves early to secure the endorsement of the Lincoln County sheriff. Indeed, by late summer, voters' mailboxes were filling up with GOP mailers claiming that Chloe would abolish the police. The attacks landed flat and ended up looking downright silly because we were several steps ahead and had already spent thousands to highlight the sheriff's endorsement.

Similarly, we anticipated Chloe's age and lack of experience in government as a key vulnerability going up against Dow, one of the most experienced legislators in Maine and the GOP Senate leader. We worked on turning Chloe's profile into a strength. We created messaging that highlighted the youthful energy and vision for the future that Chloe embodies. Chloe is the kind of success story that our aging rural communities need to lift up in order for other young people to see a future for themselves in Maine. We put Chloe's nonpartisan recognition as legislator of the year front and center in all our media and made a compelling case for the value of fresh ideas and energy in the legislature against the politics that had failed our communities for decades. The bottom line is to thoroughly analyze your team and your candidate so that you can use their significant strengths, fill in gaps before they create unnecessary challenges, and do everything possible to transform your weaknesses into strengths.

Now that we've established the foundation of strategic principles to guide us and set the critical scaffolding for the campaign, it is time to plunge headfirst into the nitty-gritty action-packed work of campaign season. We've come a long way down these dirt roads. We have a hard-earned understanding of the lay of the land. We've analyzed the successes and failures of the Democratic Party and learned from our own campaigns. From that analysis and those experiences, we've created a road map to guide us forward into this sparsely populated land of opportunity. We've completed our initial campaign build and are now ready to organize volunteers, connect with voters, and empty the toolbox to take on all the challenges of campaigning on our beautiful dirt roads.

CHAPTER 7

LIVING IT ON
THE DIRT ROADS

Our lessons up until now have focused on the strategic principles and structures that we established for our campaigns. These new ways of approaching the work fundamentally changed the way that our movements felt to our community—and they laid the groundwork for our two improbable victories in red-leaning rural America.

What really sealed our victories were the concrete day-to-day tools and tactics that we deployed to ensure that our campaigns paved a new way forward from top to bottom, inside and out. We knew what we wanted our campaigns to look like and how we wanted them to feel. Making it so was a different story. We came up with a slogan to reflect our intentions: "Vision to action!" A hand gesture was invented to pair with it: a peace sign turned upside down to make an A. We flashed it in celebration whenever we lived a moment that we had previously only dreamed could happen. It's silly, but it shows how we have been intentional about creating a vision before we launch into action so that we know that our work will achieve our goals.

This is not an exhaustive list of everything that we did. But they are the highlights that we have identified as moving us toward success. We believe that these tools can help any Democrat running in a rural area, and we are excited to share our hard-earned knowledge with you.

SET CLEAR GOALS AND COMMUNICATE CONSTANTLY

We wrote earlier about how one of the first things that we did in 2018 was pull out giant flip charts and write our big-picture vision and values down on paper together. We mentioned that we also took the time to chart out our year and create a vision for our work. We also did this regularly on a smaller scale during the campaign. This was something that we started doing in 2020, and it completely changed the way that our campaign flowed.

In 2020, we had exponentially more work to do than in 2018. We found ourselves failing to communicate and getting frustrated with each other over unspoken and unmet expectations. We realized that we needed to set aside one-on-one time to check in each week and plot out the campaign work ahead. Once we implemented this, we were more organized, more communicative, and more prepared. We started a Google Doc, titled "C&C Weekly SD13 Check-In Notes," which we used to document our meetings every week from February 28, 2020, all the way until October 26, 2020—a week before the election.

Each Monday, we set aside an hour to envision and plan for the next week, the coming two weeks, and the coming month. We each waited to share feedback, action items, and planning questions until this Monday meeting. If one of us needed to change the meeting time, we gave ample notice. We had a standing agenda that went like this:

- *Individual check-ins*
  - *What are clouds (troubles)? What's giving anxiety? What are the needs around that?*
  - *What's making you excited? How can we lift that up?*
  - *How's workload/burnout going?*
  - *Feedback for selves; feedback for each other*

Then we launched into campaign needs using this rubric:

- *Preview the coming days' immediate needs*
  - *Week immediate needs*
  - *Two-week preview*
  - *Big-picture needs*

We also set norms for how to communicate between meetings, understanding that pressing issues would inevitably arise in the time between meetings. Most of the time, we would communicate via text or quick phone calls, as Chloe was out canvassing all day while Canyon was at home. We came up with emoji codes to signal when communication was working (a rainbow) or when we felt unheard or frustrated (cauliflower). Campaigning is stressful, overwhelming, and nonstop. Although this kind of communication and planning might seem to add additional work, it was crucial to keeping our massive ship on course. Remember, we didn't have the funding to hire staff. So it was only the two of us, and Henney for the final months, responsible for all of the planning.

It's interesting to look back at our notes. On October 5, 2020, our agenda included an endorsement video from the Lincoln County sheriff, ads for the local paper, getting people to fill out absentee ballots, radio ads, GOTV preparation, and more. Setting specific goals around these enabled us to communicate clearly with the rest of our team and volunteers. During our check-in a week before Election Day, on October 26, 2020, Chloe said: "I am super-tired beyond repair but feel solid and ready for this shit show to be over." Canyon said: "Feel kinda weird. Not good or bad. Pretty much ready to escape this living hell. . . . Excruciating period that I do not care for with the election so close. Feel good about things. I think we will win."

During our 2020 State Senate campaign, we would have a virtual check-in with our whole volunteer team right after our weekly meeting with Henney. We asked how their work was going and what they needed from us. We also made sure that everyone was clear about their work for the coming week. These meetings were really exciting because our team members could see how their work contributed to the big picture, which provides additional motivation. It is crucial to put your goals front and center for yourselves and your volunteers in order to make them a reality. As the saying goes, "What you pay attention to grows."

We do our best to cultivate a culture of support that empowers people to communicate if they realize they won't be able to follow through on something, enabling others on the team to fill the gap if needed. People juggle so many balls when working on campaigns that it's inevitable some of them will drop. If there is a pattern of not doing what you commit to, regular check-ins will reveal that and provide the opportunity for feedback and coaching to work through it. Sometimes feedback and coaching aren't successful in achieving follow-through and communication, and the best decision for the success of the campaign is to cut that person from the team so that their failure doesn't impact others. We've had to do this occasionally. Although not pretty, it is essential.

SHOW APPRECIATION AND CELEBRATE SUCCESSES

Amid the stressful campaign slog, it is very important to recognize and thank your supporters regularly—voters, donors, volunteers, staff, your close team, family, and anyone else who is sending goodwill your way. No contribution to the campaign should go unacknowledged, from thirty minutes of phone banking to a thousand-dollar check. Always show appreciation.

We incorporated this into both of our campaigns. Regular community gatherings to celebrate our work gave renewed energy to our team. Chloe wrote clincher cards (which we'll discuss in depth later) to every person that she spoke with. Volunteers received a thank-you postcard, email, or phone call too. We wanted people to know that we were genuinely grateful for their time and their continued support.

This is such a basic element of our campaign vision, but you might be surprised how easy it is to forget taking time to express gratitude once the campaign heats up—unless you make sure that it's on the list of daily priorities. Acknowledging people's contributions also tells them that their actions have an impact that is concretely connected to the success of the campaign, creating an inclusive, validating politics. This is not the typical experience of campaign volunteers. It also makes it more likely that these contributors will continue to volunteer or donate in the future.

In addition to these personal touches, we created structures to facilitate broader communication of appreciation and engagement. Examples of this include Facebook groups for volunteers, an email list for supporters, group chats for staff, Instagram live events with the candidate, and so on. Keeping vibrant streams of communication flowing helps animate the campaign, energize volunteers, and demonstrate the campaign's momentum.

Lastly, celebrate campaign milestones! This is one of the easiest things to neglect as urgent tasks demand your time on the campaign trail, but it too is important for building community and keeping morale high. There is so much work being done constantly on the campaign, and it often feels mundane and exhausting. Look for excuses to pause the work and gather folks together to have fun and blow off some steam to celebrate candidate, staff, volunteer, or collective milestones. Whether it's winning a primary or having knocked on your first one hundred doors—celebrating is always worthwhile.

CAMPAIGNS AS A COMMITMENT TO PUBLIC SERVICE

Campaigns are not just about getting someone elected. They are a public service, a way for community members to support one another. Our work is about coming together as a community and understanding one another's needs. This theme has been part of both of our campaigns.

In 2018, we often met elderly folks living alone who needed help, and despite being in campaign mode we always tried to do what we could, unrelated to getting their vote. An older woman couldn't stand up long enough to wash the dishes in her sink. Chloe showed up one morning and quietly washed her dishes. We met citizens who needed help navigating a state agency, and we always found them assistance.

This ethic was put to the real test when COVID hit in 2020 during our State Senate campaign. As we discussed previously, we decided to pause campaigning and pivot our entire infrastructure toward supporting seniors in the community. One voice memo at the height of the first lockdown gives evidence of some of the need and uncertainty that we were able to help alleviate. After a day of phone banking, Chloe recorded, "I talked with a man who is eighty-six and lives in Jefferson. He lives alone, and his wife died last year. He needs food during the coronavirus crisis and is so sad. I also talked with Sarah from Nobleboro who lives alone. I asked her how she was doing, and she said she was really scared being alone and not going anywhere, just cleaning her house." Our two hundred volunteers made over 13,500 phone calls and comforted thousands of seniors in our community.

This public service continues as of this writing. We send six people from our old campaign squad to the local grocery store every week to deliver meals to residents who are quarantining or unable to leave their homes because of health conditions. We also provide rides for local folks to doctor appointments, partnering with the local hospital and social workers, as there are few other transportation options up and running in our rural community.

The point is that our campaigns are not just about us. Our public service is not political. We don't only do it for votes. We expand beyond the campaign into supporting our community because it's the right thing to do. Public service spreads our vision of community whether or not we win the election. And people notice. Someone wrote out of the blue in 2020, "You called our home at the beginning of the pandemic—when you were making sure seniors and others had what they needed. I liked that and was very impressed by it, and you. I have been a Republican for 40 years and plan to vote for you in the fall."

ABTV (ALWAYS BE TALKING WITH VOTERS)

You can send mailers and postcards. You can run Facebook ads and radio spots, and supporters can write letters to the editor. But the number-one priority every day on the campaign trail must be to talk with voters directly. This is ideally accomplished through canvassing, but it can also be achieved through phone banking, especially for volunteers who don't feel comfortable going door to door. It is vital that your infrastructure is set up to prioritize voter conversations. Your primary request from volunteers is asking them to talk with voters. Other things are important too but only after you mobilize your volunteers to have thousands of conversations. It is the only way to build relationships that are based in trust and respect.

This may seem as obvious as eating your vegetables, but it's not—especially in rural races. Case in point: Tom Perez, former DNC chair, said in 2018 that you "can't knock doors in rural America."[1] In a city, you can knock eighty doors in an hour and probably more if you're in an apartment building. In our districts, it takes five hours, *at the very least*, to knock on one hundred doors. Rural door-knocking requires much more of the candidate's time than urban door-knocking, and, by extension, it requires more volunteer capacity. But not only *can* it be done—it is *necessary* and worth every minute.

The best way to contact voters is by door-knocking. Nothing beats a face-to-face conversation. In 2018, we hosted one phone bank for volunteers who were physically unable to go knock on doors. Other than that, all of our volunteers went a-knockin'. The situation was different in 2020 with COVID. Chloe canvassed basically nonstop after for the first several months of the COVID shutdown. We were confident in Chloe being able to have safe, distanced, outdoor conversations with voters, but we didn't feel comfortable sending dozens of volunteers out into the world during the pandemic. Instead, we channeled their energy into phone banking because it was the only way to achieve our goal under the emergency conditions. We eventually integrated lit drops and canvassing into our 2020 repertoire for volunteers who were comfortable with it.

While it's vital for volunteers to canvass, the most effective relationship-building and trust-building is going to come from the candidate talking with as many voters as possible. Although it can be uncomfortable, the onus is on the candidate to build relationships with their (hopefully) soon-to-be constituents. They need to see you making the effort, saying hello, listening, and fighting hard to represent them. How you run should reflect how you will be in office.

Another important reason to prioritize talking with voters is that this is an effective way to break the cycle of "fake news" that can sink a candidacy. No one knows what to believe anymore—whether a politician's tweets or a rumor that they heard from the neighbors. One of the biggest ways to counteract this dangerous trend of political lies is by looking someone in the face and telling them your truth.

Here's a good example of the power of even a phone call from a volunteer. This is a story from one of our stalwart supporters who phone-banked with us frequently:

> Talked with a 43 year old guy who announced that he wasn't voting, that he was so depressed at the quality of people in office & the current political environment that there was nothing or nobody out there that could serve as an inspiration to him or his kids so he saw no point in voting. But I said, "Let me tell you about the young woman I've been working for as a volunteer for years because of her positive attitude about community, because she cares so much about the people of Maine & because in her short time in the Maine House she's introduced legislation that really matters." He said, "Interesting, tell me more." So I did. I told him the Chloe story & how she & her campaign were the best I'd seen in my 50+ years of doing political work in 3 different states & that Chloe has been inspiring to lots of voters who are fed up as well as even some Republicans. Then he got excited & asked whether it's possible to vote for just one person even if he wasn't currently registered & I told him he could register & vote on election day. He said, "That's what I'm gonna do! The fact that an older person is optimistic & working to elect young people is a great thing. Thanks for inspiring me!" He sure made my day!!

Our commitment to door-knocking far outpaced any other candidate's both in 2018 and 2020. In 2018, our team knocked on over ten thousand doors total for a district of around 9,000 people, returning to houses multiple times. We had conversations with 2,369 voters. (Knocking on ten thousand doors doesn't mean you talk with ten thousand people. There is a contact rate of approximately 25 percent.)

In 2020, our total number of direct voter contact attempts (canvassing and phone banking combined) in District 13 was 83,662 people. As a point of comparison, the 2018 Democratic State Senate campaign for District 13 recorded 8,799 voter contact attempts, and that was the fourth-highest of any Senate campaign in the state that year. In 2020, the second-highest number of voter contact attempts in Maine by a State Senate campaign was 34,360. Chloe herself knocked on 13,395 doors. The second-highest number of direct knocks by a candidate was 2,189. All of this effort paid off. In 2020, we had 10,249 conversations with voters, and those made all the difference.

Some have called our approach "deep canvassing," and that would be accurate. In a *Rolling Stone* article titled "Can Millions of Deep Conversations with Total Strangers Beat Trump—and Heal America?," deep canvassing is defined as "when volunteers and organizers engage in extended, empathetic conversations, with the goal of combating prejudice and shifting beliefs. (The typical door-to-door canvasser, by contrast, gives a brief spiel, asks how you're voting, and moves on.)"[2] In our case, we had never heard of "deep canvassing." We stumbled on this approach by committing ourselves to a humane and empathetic campaign in a community that had been left behind by rote transactional politics.

The power of always talking with voters is calculable if Democrats deployed this strategy across rural parts of the country. We've shown that a candidate and campaign can truly reach folks with meaningful conversations if the priority is listening and outreach. The dark side of this approach is merely to say that the good work is hard work. We can't let the hard times stop us from doing what is right.

BUILD REAL RELATIONSHIPS WITH YOUR COMMUNITY

Building real relationships is the foundation for more honest and difficult conversations that can change how we think about and interact with politics and each other. We can only meet people where they are and build an on-ramp to dialogue if we are authentic and create rapport. If you charge right in to the divisive issues of our times without that relationship of trust and mutual understanding, you'll find that there's no basis for conversation and understanding to help move people toward mutual respect and understanding.

We put this into practice during both of our campaigns. Every volunteer, no matter their age, whether or not they had volunteered on a
campaign before, or how many times they had volunteered with us, was
brought into the fold with a conversation with one of our team. They
were then brought into a community with their neighbors and lovingly
trained on how to do phone banking or canvassing. Every volunteer also
got a thank-you postcard, email, or phone call from Chloe to express
appreciation. We also made sure, to the best of our abilities, that each
volunteer activity included time to connect, meet other people, debrief,
share stories, and engage with our campaign. Every volunteer also had
the space to choose whatever role they felt comfortable with—whether
it was writing postcards or doing doors every day or finding some other
activity that they felt called to do.

This principle was even more apparent in the way that we canvassed.
As we've mentioned, one of the benefits of Maine's districts, and many
state-level districts, is that they are small enough to allow multiple visits to a voter's house. In 2018, for our primary, Chloe did eight passes
through the universe. In the 2018 general election, she did four passes
through the universe. In 2020, because the Senate district is six times
larger than the House district, Chloe did about three passes through the
universe. She talked with many people more than once, but—at the very
least—voters received two palm cards with a handwritten note reading
"Sorry I missed you—call anytime."

This approach may seem like the humane way to win trust and earn
a vote. But it is the exception. Our experience on campaigns has revealed
the way that Democratic machines view voters solely as targets and data.
Volunteers are sent out to grade voters' support of a candidate. The goal
is numbers, not meaningful conversations. No wonder voters feel used
and unheard.

THE NITTY-GRITTY OF CANVASSING

We've talked a lot about the importance of talking with voters and building relationships through canvassing. Here we will provide a more on-
the-ground view of how we canvassed, what we said, and how we handled
all the various scenarios that came our way. Our strategy evolved considerably throughout the months and years.

As we mentioned, Chloe decided to canvass solo. For expediency and
emotional well-being, it's what worked best for her. It also added some

stress. Heading down long dirt driveways by yourself can be tough because you don't know what you'll find at the end. So, for all of you canvassing on the dirt roads of America, make sure someone knows where you are canvassing that day. Chloe kept Mace in her car just in case. Make sure you pack lots of food and water to keep you going. Get your favorite music going. Wear comfortable clothes and shoes that will support your body and mind. Chloe kept her palm cards in the pocket of her car door and a Sharpie in her pocket for writing notes on the cards.

In many rural places, "no trespassing" signs abound. For the most part, we respected these and would not enter the property. Instead, Chloe would mail them a handwritten postcard saying that she tried to stop by, wanted to respect their private property, and welcomed a phone call anytime. We also asked our volunteers to follow this protocol.

When you get to the house, keep an eye out for loose dogs or anything that might signal the need for caution. Chloe wouldn't get out of the car if a dog was loose and there was no owner in sight. One time, Chloe was deep in the woods trying to find a trailer. She got out of the car and walked around to the front door of the trailer only to find dozens of shotgun shells, tons of marijuana plants, and dogs viciously barking inside. She immediately left. For the most part, though, houses will look safe and approachable.

Before you go to the front door, make sure you know the name of the voters you're expecting to meet there. Walk up to the front door and knock loudly and with confidence. Chloe would often yell "Hello!" as she walked up the front door, to avoid startling anyone. This turned into a really nifty trick: it helps you find folks who are outside and won't hear you knock.

As the saying goes, people will remember how they felt when they met you, not what you said. When you meet the voter, say hello with a big, kind smile. Here's what Chloe's script looked like:

CHLOE: "Hi there. I'm Chloe Maxmin, and I'm running for State Senate. Are you Joe?"

JOE: "Yes, I am."

CHLOE: "Hi, Joe. It's so nice to meet you. I was just stopping to see if you have any thoughts or questions as we head toward the election in November."

Joe and Chloe chat for a while.

CHLOE: "Well, thank you so much for your time. Here is my card with my cell phone on it. Please feel free to reach out anytime. Can I count on your vote in November?"

Joe, hopefully, says yes.

A couple of notes here about things learned after hours of practice and refining. First, make sure you introduce yourself and say that you are running for office before you ask the person who they are. You're a stranger who just showed up on their front porch, so introduce yourself to take tension out of the conversation. Second, always smile and have a friendly demeanor. Third, ask what they have on their mind instead of telling them what's on yours. This is key. It immediately opens the door for voters to share their thinking.

Lastly, make sure that you explicitly ask if you can count on their vote. Chloe didn't do this at the beginning of her canvassing career because it felt too awkward. The result was campaign data that were unreliable since we didn't know if people were supporting, undecided, or opposing. One day when Canyon accompanied Chloe canvassing, he encouraged her to ask. It completely changed the game. Our data was more accurate. Also, when you are the candidate or canvassing for a candidate you believe in, it is appropriate to project confidence. It turns out that voters like it when you're honest, strong, and self-assured. They're more likely to respond to a confident question than to a conversation with a weak conclusion.

If the person isn't home, write a note on your palm card and leave it at their door. If someone answers, but it's not the person on your list, talk with them! Get their name, look them up in the voter database when you get home, and mark down whether they are a supporter or not. In rural communities, word travels fast. A good conversation with *anyone* can go a long way toward building your reputation as someone who is kind and listens.

Not every conversation is as easy and straightforward as the one with Joe above. Sometimes folks can talk for a really, really long time, and all you can think about is how many doors you have left to do before you can go home. In that case, Chloe would politely intervene and say that she had to get home, encouraging the person to call her for further discussion. You will inevitably find folks who yell at you or are rude. Chloe's approach was to say something like, "I am willing to have a kind, calm conversation with you, but I do not deserve to be yelled at and will not stand for it." If they don't calm down, you say good-bye, thank them, and leave.

Lastly, there will always be conversations that are difficult to engage in because they conflict with your values. You'll have to decide on your approach. Chloe often found that listening and staying calm helped her better understand viewpoints that were different than her own. She might listen, offer her own opinion, and then politely leave instead of asking someone for their vote. Other times, Chloe would fight back harder if the conversation became personal or extremely offensive. It is a learning curve, and there's no one-size-fits-all approach.

HOST LOTS OF COMMUNITY EVENTS

Creating space for the community to come together was one of the guiding visions of our campaigns. In 2018, our canvasses started and ended with a gathering over food, music, and conversation. We launched our 2020 campaign with a potluck and sharing circle where everyone in the room—about a hundred people—had the opportunity to speak and hear others. Volunteers cannot just be faceless cogs in the machine of a meaningful campaign. Campaigns must be a space of inclusion, self-expression, relationship, and fun. We knew all of our volunteers by first name and made a point of creating space in each of our campaign events for relationship-building. Every person has a story that brought them to give their time to this work. Sharing those stories in public creates a sense of camaraderie and connectedness that draws people deeper into the work together. Every gathering, from a canvass to a house party, is an opportunity to build community.

House parties are one of the best, most intimate events for gathering folks in the community. A hallmark of grassroots campaigning, these get-togethers were huge successes in our primary race in 2018. We hosted four house parties in the spring, each with around two dozen guests. The host would invite their friends to join. These were an opportunity to learn about Chloe. More importantly, they were a chance to bring people into the campaign fold by explaining the importance of volunteering and signing people up for letters to the editor, sign painting, canvassing, and anything else that they wanted to contribute. Everyone got acquainted with one another—and Chloe and Canyon—in a casual setting over refreshments in the comfort of a volunteer's home.

Larger community celebrations are another hallmark of our campaigns. We would host these at the North Nobleboro Community Center or, as with our 2018 post-election celebration, at a local business. Often overlooked in favor of more pressing concerns, celebrations can play an instrumental role in creating and maintaining a vibrant, upbeat campaign culture. These are larger open-invitation events meant to be as much a community gathering as an opportunity to learn about our campaign.

The year 2020 was different, of course, due to COVID. Yet we still found ways to bring the community together. Bringing folks together from across the district in our mutual-aid effort was instrumental in building bonds and community from the outset. Our COVID phone-banking Zoom calls were often filled with laughter and hope in such a dark time. In the early summer, we held virtual house parties across the district to give folks a chance to get together on Zoom and hear from Chloe as well as ask questions about the campaign. In August, we organized volunteer launches at four hubs across the district. Democrats in various towns organized small outdoor gatherings as well, giving Chloe, other candidates, and local Democrats a chance to safely come together in person.

Campaigns should actively facilitate connection between individuals and communities, as well as foster a sense of being part of something bigger than oneself. If this is done well, it is not only a key to successful campaigning but also a lasting contribution to the people and communities in which the campaign organizes. Every campaign should be an invitation for people to come together and find something of themselves in strangers who are drawn to a common cause.

INCLUSIVE, FUN, AND PERSONAL
VOLUNTEER TRAININGS

Chloe remembers one particular experience volunteering on Hillary Clinton's 2016 campaign in Maine. She was sent to a stretch of suburban road in southern Maine, knocking on doors alone in the rain, talking with voters who had already been contacted multiple times. At the end of her shift, she arrived at the campaign office. Only one staffer was there. The staffer took Chloe's clipboard without an inkling of interest in how it went. Chloe grabbed the world's worst cookie and left. This is pretty par for the course on campaigns, and it's not a great way to engender hope or spirit in politics. How can we build anything sustainable or powerful with campaigns like this?

We did our own volunteer trainings for canvass days and phone banks, and we put a lot of intention into them. Communicating our philosophy and approach to rural campaigning was fundamental to the experience of both volunteers and the voters with whom they would connect. We were out to do things differently, and for volunteers to embody that spirit in public and at doors, we knew that these trainings needed to provide a lot more than the typical session. Our trainings had soul. Chloe made a Spotify playlist with Bruce Springsteen, Garth Brooks, and all our favorite country songs. We gathered at the North Nobleboro Community Hall and started by hearing each other's stories of why they were there. Most had never volunteered for a campaign in their lives, and many were there because they had met Chloe when she showed up knocking at their door.

Then we talked with volunteers about our experiences canvassing and the importance of listening, values, and searching for common ground. We talked more about how interactions should feel than what they should sound like. We gave everyone talking points and a sample script to fall back on if they were nervous, but we encouraged them to toss those aside and go from the gut. We wanted to prepare our volunteers to have real conversations with voters instead of merely regurgitating talking points and marking people down as supporters or not. We invited volunteers with canvassing experience to share their insights and best practices with newcomers. We emphasized the importance of making good eye contact and listening to understand, not merely to persuade. We impressed upon people that they need not be policy experts or even Chloe experts but rather just needed to be honest, earnest representatives of the campaign—to ask questions and answer honestly if they weren't sure about something. "I don't know what Chloe's stance is on the CMP corridor, but I can give you her phone number or have her call you to talk about it" is a perfectly fine answer. Recording accurate data about where each voter stands is a vital part of canvassing, so we made sure that people got comfortable asking directly whether voters planned to vote for Chloe or not and understood how to record their responses. "Be kind to *everyone*," Chloe would often repeat. "This movement isn't about a political party . . . it's about the well-being of our community, homes, and families. If they're mean to you, say 'thank you for your time,' smile, and leave."

Everyone practiced their script with a partner while we stood by to answer any questions. Then off they went. Each canvasser was accompanied by a driver for moral support so that no one would burn out after a single lonely shift and never return. Another benefit of using drivers is that it is an excellent entry-level role for volunteers who want to participate but are timid about talking with strangers. Driving canvassers around and seeing them have conversations with voters demystifies the process and makes it appear considerably less frightening. Drivers often eventually volunteer to become canvassers.

Once volunteers finished a shift, they would meet back at the old community hall. Often, we would bring baseball gloves, and people would play catch or kick a soccer ball as we waited for others to return. We broke out seltzers and food while gathering together to debrief. This process was essential to build community, celebrate the conversations that went well, air out the painful encounters, learn from one another's experiences, and simply have fun together. The feedback was immediate. One experienced local activist said that our canvassing trainings were the best she had seen in her decades of doing political work.

HANDWRITE CLINCHER CARDS

As we hope is clear by now, one of our biggest goals for a new politics in rural America is to build real relationships with voters. There are so many ways to do this beyond knocking on a door, and one of them is writing clincher cards. This is a campaign term for handwritten postcards sent to everyone you talked with while door-knocking to clinch (it is hoped) their vote. They are a kind and simple way to express gratitude for a conversation, reflect on the ideas you exchanged, and share your contact information again.

Clinchers are a key part of our campaigns. We are genuinely grateful that people take the time to talk with us, share their stories, and hear about our work. That deserves a handwritten thank-you card. Every night, throughout both campaigns, Chloe wrote a postcard to each person contacted that day. If we talked with someone twice, they received two cards. We want people to feel appreciated and heard.

We felt that it was important to immediately write and send a postcard to reinforce the conversation. Postcards were only written to people who said that they would support Chloe or folks who were still undecided. To conserve resources and focus on the relationships where there was room for growth, we didn't write cards to folks who said that they would not support us.

Like so many other parts of our campaign, people took notice of our handwritten and genuine approach. An email came in one day: "Taking a break from the recording studio projects to thank you for taking the time/energy to send me a handwritten postcard. Very classy and impressive! Some of my friends have expressed the same sentiment and you won their vote and support. I voted for you last week absentee." In 2020, Chloe wrote almost five thousand postcards. It's time-consuming, but it's worth it.

DESIGN AND WRITE MEMORABLE PALM CARDS

A palm card is a flyer-sized piece of literature that serves as an introduction to the candidate and your campaign. Palm cards are left on doors while canvassing and given out at events. Usually, these cards feature poll-tested consultant favorite phrases like "for good jobs" and "for affordable healthcare." Boilerplate. Ours, by contrast, were substantive and a genuine introduction to our work and Chloe's story. Like our mailers, we made these ourselves instead of outsourcing them to consultants, and so they looked—and were—different and authentic. Voters commented on them frequently.

When we first thought about designing palm cards with the consultants in early 2018, their plan was to print thousands of cards that would serve us for the entire campaign season. We did not like this one-size-fits-all approach. Instead, we printed a different palm card for each round of canvassing and tailored them for each constituency. We printed palm cards specifically for the primary, for example. For the general election, we printed palm cards with different coloring and messaging to reflect the range of hard-core Trump supporters to moderate Democrats we spoke with. In 2020, since the district was so big, we created palm cards for different regions, making sure to list towns in that region on the front of the card instead of naming a town over an hour away.

We also matched the content of the palm cards with the phase of the campaign. As with mailers, the various rounds of palm cards should have a strategic arc. We began with Chloe's story and vision in the first round of cards, moving on to a focus on endorsements and quotes from community members' letters to the editor in later versions. Depending on the field plan, we would often print slightly different versions to speak to different constituencies based on who we were canvassing. Persuadable moderate and conservative voters would get a version that highlighted Chloe's bipartisan work and emphasized conservative value frameworks such as loyalty and tradition. For low-turnout Democrats, we might highlight Obama's endorsement rather than an endorsement from the former chair of the Lincoln County Republicans.

Lastly, we always put a personal touch on palm cards that were left at doors of voters who weren't home. Whether it was Chloe or a volunteer doing the knocking, we always left a handwritten note either directly on the card or attached via a sticky note with Chloe's phone number and a short message like "Sorry to miss you" or "Call anytime!" These cards are often the first thing voters will see from the campaign, so it's important to stick the landing and make the cards an invitation to further conversation.

FLOOD THE PAPERS WITH LETTERS TO THE EDITOR

Letters to the editor played a huge role in our campaign. In our neck of the woods, local papers are still printed and widely read. From reporting on the friendly llama that visits senior care facilities to documenting commercial fishers' protests against offshore wind development, our local papers spread news far and wide. For both campaigns, we had LTEs printed almost every week throughout the campaign. Sometimes we'd have four or five in one issue of a paper, which made it impossible to ignore our success and traction across the district.

The letters were effective for two reasons. First, they are a wonderful way to engage volunteers who don't have a lot of time on their hands but want to contribute. They can quickly write a hundred words and submit it to the papers. We had volunteer leaders from our team offer help with editing as well as a messaging guide. The rest was up to them to craft a meaningful letter.

Second, it makes a big difference in a tight-knit rural community when people see their neighbors and friends standing up for a candidate. It makes them feel like they can too. Chloe always heard about the letters when knocking on doors. One person told her, "I saw all your letters in the paper. I think you're going to win!" We also heard: "I saw that Bob supports you. I've known him for years!"

Your community might not have a local printed paper. Can you rely on a local online paper? Or even a statewide paper? You could also use letters to the editor on Facebook feeds, Instagram posts, or other community forums. Adapt the lessons from this section to the channels that are available to you.

A THOUGHTFUL AND CREATIVE MAILER PROGRAM

When you knock on doors, typically a quarter to a third of people are at home or answer the door. Even when people are home, you will only have deep conversations with a small percentage. There remains a lot of work to do to introduce the candidate. That is where mailers come in. A well implemented direct-mail program is crucial to deliver your story and message directly to the voters you need to reach. Mail is one of the easiest ways to communicate directly with everyone in your persuasion universe to introduce the candidate and deliver a coherent narrative over the course of many weeks.

We're probably all familiar with this perennial campaign tactic. We get glossy, corporate-looking pieces of paper in our mailboxes that seem to either paint one candidate in an abnormally good light or bash the other one in unfair ways. It has become a dirty business. Most campaigns outsource their mailer program to consultants who create the same type of junk cycle after cycle. This is for a couple of reasons. First, it is challenging and time-consuming to figure out how to send mail to thousands of people economically. And second, the messaging and design of a professional mailer isn't easy to craft.

We felt very strongly about doing our own mailers. We saw potential in this method of reaching voters, and the only way that we could fulfill the dream of an authentic mail program was by taking it into our own hands. We figured out how to mail them out, and we designed them ourselves. As a result, we were able to reach 20 percent more voters than if we had outsourced them, and for half the cost. And, more importantly, our mailers looked and felt profoundly different from all the other consultant-produced mailers that filled people's mailboxes.

We heard wonderful feedback about our mailers from voters. A Republican man told Henney at his door days before the election: "You know, I've been reading every single one of those mailers I've gotten, and I think I'm gonna vote for her." Another voter emailed out of the blue: "Your gigantic post card crashed into my mail box a few days ago. I have never read anything like it. Genuine, authentic, credible, persuasive."

The first step is to plan at the outset how many pieces you can afford to send and budget it out, working backward from the final piece right before Election Day. Call all the printers in the region to get quotes for the printing and mailing price. Most printers have their own USPS commercial mail permit. Some will up-charge you for postage, and some will just take the profit from printing and mail at cost. Negotiate to get the best price. Can the printer give a discount based on the total number of pieces you'll be printing if you commit to using them for the entirety of the mail program, including palm cards and clincher cards? Can you save money by doing black and white on one side or going with pieces of a different size?

Once you know how many mail pieces you'll be sending, create your plan for the narrative arc and frequency of mailings. Each piece should follow from the previous one and set up the next one, while also having a discrete purpose and standing on its own. You're telling a story with each one, weaving a tale together.

In our mailers, as elsewhere in the campaign, we emphasized stories and values over policy. We sent eight mailers in all in 2020, sending them a little less frequently than once a week for the two and a half months leading up to the election. We generally stuck to the plan as crafted from the outset, but—because we did it ourselves—we were also able to make changes on the fly. Hearing at the doors how much Chloe's commitment to positive campaigning was resonating, we worked that into nearly every mailer. Seeing GOP attacks claiming Chloe would abolish the police, we reemphasized the endorsement of the local sheriff.

Some other helpful tips: Good photos are crucial. They should show the candidate in the community interacting with people. They should be professional, bright, and reinforce the message of the mailer. Keep your campaign colors and fonts consistent across mailers and all campaign materials. We considered using handwritten text for the mailers, but Chloe's handwriting is hopeless, and using someone else's felt disingenuous. We settled on a font with a handwritten feel. While copying the corporate mailers that fill your trashcan is not a good idea, make sure you do not throw graphic design out the window. If the mailers look different, that's great, but they also need to look good. The front should be simple, attractive, and get the key message across in an instant. The back can go into significantly deeper detail, an invitation for the voter to learn something new about the campaign. When designing mail pieces, think about what different folks will get out of it depending on whether they look at it for one second, ten seconds, or thirty seconds or more.

While a mailer is obviously nowhere near as impactful as a face-to-face conversation, it is an effective way to keep the campaign on voters' radars consistently. Even for voters who only glance at it for a moment as they toss it in the trash, it can still serve to reinforce the message and presence of the campaign. For more engaged voters, it is an opportunity to further flesh out the candidate's story, values, and platform. It also primes voters for conversations at the doors and reinforces those in-person interactions.

FREQUENT EARNED MEDIA COVERAGE

Earned media refers to media coverage that the campaign does not pay for. Usually, campaigns pay for ads in the local paper or on Facebook. But the best media coverage is the stuff that comes naturally. Any event or milestone can be used to get yourself in the local news. Some examples of opportunities to generate earned media are campaign launches, town halls and rallies, big volunteer events, fundraising or voter contact milestones, and endorsements. Turn it into a press release, send it off to the local paper, and soon see it in print.

Here's an example of a campaign press release that we sent to newspapers and radio stations in early October announcing Lincoln County sheriff Todd Brackett's endorsement:

—FOR IMMEDIATE RELEASE—

Contact: Chloe Maxmin [phone number and email included]

Lincoln County Sheriff Todd Brackett Endorses
Chloe Maxmin for State Senate

Todd Brackett, the Sheriff of Lincoln County, has endorsed Representative Chloe Maxmin (Democrat-Nobleboro), candidate for State Senate District 13. Brackett began his career in law enforcement over 30 years ago and is the most senior sheriff in the state, having served Lincoln County for over 18 years.

"Chloe Maxmin is a problem-solving powerhouse who unites people around solutions," said Brackett. "We need her courageous leadership for the critical times ahead."

Maxmin thanked Brackett for his leadership on behalf of Lincoln County. "Todd's commitment to our communities is truly extraordinary," said Maxmin. "His compassion, integrity, and leadership in his jail diversion program and alternative sentencing program were ahead of the times in seeking treatment for people with mental illness and addictions rather than jail sentences. I have enormous respect for Todd and am deeply humbled to receive his endorsement."

Brackett pointed to Chloe's work as a State Representative and her ability to work across the aisle as reasons for his support. "Chloe's work in the Legislature speaks for itself," Brackett said. "She is a solutions-oriented leader who takes her job seriously and has a unique ability to bring everyone to the table to work through the very real issues facing our community. Please join me in voting for Chloe Maxmin on Nov 3rd."

Maxmin was elected to the State House in 2018 with bipartisan support. In September she was recognized as the 2020 Legislator of the Year by the nonpartisan Maine Council on Aging for her work supporting seniors through the COVID pandemic.

State Senate District 13 includes all of Lincoln County except Dresden, plus the towns of Windsor and Washington.

Campaigns have a much better chance of garnering earned media if they actively work on developing relationships with reporters, hosts, and editors and send timely press releases. For things that you can control the timing of, such as notable endorsements from local leaders, it's important to think about the most effective timing for each and spacing between them. You don't want to use up all your big announcements in August and then have nothing big to say until November. Space out the media blasts. Letters to the editor can fill the moments in between.

HAVE A PAID MEDIA STRATEGY

Media buys are one of the primary tactics that most traditional campaigns invest in to try to win: TV, radio, newspaper, social media, and digital ads. They're not targeted, but they get your name out there. As is surely evident by now, our campaigns were fueled by our passion for the grassroots elements of campaigning. Carefully identifying persuadable voters and then devoting all the time and money we can muster to make direct contact with them is our bread and butter. Face-to-face conversations come above all else, supplemented with calls and postcards from volunteers, targeted direct mail, and clinchers from the candidate. We could not have won over the voters necessary to flip these districts without innovating and going all out in those areas. Yet we didn't abandon traditional tactics completely. Here's a brief look at how we approached paid media.

Television ads were prohibitively expensive with the small Clean Elections budgets that we were operating with—and they are often out of reach for progressive candidates mounting long-shot candidacies in rural areas. So, instead, we paid to promote our video ads on social media. As we've mentioned, we had a volunteer who did video work professionally. He graciously volunteered his time to produce an excellent campaign video in 2020, and other volunteers did the same in 2018. Television ads certainly make sense if you have the budget for it, but this is also an area where you can save a ton of money if you're able to produce ads in-house and make the media buys yourself.

In rural areas, a lot of people still listen to the radio. Folks log lots of time in the car getting from place to place, households without access to high-speed internet can't use streaming services, and many older folks enjoy it as a familiar form of media. Thus, we spent more than most campaigns on radio, putting about 10 percent of our total budget toward it. We used the audio from our video ad for one radio spot and endorsement messages from the sheriff and former county GOP chair for the other. Then we decided to pay the party consultants a nominal fee to place the ads and handle communications with radio stations.

Local newspapers, though struggling with declining revenue, still have large followings in most small towns. Like radio, these can be especially effective for reaching the older demographic. In District 13, there are still several print newspapers. The *Lincoln County News* is the biggest and serves basically the entire district, with a robust readership. The suggested campaign budget from the SDCC surprisingly didn't include anything for newspaper ads. Rather than spend nearly 20 percent of our budget on digital ads as suggested, we put most of that money into newspaper ads that we designed ourselves and purchased directly.

Social media advertising is a rapidly changing area, and it's worth investing some time to understand its complexities. We saw a marked decline in the effectiveness of Facebook ads in 2020 compared to 2018, though we still put thousands of dollars into pushing video ads out on Facebook pages and boosting certain posts. We also enlisted volunteer leaders to help keep an active, organic presence on Facebook and Instagram, regularly posting updates, letters to the editor, photos with campaign messages, and so on. As social media usage changes from year to year, it's important to maintain an understanding of which platforms are being most used by the demographics that your campaign needs to reach.

Digital ads, much like yard signs, can be somewhat useful for boosting name recognition but generally aren't worth spending too much money on, in our opinion. For those who aren't familiar, digital ads are the kind of ad that appear across most websites—often as a small square on the side or as a short video pop-up. There isn't a whole lot of research on their effectiveness, but, for the purpose of persuading voters to support a candidate, their effectiveness in getting through to people who are focused on something else (whatever it is that brought them to the page) is likely limited.

GET OUT THE VOTE!

Elections ultimately come down to which campaign can get more of its supporters to go out and vote. Get Out the Vote! (GOTV) is the final sprint to the finish line. It is exhilarating, exhausting, and can make or break a campaign. In a country that sees staggeringly low rates of voter turnout, an excellent GOTV effort can move the needle by several percentage points or more. GOTV takes place over the several days leading up to an election. In states with early voting, it begins even earlier. Either way, it is something that needs to be planned for months in advance.

The goal of GOTV is to contact as many of your supporters and likely supporters as possible to ensure that they have a plan to vote and will follow through on that plan. The approximate number of voters that will be in your GOTV universe and the number of volunteers necessary to reach them all should be calculated well in advance. This universe is all of the people the campaign has spent months and months identifying and persuading who have indicated support, as well as Democratic voters with sporadic voting histories who may need extra encouragement to get to the polls.

You should aim to do at least two passes of the GOTV universe if possible: one pass over the Saturday, Sunday, and Monday before Election Day, and a final entire pass on Election Day itself. This requires an enormous amount of volunteer capacity, which means it's a good idea to begin recruiting folks weeks or even months in advance. Emphasize to volunteers the vital importance of GOTV, and explain that it is the most exciting time in the campaign and the easiest doors to knock because it should be entirely supporters. Start lining up volunteers early. We asked as early as August. Try to get people to sign up for a shift every day of GOTV, multiple shifts if they are willing. Print out sign-up sheets and bring them along to every event throughout the fall.

For GOTV, more than any other time in the campaign, it is vital to be in communication with the state party, other campaigns, and any other organizations conducting GOTV activities to ensure that everyone is coordinating as well as possible. In some cases, it might make sense for campaigns to join efforts and pool volunteers to GOTV for multiple candidates. In some cases, the local and state party organizations may be so well organized with their GOTV that the campaign can continue doing persuasion canvassing up until the very end. In other cases, there may not be anybody else doing GOTV at all in your district, in which case a herculean GOTV operation is required. As much as possible, communicate with all other candidates, campaigns, organizations, and volunteers to minimize overlap. It's very frustrating for a voter to have multiple volunteers a day knocking on their door pestering them. Share data, and use everyone's resources as effectively as possible.

For both of our campaigns, we ran our own GOTV effort in part or whole, in parallel to the state and local Democrats' efforts. We coordinated with them, but we did trainings on our own. Volunteers went to houses that had Trump signs and flags to follow up with conservative voters who were supporting Chloe. Those relationships and conversations with voters who don't typically vote Democrat are unique, and they aren't on the radar of the Democratic Party's GOTV game plans. In 2018, we had enough volunteer capacity to cover our district entirely, and we made multiple passes. In 2020, we were able to continue doing "persuasion" conversations—convincing people to vote for Chloe—until Election Day because so many Democrats had voted early, with party organizers covering the rest. This is a rare luxury in campaigning. It only took a fraction of our volunteer capacity to reach all of the non-Democrats that we had identified as supporters.

We hope that these last three chapters have provided some insight into the behind-the-scenes of our campaign, our thinking, approach, strategy, and day-to-day realities. These strategies are tried and true, having succeeded on two rural red campaigns that no one thought a Democrat could win. Now it's your turn to take them and run. Above all, remember that campaigns are about relationships with your voters and your volunteers. Treat those relationships with the kindness and care that they deserve. In an age where it's hard to believe anything that you read or hear, you can always count on the power of honesty, respect, and authenticity.

EPILOGUE

This book came from love. It began with the love of our rural towns that cared for us, called us back home, and taught us so much about the world. The dirt roads, fields, mountains, lakes, rivers, and woods grounded us in place. The people who raised us showed us the power of kindness, independence, community, dialogue, and acceptance. There were times when it was hard to remember our purpose. There were times when the journey felt too challenging. But we knew that there was something rumbling on the dirt roads that was deep, yearning to be heard and appreciated.

This book also came from love for the Democratic Party. Many, including us, have felt lost in the party, where the voices of elite and corporate interests became too loud for our voices to be heard. But our future relies on the Democratic Party reinventing itself to stand firmly on its ostensible core values: equal opportunity and justice for all. These values, as we have shown, can and do resonate in rural communities. The Democrats have all but abandoned these corners of our country, surrendering these critical territories to the violence, division, and cynicism fostered and sown by Trump and his right-wing networks.

We must rise to the challenge of reimagining a Democratic Party committed to representing all. This too is a work of love—love for our communities and the diversity of our people. If we are to combat narratives of white supremacy, we must tell our own stories that resonate with rural people and call upon the values, struggles, and hopes we share. It's time to invest in state and local politics and develop well-organized state parties in order to build durable power. These reforms should be complemented by rebuilding our base, as Democrats show up in every community and on every dirt road to listen, forge relationships, and develop the conditions for trust to grow. This is what everyone deserves.

Last but certainly not least, this book came from the love of the movements, campaigns, mentors, and fellow organizers who showed us the meaning of people power. These spaces are our "political home," as adrienne maree brown described it, places "where we ideate, practice and build futures we believe in, finding alignment with those we are in accountable relationships with, and growing that alignment through organizing and education. Political home is where we solidify our critiques and generate solutions for human and planetary futures that, with practice and time and a functional government, become viable enough to scale."[1] These spaces have both pushed and nurtured us to grow into the organizers we have become and are still becoming. From the blockades, marches, and protests to canvass days, celebration parties, and GOTV weekends: the truly renewable, never-ending, eternal power in our world today is the power of the people. Together, we do the real enduring work. The world will change because of us, together.

We wrote this book with a deep sense of urgency. The biggest questions of our time depend on political action being taken within months and years, not decades. Can we mitigate the climate crisis and exercise compassion across borders? Can our society dismantle systemic racism and challenge xenophobia? Can we save our agricultural lands and working waterfronts? Can we ensure that all children in the United States grow up with equitable access and opportunity, no matter their zip code? If we care about LGBTQIA+ rights, climate justice, racial justice, economic justice, education reform, prison abolition, regenerative agriculture, saving the lobsters, affording the next visit to the doctor, healthy food, and a stable society today and tomorrow, then it is time to take matters into our own hands.

We and our politicians need to stand on the right side of history. There is too much at stake to sit by and hope that the world goes our way.

Who decides who sits in elected office? Who holds politicians accountable to their promises, our tax dollars, and the will of the people? We do. The people, the voters, the citizens are the ones who decide where our country will go. We elect the politicians who decide so much of our fate. We vote on referenda and initiatives that change what is possible. We hold deep power, and it is time to wield it.

How we use our power as citizens is just as important as whether we use it at all. We're too used to voting once every year (or four), reading headlines, signing an online petition here and there, and then hoping all will go well. But now there is too much at stake to engage only at this bare minimum. We must think deeply about how we're using our collective power to build a better world for all who live here. This work requires stretching our hope, deepening our commitment, and stepping into new ways of relating to the world and society.

It is time that we all accept responsibility to build and support inclusive movements that welcome all perspectives and backgrounds. We need to focus on communities that have been left behind, to expand from the margins. We need to draw on the power of human relationships and to show up, listen to one another, find common ground, and discover how we forge a better, sturdier path together.

This book redefines campaigns as social movements that build a necessary bridge between people power and electoral politics. We need a Democratic Party that can inspire and support such campaigns in which political power is rooted in community, based in relationships, and built to last. We must build social movements that exert pressure on decision makers from the outside and wield power on the inside. Our theory of change must include running for office, volunteering on campaigns, hosting house parties, canvassing, working with local Democrats, and digging deep into politics beyond just a single candidate or election. Politics is our long-term work. It is our biggest work of love.

We committed ourselves to the dirt road revival and to share our discoveries with you because we recognize that the pain that is evident in our rural districts has come to define much of US politics. There is power in the disproportionate influence of the rural vote. It contributed to electing one of the most dangerous presidents in US history. The rural vote is defining state legislatures and local politics across this country. But there is also power in the untold stories of rural people, in their frustration and search for a better life, in the wisdom that dwells at the crossroads of independence and interdependence.

We hope that this book has shown the urgent need for a dirt road revival and provided a foundation for you to make it happen. Our aim hasn't been just to catalogue the problems but also to lay out the solutions and distill them, providing practical details that empower you to catalyze a dirt road revival in your own communities. We think of this book as our word tent, infinitely extending the well-worn spaces of our beloved North Nobleboro Community Hall, welcoming all of you with good company, joyful music, and tables bent under the weight of crockpots and platters piled high with our neighbors' home cooking.

The dirt road revival will take years to realize. We will slowly but surely watch our efforts take hold and change the political landscape. We are in it for the long haul, and we have each other as support along the way. We're only going to get where we need to go if we are committed to steady, sustained, durable strategies that lovingly create movements and relationships at every campaign event, training, teach-in, forum, and debate. A true revival across the country needs all of us to show up.

This book begins that journey as we start down the dirt roads together. It's a journey that will take us to many houses, winding through woods and fields, mountains, farmland, and desert. It awes us with its beauty and braces us for what lies just over the next hill. It reminds us that we are not alone. As the dust settles on the past, the road ahead beckons. We know where we need to go together, creating the possibility for community, hope, and understanding at every door, with every conversation, clincher card, smile, wave, and handshake. Now, it's your turn to take the wheel.

ACKNOWLEDGMENTS

CANYON THANKS . . .

Deepest gratitude first and foremost to my family. To Mom and Dad, for devoting everything to building our family, for educating us, and for all the adventures. I can't imagine a better childhood. Thank you for instilling a lifelong love of learning, outdoor adventure, striving for change, and fostering meaningful relationships. Mom, queen of wildcamp, thank you for your endless visioning, support in every endeavor, adventurous spirit, playfulness and smack talk, outspokenness, listening, and holding all of us close with so much care. Dad, thank you for showing up without fail—from Divest Harvard blockades, to tennis tournaments, to 4:00 a.m. airport rides, to late-night aid stations—for modeling incredible resourcefulness, memory keeping, sense of humor, and for countless books read aloud and back rubs exchanged. Cricket, thank you for the hikes, songs, fierce support, and encouraging me to sing even though I'm terrible at it. Dave, thank you for many of the fondest days of my life, on the Chattooga and beyond. Autumn, thank you for all the ways in which you look after the world and each of us with the full magic of your being, for your earth-shaking poetry, and Rowan! Dear nephew, you light up our world. Forest, there's nothing I cherish more than our mountain of exquisite life touchstones collected together over the past decade—thank you for your truly immeasurable support and believing so big in me on every front. Rivers, thank you for all our adventures together, your humble trailblazing as you transform all you touch with your creativity, work ethic, and vision, and for being a best friend from the early Stehekin days to now. Auntie Sue—Suzanne Severin—thank you for being a hugely integral, fun part of my life. And thank you to

Libby and Doug Hedstrom, Mike Severin, and Linn and Fleur Larsen for all the great memories created and love shared through the years.

To my dear friends, mentors, and chosen family without whose love and support throughout it all this book never could have come to be—y'all are the best! Nic Brow, Camilla Gibson, Grace Chen, and George Mills, cheers to all the light you've shined on every step of the journey. Huge appreciation also to William Dean, Caroline Cox, Joey Wraithwall, Emily Savage, Jon Raduazzo, David Roche, Jake Maxmin, Laura Yale, Brett Roche, Elliot Ross, Joey Schusler, Kellar Mackoviak, Raven Berman, Jeff Berman, and Josette Pelletier.

To Chloe. Soul sister, *caminante*—for your love, courage, and vision, forging the trail with every step forward, plunging us deeper and deeper into the most uncertain, challenging, meaningful endeavors of my life. You are the embodiment of the maxim "believe," and your unsurpassed integrity and fierce loyalty to your people and principles are beyond measure. Our friendship is one for the ages. Here's to a lifetime of belly-aching laughs, tears, changemaking, tomfoolery, adventures, and good trouble together.

To Shoshana—Mama Z—for giving me family and home away from home and playing an integral role in the book and both campaigns every step of the way. Always there with whatever the situation demands—from red strikethrough, to champagne, to tissues, to feasts, to campaign communications czaring, to life counsel.

To James Henney Sullivan. "Henney is coming, Henney is coming!" This mantra carried our weary spirits through the dog days of the 2020 campaign, knowing that as the leaves turned you would appear to help us make it up the slope of Mount Doom. From the early tandem days, to FOP, to a mini lifetime of Divest Harvard, to Bernie 2016, to now, and every precious slice of life we've shared in between, it's all been very exciting! This book would not exist without you.

To the incomparable John deVille for sage counsel and friendship through the years. From learning me about history, philosophy, and writing, to emergency Zoom huddles on the campaign trail, to tarot storytelling, bonfire stogies, and good-natured ribbing, to lending your discerning eye to chapters of this book.

To Julia Buckner for being a mentor and friend, opening my eyes to the power and potential of state politics on my home turf in North Carolina, and giving valuable perspective and feedback on this book.

To Ana Maria Spagna for years of slinging Word documents back and forth, helping make a writer out of me against the odds.

A large debt of gratitude accrued to Sam Sokolsky-Tifft for your 4:00 a.m. time-stamped edits, clarifying conversations and encouragement, feedback on chapter drafts, and editing support to the very end. Can't imagine the past decade without you, my dear friend—here's to all the adventures between now and 108!

Vince Cooper, brother, thank you for taking the time to read our early work conceptualizing the book and bringing your down-home rural Ohio sensibilities to bear on it. Most importantly, thank you for being one of the best dang friends a person could ask for. Your imagination and vision are a gift. The rest of the world wears bifocals.

To all the organizers, movement elders, and mentors who helped me find my path. In particular, for illuminating the way forward as I learned how to organize, thank you Marshall Ganz and Timothy P. McCarthy.

CHLOE THANKS . . .

I've lovingly read the acknowledgments in every book that I've ever picked up. I appreciate the care for each name, imagining the conversations and relationships that played out behind the scenes. I also marvel at the movement behind any book project and all the pieces that fit together to make it happen.

Although it is a bit surreal, I am honored to write these words today and express gratitude to all who have supported me, Canyon, and our vision. We wrote this book after we won our State Senate campaign in November 2020, but we have been documenting our work since 2018. It has been a long journey, one that started with a dream, launching into the unknown. Slowly but surely, everything came into focus. Dream became reality.

To start, I want to thank my family. To my dad, Jim Maxmin, who was the first person to tell me that it was okay to build my life in a town of 1,600 people. He believed that great things are possible in Nobleboro, Maine. My love for home came from him. He is not here today to read this book, but it is in his honor.

To Mom, Shoshana Zuboff, who spent hours poring over every word and phrase of our manuscript. Thank you for your loving guiding hand, the care and attention that you so graciously gave to this book. Your steady presence makes me feel safe and supported in this world, and it is the greatest gift that I could ever ask for. I love you so much.

To Jake, my brother, who was the first person to put up signs on Election Day in November 2018 in front of the polls. I wasn't there to help him, but when I arrived, I drove through a Chloe tunnel as dozens of signs led the way to the polls. Jake built a beautiful firepit for campaign gatherings, a space that ultimately gave home to our Election Night party in 2020. Thank you, Jake, for your abiding love. Forever best friends.

To Pachi and Elsie, who taught me the power of infinite love and kindness.

With grace and gratitude to Bill, whose bright light and loving wisdom protected me when I felt outnumbered. We dive deep.

Saving the best for last: to Canyon. There are no words to express how grateful I am to have you in my life. From that first bus ride in Cambridge to writing the last words of this book—it is a journey that I never could have fathomed. I am the luckiest person on earth to find someone like you, a best friend, a co-conspirator, a co-coordinator, campaign manager, political genius, coauthor. Our friendship feels like the stuff of fairy tales. It has been the honor of a lifetime to watch your creative free mind infiltrate the most stalwart systems and bend them toward your empathy, righteousness, and sense of community. I can't wait for all that is to come.

TOGETHER, WE THANK . . .

We had almost given up hope on finding a publisher after over a dozen agents rejected our book proposal. It was Laura Gross who took a chance on our vision, advocated for the book, and connected us with Beacon Press. Laura, you were there first. Your faith and support changed our lives.

To Joanna Green, our editor at Beacon Press, who gave us the opportunity to put a book out into the world. You took a chance on us, helped us formulate our vision for the book, and navigated us through the complexities of book writing at an epic pace, kindly pushing us from jumbled drafts to professional manuscript.

The transformation of *Dirt Road Revival* wouldn't be complete without Will Myers, who helped us organize, structure, and finalize the book. With the perfect balance of critique and praise, the book took its final form because of Will.

To Forest Woodward for all you did to document the campaigns and help sow the seeds for the book and for the film. Thank you Anya Miller Berg, Gnarly Bay, Laura Yale, Aidan Haley, and the whole *Rural Runner* team for your support.

To Ben Davis for your wisdom, belief in our work, and all the support that helped make this book possible.

Enormous gratitude to the Wend Collective for supporting our work. There is a deep need for greater and more diverse representation in our public service

We also want to thank John deVille, Julia Buckner, Anthony Flaccavento, Jane Kleeb, and Erica Etelson, whose expertise in rural politics helped us complete the first chapters. Their knowledge and insight fine-tuned the facts, figures, and history that lay the groundwork for our campaigns.

Finally, to all those in District 88 and District 13 (and beyond) who joined our campaigns: thank you. This book belongs to you. None of this is possible without the kindness, compassion, and optimism of our community. We knew that politics needed another way forward, and we built something better, together.

NOTES

PREAMBLE: A HANDSHAKE

1. Who do we mean when we say "the Democratic Party"? The landscape is quite vast. At the national level, the Democratic National Committee (DNC) is the overarching umbrella organization that officially houses the party. Then there are subcommittees that oversee certain parts of the party's agenda. The Democratic Senatorial Campaign Committee (DSCC) is responsible for US Senate races. The Democratic Congressional Campaign Committee (DCCC) pursues US House of Representatives seats, and the Democratic Legislative Campaign Committee (DLCC) is in charge of winning state legislatures. There are also presidential campaigns that carry the mantle of the party every four years.

Then there are the state parties. We will use Maine as an example. In Maine, we have the state Democratic Party. Then there are the Senate Democratic Campaign Committee (SDCC) to oversee State Senate elections and the House Democratic Campaign Committee (HDCC) to take on Maine House of Representative contests. And then there are county Democrat groups; our race was supported by the Lincoln County Democrats, for example.

When we refer to the Democratic Party, we are referring to the national and state committees and organizations that support candidates and campaigns across the country. Sometimes we'll focus on a certain committee, and we'll let you know when we use more specific terminology. But the pitfalls that we're about to lay out for you are seen across the spectrum.

CHAPTER 1: DOWN THE DIRT ROAD—WHAT'S UP WITH RURAL AMERICA?

1. Danielle Kurtzleben, "Rural Voters Played a Big Part in Helping Trump Defeat Clinton," NPR, November 14, 2016, https://www.npr.org/2016/11/14/501737150/rural-voters-played-a-big-part-in-helping-trump-defeat-clinton.

2. "Urban Areas Facts," US Census Bureau, last revised March 30, 2021, https://www.census.gov/programs-surveys/geography/guidance/geo-areas/urban-rural/ua-facts.html.

3. Justices Roberts and Alito were nominated during George W. Bush's second term, the lone Republican popular-vote victory since 1988. However, the point remains that if Bush had not been elected as president in 2000 with a minority of the popular vote, he obviously would not have had a second term in which to appoint the justices.

4. Rebecca R. Ruiz, Robert Gebeloff, Steve Eder, and Ben Protess, "A Conservative Agenda Unleashed on the Federal Courts," *New York Times*, March 14, 2020, https://www.nytimes.com/2020/03/14/us/trump-appeals-court-judges .html.

5. Andrew Daniller, "A Majority of Americans Continue to Favor Replacing Electoral College with a Nationwide Popular Vote," Pew Research Center, January 28, 2021, https://www.pewresearch.org/fact-tank/2020/03/13/a-majority -of-americans-continue-to-favor-replacing-electoral-college-with-a-nationwide -popular-vote.

6. Robert Reich, "Trump Assaulted American Democracy—Here's How Democrats Can Save It," *Guardian*, October 25, 2020, https://www.theguardian .com/commentisfree/2020/oct/25/donald-trump-supreme-court-amy-coney -barrett-senate-joe-biden-democrats-republicans.

7. Emily Badger, "How the Rural-Urban Divide Became America's Political Fault Line," *New York Times*, May 21, 2019, https://www.nytimes.com/2019 /05/21/upshot/america-political-divide-urban-rural.html.

8. Jonathan Rodden, *Why Cities Lose: The Deep Roots of the Urban-Rural Political Divide* (New York: Basic Books, 2019), 1.

9. Holly Bailey, "Still Traumatized from 2016 Loss, Democrats Weigh How Much to Reach Out to Rural America," *Washington Post*, May 16, 2019, https://www.washingtonpost.com/politics/should-democrats-bother-reaching -out-to-rural-america/2019/05/07/23c80a16–6db4–11e9–8f44-e8d8bb1df986 _story.html.

10. Katrina van den Heuvel, "Have Democrats Learned Their Lesson? There's Reason for Hope," *Washington Post*, November 7, 2017, https://www.washington post.com/opinions/have-democrats-learned-their-lesson-theres-reason-for-hope /2017/11/07/cab3e78c-c315–11e7-aae0-cb18a8c29c65_story.html.

11. Ezra Klein, "Democrats, Here's How to Lose in 2022. And Deserve It," *New York Times*, January 21, 2021, https://www.nytimes.com/2021/01/21 /opinion/biden-inauguration-democrats.html.

12. Jane Kleeb, *Harvest the Vote: How Democrats Can Win Again in Rural America* (New York: HarperCollins, 2020), 13.

13. "Wide Gender Gap, Growing Educational Divide in Voters' Party Identification," Pew Research Center, August 28, 2020, https://www.pewresearch.org /politics/2018/03/20/wide-gender-gap-growing-educational-divide-in-voters -party-identification.

14. Thomas Frank, *What's the Matter with Kansas? How Conservatives Won the Heart of America* (New York: Metropolitan/Owl Books, 2005), 13–14.

15. Robert Wuthnow, *The Left Behind: Decline and Rage in Rural America* (Princeton, NJ: Princeton University Press, 2018), 97.

16. Alexandra Kanik and Patrick Scott, "The Urban-Rural Divide Only Deepened in the 2020 US Election," *City Monitor*, November 13, 2020, https://

NOTES **167**

citymonitor.ai/government/the-urban-rural-divide-only-deepened-in-the-2020
-us-election.

17. Bill Bishop, "One More Time: Rural Voters Didn't Desert Dems in 2008," *Daily Yonder*, May 31, 2018, https://www.dailyyonder.com/one-time -rural-voters-didnt-desert-dems.

18. Pew Research Center, "Wide Gender Gap, Growing Educational Divide in Voters' Party Identification."

19. "Changes in State Legislative Seats During the Obama Presidency," Ballotpedia, n.d, https://ballotpedia.org/Changes_in_state_legislative_seats _during_the_Obama_presidency.

20. "Changes in State Legislative Seats During the Obama Presidency," Ballotpedia.

21. Lazario Gamio, "Urban and Rural America Are Becoming Increasingly Polarized," *Washington Post*, November 17, 2016, https://www.washington post.com/graphics/politics/2016-election/urban-rural-vote-swing.

22. Gamio, "Urban and Rural America Are Becoming Increasingly Polarized."

23. Kanik and Scott, "The Urban-Rural Divide Only Deepened in the 2020 US Election."

24. Tim Marema, "Trump Maintains His Large Rural Margin; Democratic Vote Grows the Most in Mid-Sized and Large Metros," *Daily Yonder*, November 10, 2020, https://dailyyonder.com/trump-maintains-his-large-rural-margin -democratic-vote-grows-the-most-in-mid-sized-and-large-metros/2020/11/09.

25. Tim Marema, Tim Murphy, and Bill Bishop, "In Georgia, Atlanta Suburbs Deliver for Biden, but Extra Rural Votes Are Part of His Lead," *Daily Yonder*, November 10, 2020, https://dailyyonder.com/in-georgia-atlanta-suburbs -deliver-for-biden-but-extra-rural-votes-are-part-of-his-lead/2020/11/08; Tim Murphy, Bill Bishop, and Tim Marema, "Modest Gains in Rural Votes Help Biden Flip Michigan and Wisconsin," *Daily Yonder*, November 6, 2020, https:// dailyyonder.com/modest-gains-in-rural-votes-help-biden-flip-michigan-and -wisconsin/2020/11/05.

26. Phil McCausland, "Rural Hospital Closings Cause Mortality Rates to Rise, Study Finds," NBCNews.com, September 6, 2019, https://www.nbcnews .com/news/us-news/rural-hospital-closings-cause-mortality-rates-rise-study -finds-n1048046.

27. Adam Harris, "The Education Deserts of Rural America," *Atlantic*, September 4, 2019, https://www.theatlantic.com/education/archive/2019/07 /education-deserts-across-rural-america/593071.

28. "Farming and Farm Income," USDA ERS—Farming and Farm Income, May 10, 2021, https://www.ers.usda.gov/data-products/ag-and-food-statistics -charting-the-essentials/farming-and-farm-income.

29. Olugbenga Ajilore and Zoe Willingham, "Redefining Rural America," Center for American Progress, July 17, 2019, https://www.americanprogress .org/issues/economy/reports/2019/07/17/471877/redefining-rural-america.

30. Monica Anderson, "For 24% of Rural Americans, High-Speed Internet Is a Major Problem," Pew Research Center, September 10, 2018, https://www .pewresearch.org/fact-tank/2018/09/10/about-a-quarter-of-rural-americans -say-access-to-high-speed-internet-is-a-major-problem.

31. Anne Case and Angus Deaton, *Deaths of Despair and the Future of Capitalism* (Princeton, NJ: Princeton University Press, 2020).

32. Will Wilkinson, "Has Trump Handed Democrats an Opening in Red America?," *New York Times*, May 23, 2019, https://www.nytimes.com/2019/05/23/opinion/trump-rural-america.html.

33. Kim Parker, Juliana Menasce Horowitz, Anna Brown, Richard Fry, D'Vera Cohn, and Ruth Igielnik, "What United and Divides Urban, Suburban and Rural Communities," Social and Demographic Trends Project, Pew Research Center, May 30, 2020, https://www.pewresearch.org/social-trends/2018/05/22/what-unites-and-divides-urban-suburban-and-rural-communities.

34. "Older Population in Rural America," US Census Bureau, May 26, 2021, https://www.census.gov/library/stories/2019/10/older-population-in-rural-america.html.

35. Don Carrigan, "Maine's Shortage of Young People Is a Big Problem, Experts Say," *News Center Maine*, February 17, 2017, https://www.newscentermaine.com/article/news/community/maines-shortage-of-young-people-is-a-big-problem-experts-say/97-409040927.

36. *1990 Census of Population, General Population Characteristics, Maine* (Bureau of the Census, 1990), https://www2.census.gov/library/publications/decennial/1990/cp-1/cp-1-21.pdf.

37. Robert Wuthnow, *Small-Town America: Finding Community, Shaping the Future* (Princeton, NJ: Princeton University Press, 2013), 54.

38. Joseph Booth, "Our Changing Landscape," US Census Bureau, December 8, 2016, https://www.census.gov/library/visualizations/2016/comm/acs-rural-urban.html.

39. Wuthnow, *The Left Behind*, 28.

40. Patrick J. Carr and Maria Kefalas, *Hollowing Out the Middle: The Rural Brain Drain and What It Means for America* (Boston: Beacon Press, 2011).

41. Rodden, *Why Cities Lose*, 78–79.

42. "Wide Gender Gap, Growing Educational Divide in Voters' Party Identification," Pew Research Center.

43. Clara Hendrickson, Mark Muro, and William A. Galston, "Countering the Geography of Discontent: Strategies for Left-Behind Places," Brookings, November 19, 2018, https://www.brookings.edu/research/countering-the-geography-of-discontent-strategies-for-left-behind-places.

44. Carrigan, "Maine's Shortage of Young People Is a Big Problem, Experts Say."

45. Wuthnow, *The Left Behind*, 67–68.

46. Jeffrey Goldberg, "The Places Where the Recession Never Ended," *Atlantic*, November 12, 2019, https://www.theatlantic.com/magazine/archive/2019/12/tara-westover-trump-rural-america/600916.

47. "Wide Gender Gap, Growing Educational Divide in Voters' Party Identification," Pew Research Center.

48. Wuthnow, *The Left Behind*, 93.

49. Wuthnow, *The Left Behind*, 4.

50. Kleeb, *Harvest the Vote*, 179.

51. Quoted in Benjamin Barber, "Political Scientist Angie Maxwell on Countering the 'Long Southern Strategy,'" *Facing South*, January 22, 2021, https://

www.facingsouth.org/2021/01/political-scientist-angie-maxwell-countering
-long-southern-strategy.

52. Luke Darby, "72 Percent of All Rural Hospital Closures Are in States
That Rejected the Medicaid Expansion," *GQ*, July 30, 2019, https://www.gq
.com/story/rural-hospitals-closing-in-red-states.

53. Quoted in Zack Stanton, "How the 'Culture War' Could Break Democracy," *Politico*, May 21, 2021, https://www.politico.com/news/magazine/2021
/05/20/culture-war-politics-2021-democracy-analysis-489900.

54. Barber, "Political Scientist Angie Maxwell on Countering the 'Long
Southern Strategy.'"

55. Jon Tester and Aaron Murphy, *Grounded: A Senator's Lessons on Winning Back Rural America* (New York: Ecco, 2021), 342.

56. Barber, "Political Scientist Angie Maxwell on Countering the 'Long
Southern Strategy.'"

57. Bill Hogseth, "Why Democrats Keep Losing Rural Counties Like Mine,"
Politico, December 1, 2020, https://www.politico.com/news/magazine/2020/12
/01/democrats-rural-vote-wisconsin-441458.

58. Barber, "Political Scientist Angie Maxwell on Countering the 'Long
Southern Strategy.'"

59. Howard Berkes, "Rural America to Obama: Remember Us," NPR,
https://www.npr.org/templates/story/story.php?storyId=97307012.

60. Thomas Frank, *Listen, Liberal, or, Whatever Happened to the Party of
the People?* (New York: Metropolitan, 2016).

61. "Hillary Clinton: 'America Has Never Stopped Being Great,'" BBC
News, February 28, 2016, https://www.bbc.com/news/av/election-us-2016
-35680694.

62. Dominique Mosbergen, "Joe Biden Promises Rich Donors He Won't
'Demonize' the Wealthy if Elected President," *Huffington Post*, June 19, 2019,
https://www.huffpost.com/entry/joe-biden-wont-demonize-the-rich_n
_5d09ac63e4b0f7b74428e4c6.

63. Wuthnow, *The Left Behind*, 162.

CHAPTER 2: HOW DEMOCRATS LEFT RURAL AMERICA IN THE REARVIEW

1. "About the Democratic Party," Democratic National Committee, democrats
.org/who-we-are/about-the-democratic-party, accessed August 31, 2021.

2. Bill Bishop and Tim Marema, "'Blue Wave' Has Been a Trickle Outside
Largest Cities," *Daily Yonder*, July 17, 2019, https://dailyyonder.com/blue-wave
-trickle-outside-largest-cities/2018/05/09.

3. Jonathan Rodden, *Why Cities Lose: The Deep Roots of the Urban-Rural
Political Divide* (New York: Basic Books, 2019), 7.

4. Katherine J. Cramer, *The Politics of Resentment: Rural Consciousness in
Wisconsin and the Rise of Scott Walker* (Chicago: University of Chicago Press,
2016), 5.

5. Cramer, *The Politics of Resentment*, 66.

6. Ross Benes, *Rural Rebellion: How Nebraska Became a Republican
Stronghold* (Lawrence: University Press of Kansas, 2021), 66.

7. Cramer, *The Politics of Resentment*, 59.

8. Jane Kleeb, *Harvest the Vote: How Democrats Can Win Again in Rural America* (New York: HarperCollins, 2020), 108.

9. Rodden, *Why Cities Lose*, 1.

10. Nick Hillman, "Party Control in Congress and State Legislatures (1978–2016)," February 1, 2017, University of Wisconsin, School of Education, https://web.education.wisc.edu/nwhillman/index.php/2017/02/01/party-control-in-congress-and-state-legislatures.

11. "Under Obama, Democrats Suffer Largest Loss in Power since Eisenhower," *Quorum*, June 9, 2020, http://www.quorum.us/data-driven-insights/under-obama-democrats-suffer-largest-loss-in-power-since-eisenhower.

12. "Historical Partisan Composition of State Legislatures," Ballotpedia, https://ballotpedia.org/Historical_partisan_composition_of_state_legislatures.

13. "Republicans Now Control More State Legislatures Than Any Point in U.S. History," *Quorum*, November 16, 2020, https://www.quorum.us/data-driven-insights/republicans-now-control-more-state-legislatures-than-any-point-in-u-s-history.

14. Benes, *Rural Rebellion*, 91.

15. Matthew Yglesias, "The Democratic Party's Down-Ballot Collapse, Explained," *Vox*, January 10, 2017, http://www.vox.com/policy-and-politics/2017/1/10/14211994/obama-democrats-downballot.

16. Quoted in Emma Green, "The Ideological Reasons Why Democrats Have Neglected Local Politics," *Atlantic*, January 4, 2017, http://www.theatlantic.com/politics/archive/2017/01/the-ideological-reasons-why-democrats-have-neglected-local-politics/512024, brackets in original.

17. Amanda Litman and Ross Morales Rocketto, "Democrats' Myopic Focus on Just Winning the White House," CNN, January 15, 2020, https://amp.cnn.com/cnn/2020/01/15/opinions/democratic-party-myopic-white-house-focus-litman-rocketto/index.html.

18. Tim Murphy and Bill Bishop, "Barack Obama's Vote in the Cities Overwhelmed Rural," *Daily Yonder*, July 18, 2019, https://dailyyonder.com/barack-obamas-vote-cities-overwhelmed-rural/2008/11/19.

19. "Where Obama Did Better—and Where He Did Worse," *Washington Post*, November 7, 2012, http://www.washingtonpost.com/wp-srv/special/politics/obama-better-or-worse.

20. Reid Wilson, "Perspective: Democrats Had a Decade to Consolidate Power. They Blew Their Chance," *Washington Post*, November 6, 2020, http://www.washingtonpost.com/outlook/2020/11/06/democrats-republicans-redistricting-state-legislatures-flip.

21. "Maine Legislature Votes on Medicaid Expansion: VoteTrac," *Portland Press Herald*, June 20, 2014, https://www.pressherald.com/interactive/maine_senate_vote_results_for_medicaid_expansion_proposal__votetrac.

22. "Status of State Medicaid Expansion Decisions: Interactive Map," Kaiser Family Foundation, June 7, 2021, http://www.kff.org/medicaid/issue-brief/status-of-state-medicaid-expansion-decisions-interactive-map.

23. Alex Tausanovitch, "The Impact of Partisan Gerrymandering," Center for American Progress, October 1, 2019, http://www.americanprogress.org/issues/democracy/news/2019/10/01/475166/impact-partisan-gerrymandering.

24. Jay J. Chaudhuri, "The Most Important Pledge Democratic Presidential Candidates Can Make," *The Hill*, June 19, 2019, https://thehill.com/blogs/congress-blog/politics/449421-the-most-important-pledge-democratic-preside ntial-candidates-can.

25. Alex Kotch and Mary Bottari, "Tax Forms Reveal Koch Brothers Spent Millions to Shape State Politics in 2017," *Truthout*, February 25, 2018, https://truthout.org/articles/tax-forms-reveal-koch-brothers-spent-millions-to-shape-state-politics-in-2017.

26. Meaghan Winter, "Think America's Fate Hinges on the 2020 Presidential Race? You're Forgetting Something," *Guardian*, September 23, 2019, http://www.theguardian.com/commentisfree/2019/sep/23/think-americas-fat e-hinges-on-the-2020-presidential-race-youre-forgetting-something.

27. Benes, *Rural Rebellion*, 11.

28. Cramer, *The Politics of Resentment*, 183.

29. Alexandra Kanik and Patrick Scott, "The Urban-Rural Divide Only Deepened in the 2020 US Election," *City Monitor*, November 13, 2020, https://citymonitor.ai/government/the-urban-rural-divide-only-deepened-in-the-202 0-us-election.

30. Quoted in Diane Hessan, "Understanding the Undecided Voters," *Boston Globe*, op-ed, November 21, 2016, https://www.bostonglobe.com/opinion/2016/11 /21/understanding-undecided-voters/9EjNHVkt99b4re2VAB8ziI/story.html.

31. Jon Tester and Aaron Murphy, *Grounded: A Senator's Lessons on Winning Back Rural America* (New York: Ecco, 2021), 344.

32. Benes, *Rural Rebellion*, 4–5.

33. Tester and Murphy, *Grounded*, 342.

34. Julia Terruso, "Pa. Counties Where Bernie Sanders Beat Hillary Clinton in 2016 Are Full of Warning Signs for Him Now," *Philadelphia Inquirer*, March 17, 2020, http://www.inquirer.com/politics/pennsylvania/pa-bernie-sanders -hillary-clinton-2016–2020–20200312.html.

35. Tim Marema and Bill Bishop, "Sanders' Rural Support Drops from 2016 in Michigan, Other States," *Daily Yonder*, June 2, 2020, https://dailyyonder .com/sanders-rural-support-drops-from-2016-in-michigan-other-states /2020/03/11.

36. Danielle Kurtzleben, "Here's How Many Bernie Sanders Supporters Ultimately Voted for Trump," NPR, August 24, 2017, https://www.npr.org/2017 /08/24/545812242/1-in-10-sanders-primary-voters-ended-up-supporting -trump-survey-finds.

37. Kleeb, *Harvest the Vote*, 114.

38. Robert Wuthnow, *The Left Behind: Decline and Rage in Small-Town America* (Princeton, NJ: Princeton University Press, 2019), 4–6.

39. Tester and Murphy, *Grounded*, 346.

40. Cramer, *The Politics of Resentment*, 7.

41. Cramer, *The Politics of Resentment*, 205.

42. Jennifer Finney Boylan, "Mainers Are 'Disappointed,' Too, Susan Collins," *New York Times*, July 9, 2020.

43. "Maine Senate 2020 Race," OpenSecrets, n.d, http://www.opensecrets .org/races/summary?cycle=2020&id=MES2.

44. Ellen Barry, "The Democrats Went All Out Against Susan Collins. Rural Maine Grimaced," *New York Times*, November 17, 2020, http://www.nytimes.com /2020/11/17/us/maine-susan-collins.html?auth=login-email&fbclid=IwAR1xiu Gbo6KjbcEV4iPvNyvcM1JEWuirfoejI5J5Lc1Jq9K82gDZ9ejFyTI&login=email.

45. Nathan Bernard, "How Sara Gideon Lost to Collins the Day After She Entered the Race," *Mainer*, December 18, 2020, https://mainernews.com/how -sara-gideon-lost-to-collins-the-day-after-she-entered-the-race.

46. Micah L. Sifry, "Obama's Lost Army," *New Republic*, February 9, 2017, https://newrepublic.com/article/140245/obamas-lost-army-inside-fall -grassroots-machine.

47. Clio Chang, "Obama Lost His Grassroots Army. Will Bernie Keep His?," *Vice*, February 27, 2020, http://www.vice.com/en/article/k7enmy/obama -lost-his-grassroots-army-will-bernie-keep-his.

48. Jane Kleeb, *Harvest the Vote: How Democrats Can Win Again in Rural America* (New York: HarperCollins, 2020), 77.

49. Tester and Murphy, *Grounded*, 344.

50. "Rural Objective PAC—Battleground States," YouGov Blue, n.d., https://actionnetwork.org/user_files/user_files/000/059/832/original/Rural Objective_toplines.pdf.

51. Joy Cushman, "The Trump Campaign Knows Why Obama Won. Do Democrats?," *New York Times*, August 30, 2019, http://www.nytimes.com /2019/08/26/opinion/republicans-obama-campaign-playbook.html.

52. Derek Thompson, "Why Big-City Dominance Is a Problem for Democrats," *Atlantic*, November 26, 2020, http://www.theatlantic.com/ideas/archive /2020/11/why-big-city-dominance-problem-democrats/617161.

53. Ben Lilliston, "The Legacy of Lost Credibility in Fly Over Country," Institute for Agriculture and Trade Policy, November 30, 2016, http://www.iatp .org/blog/201611/the-legacy-of-lost-credibility-in-fly-over-country.

54. Quoted in "Trump Organization Executives Under Investigations," Transcripts: 9/7/2018, *All In with Chris Hayes*, MSNBC, September 17, 2020, https://www.msnbc.com/transcripts/all-in/2018-09-07-msna1143041.

55. Matt L. Barron, "Book Review: 'Harvest the Vote—How Democrats Can Win Again in Rural America,'" *Daily Yonder*, June 2, 2020, https://dailyyonder .com/book-review-harvest-the-vote-how-democrats-can-win-again-in-rural -america/2020/02/14.

56. Matt Hildreth, "'Don't Mistake Your Consultants for Your Constituents.' That's My Number One Tip for Democrats Running in Rural America," Twitter, May 10, 2021, https://twitter.com/mhildreth/status/1391818907477024770.

57. Cheri Bustos and Robin Johnson, *Hope from the Heartland: How Democrats Can Better Serve the Midwest by Bringing Rural, Working Class Wisdom to Washington*, Executive Summary, Cher PAC, Washington, DC, January 10, 2018, available at *Medium*, https://medium.com/@cherpacpress/hope-from-the -heartland-how-democrats-can-better-serve-the-midwest-by-bringing-rural -working-e5ff746f9839.

58. Nathan Bernard, "How Sara Gideon Lost to Collins the Day After She Entered the Race," *Mainer*, December 18, 2020, https://mainernews.com/how -sara-gideon-lost-to-collins-the-day-after-she-entered-the-race.

59. Thomas Frank, *What's the Matter with Kansas? How Conservatives Won the Heart of America* (New York: Metropolitan/Owl Book, 2005), 252.
60. "Our Mission," Campaign Workers Guild, n.d., https://campaignworkers guild.org/what-we-do.
61. George Gao, "The Up and Down Seasons of Political Campaign Work," Pew Research Center, May 30, 2020, http://www.pewresearch.org/fact-tank /2014/11/17/the-seasonal-nature-of-political-campaign-work.

CHAPTER 3: HOUSE DISTRICT 88
1. Reid Wilson, "The 10 Counties That Will Decide the 2020 Election," *The Hill*, September 5, 2019, https://thehill.com/homenews/state-watch/459832-the -10-counties-that-will-decide-the-2020-election.

CHAPTER 4: LUCKY DISTRICT 13
1. "2019 MCOA Award Recipients," in "Annual Awards," Maine Council on Aging, n.d., http://mainecouncilonaging.org/annual_awards.
2. "What Is a 'Push' Poll?," American Association for Public Opinion Outreach, https://www.aapor.org/Education-Resources/Resources/What-is-a-Push -Poll.aspx.
3. Bill Nemitz, "It's Time to Shove Back Against 'Push Polls,'" *Portland Press Herald*, October 1, 2020, https://www.pressherald.com/2020/10/02/bill -nemitz-its-time-to-shove-back-against-push-polls.
4. Caitlin Andrews, "Maine GOP Campaign Arm Paid for Shadowy Poll Hitting Democratic Legislative Candidate," *Bangor Daily News*, October 14, 2020, https://bangordailynews.com/2020/10/14/politics/maine-gop-campaign -arm-paid-for-shadowy-poll-hitting-democratic-legislative-candidate.

CHAPTER 5: STRATEGIC PRINCIPLES
1. Marshall Ganz and Emily S. Lin, "Learning to Lead: A Pedagogy of Practice," in *Handbook for Teaching Leadership: Knowing, Doing, and Being*, ed. Scott Snook, Nitin Nohria, and Rakesh Khurana (Los Angeles: SAGE, 2011), 353–66.
2. Anthony Cilluffo and Richard Fry, "Gen Z, Millennials and Gen X Outvoted Older Generations in 2018 Midterms," Pew Research Center, August 14, 2020, https://www.pewresearch.org/fact-tank/2019/05/29/gen-z-millennials -and-gen-x-outvoted-older-generations-in-2018-midterms.
3. "Pelosi Concerned Outspoken Progressive Flank of Party Could Harm Democrats' Reputation as Ineffectual Cowards," *The Onion*, July 25, 2019, https://politics.theonion.com/pelosi-concerned-outspoken-progressive-flank -of-party-c-1836707083.
4. Clare Foran, Manu Raju, Sunlen Serfaty, and Ashley Killough, "Dispute Between Pelosi and 'the Squad' Has House Democrats Pleading for Unity," CNN Politics, July 25, 2019, https://www.cnn.com/2019/07/12/politics/pelosi -alexandria-ocasio-cortez-house-democrats/index.html.
5. Anthony Cilluffo, "5 Facts About Student Loans," Pew Research Center, January 13, 2021, http://www.pewresearch.org/fact-tank/2017/08/24/5-facts -about-student-loans.

6. Ana Hernandez Kent, William Emmons, and Lowell Ricketts, "Are Millennials a Lost Generation Financially?," Federal Reserve Bank of St. Louis, August 4, 2020, https://www.stlouisfed.org/on-the-economy/2019/december/millennials-lost-generation-financially.

7. "Institute of Politics Spring 2018 Youth Poll," Institute of Politics, Harvard Kennedy School, 2018, http://iop.harvard.edu/spring-2018-poll.

8. Ronald Brownstein, "Millennials to Pass Baby Boomers as Largest Voter-Eligible Age Group, and What It Means," CNN Politics, July 25, 2017, https://www.cnn.com/2017/07/25/politics/brownstein-millennials-largest-voter-group-baby-boomers/index.html.

9. Drew DeSilver, "Millennials, Gen X Increase Their Ranks in the House, Especially Among Democrats," Pew Research Center, July 27, 2020, https://www.pewresearch.org/fact-tank/2018/11/21/millennials-gen-x-increase-their-ranks-in-the-house-especially-among-democrats; "Estimated Generations of Legislators Revised (Percentages of Valid Data)," National Conference of State Legislatures, 2015, http://www.ncsl.org/Portals/1/Documents/About_State_Legislatures/Generations_Rev1.pdf.

10. "Public Highly Critical of State of Political Discourse in the U.S.," Pew Research Center, June 19, 2019, https://www.people-press.org/2019/06/19/public-highly-critical-of-state-of-political-discourse-in-the-u-s.

11. Jessie Spector, "Maxmin Believes in Maine People," *Kennebec Journal and Morning Sentinel*, October 25, 2018, https://www.centralmaine.com/2018/10/26/maxmin-believes-in-maine-people.

12. Colin Campbell, "Democrat Says Chuck Schumer Told Him to Spend Campaign in 'Windowless Basement,'" *News & Observer* (Raleigh, NC), October 8, 2019, https://www.newsobserver.com/news/politics-government/article235912452.html.

13. Anne Truitt, *Daybook: The Journal of an Artist* (New York: Pantheon Books, 1982).

14. Jonathan Haidt, *The Righteous Mind: Why Good People Are Divided by Politics and Religion* (New York: Penguin, 2013).

15. A possible sixth foundation is being researched, "Liberty/oppression," which concerns "the resentment people feel toward those who dominate them and restrict their liberty," Moralfoundations.org.

16. Nathan Bernard, "How Sara Gideon Lost to Collins the Day After She Entered the Race," *Mainer*, December 18, 2020, https://mainernews.com/how-sara-gideon-lost-to-collins-the-day-after-she-entered-the-race.

17. Marshall Ganz, "Leading Change: Leadership, Organization, and Social Movements," 2010, originally published as chapter 19 of *Handbook of Leadership Theory and Practice: A Harvard Business School Colloquium*, https://marshallganz.usmblogs.com/files/2012/08/Chapter-19-Leading-Change-Leadership-Organization-and-Social-Movements.pdf.

18. Naomi Klein, Twitter, February 4, 2020, https://twitter.com/NaomiA Klein/status/1224695162921783297.

CHAPTER 6: CAMPAIGN BUILD

1. Courtney Kennedy and Hannah Hartig, "Response Rates in Telephone Surveys Have Resumed Their Decline," Pew Research Center, May 30, 2020, https://www.pewresearch.org/fact-tank/2019/02/27/response-rates-in-telephone -surveys-have-resumed-their-decline.

CHAPTER 7: LIVING IT ON THE DIRT ROADS

1. Quoted in "Trump Organization Executives Under Investigations," Transcripts: 9/7/2018, *All In with Chris Hayes*, MSNBC, September 17, 2020, http://www.msnbc.com/transcripts/all-in/2018-09-07-msna1143041.

2. Andy Kroll, "Can Millions of Deep Conversations with Total Strangers Beat Trump—and Heal America?," *Rolling Stone*, July 15, 2020, https://www .rollingstone.com/politics/politics-features/deep-canvassing-joe-biden-donald -trump-2020-presidential-election-coronavirus-1028034.

EPILOGUE

1. adrienne maree brown, "Strategy and Kamala Feels," August 12, 2020, http://adriennemareebrown.net/2020/08/12/strategy-and-kamala-feels.